SHARIʿA IN THE MODERN ERA

Written by the Qadi (judge) of the Jerusalem Shariʿa Court and former director of the Shariʿa Court system in Israel, this book offers a unique perspective on the religious law of Muslim minorities living in the West. Specifically, it explores the *fiqh al-aqalliyyat* doctrine of religious jurisprudence developed by modern Islamic jurists to resolve the challenges of maintaining cultural and religious identity in majority non-Muslim societies. The author examines possible applications across numerous cultural and geographical contexts, answering questions such as: What are the rules for assuming political and public roles? And should one deposit money that incurs interest? Building on a growing scholarship, this book aims to resolve points of view and facets of religious law that have been neglected by previous studies. Accessibly written, *Shariʿa in the Modern Era* is designed to promote cross-cultural understanding among readers of all faiths.

IYAD ZAHALKA is the judge of the Shariʿa Court of Jerusalem, holds a PhD in Muslim Minority Jurisprudence from the Hebrew University in Jerusalem, and serves as a lecturer at the Hebrew University of Jerusalem, Tel Aviv University, and Bar-Ilan University. Drawing on his experience as the former director of the Israeli Shariʿa Court system, Zahalka's work focuses on the tension between minority identity and integration in Western society. He is the author of *Guide to Shariʿa Law* (2008) and *Shariʿa Courts between Identity and Adjudication* (2009).

SHARIʿA IN THE MODERN ERA

Muslim Minority Jurisprudence

IYAD ZAHALKA

Translated by

OHAD STADLER and CECILIA SIBONY

CAMBRIDGE
UNIVERSITY PRESS

CAMBRIDGE
UNIVERSITY PRESS

University Printing House, Cambridge CB2 8BS, United Kingdom

Cambridge University Press is part of the University of Cambridge.

It furthers the University's mission by disseminating knowledge in the pursuit of education, learning and research at the highest international levels of excellence.

www.cambridge.org
Information on this title: www.cambridge.org/9781107114586

First published 2016

A catalogue record for this publication is available from the British Library

Library of Congress Catalouging in Publication Data
Zahalka, Iyad, 1969– author.
[Shariʿah be-'idan ha-moderni English]
Shariʿa in the modern era : muslim minorities jurisprudence / Iyad Zahalka.
pages cm
ISBN 978-1-107-11458-6 (hardback)
1. Islamic law – Non-Islamic countries. 2. Muslims – Non-Islamic countries. I. Title.
KBP69.5.Z34 2016
340.5′9–dc23 2015030768

ISBN 978-1-107-11458-6 Hardback

This book is dedicated to my dear parents,
Suad and Ahmad Zahalka

CONTENTS

ACKNOWLEDGMENTS

I wish to thank my family, my wonderful wife Fayroz and my children, Abed Allah, Rana, Ruba, and Reema, for their continuous and unconditional love and support. I wish to acknowledge the tremendous work and commitment of the translation team. Ohad Stadler and Cecilia Sibony traversed three languages in order to bring my manuscript to the English reader, and language editor Rebecca Sacks expertly and attentively ensured the quality of the content in English.

A warm thank you to the Cambridge University Press team and particularly, to John Berger, senior editor at Cambridge University Press, whose recognition of the potential of the project, time, advice, and commitment contributed immensely to the final published book. I also wish to extend a sincere thank you to project manager Kanimozhi Ramamurthy of Newgen Knowledge Works for her dedicated, thorough, and hard work, copy editor of the manuscript Laura Lawrie, and production editor at Cambridge Helen Francis.

A special thank you to Professor Ron Shaham, head of the Islamic and Middle Eastern Studies Department at Hebrew University, who served as advisor of my PhD, and the members of the Dissertation Committee, Professors Yitzhak Reiter, Isaac Hasson, and Michael Karayanni. I wish to thank Dr. Ido Shahar who generously reviewed the manuscript, volunteering his knowledge and insight, and Dr. Aisha Musa, Assistant Professor of Religion and Middle East and Islamic Studies at Colgate University, for expertly advising on Islamic religious terminology in English and transliteration. I wish to thank Professor Jonathan Price for his support and encouragement of the publication of the book, Dr. Uriyah Shavit for his insightful comments, Shammai Fishman for aiding in the location of sources and translation from English, and Dr. Muhammad al-Atawneh for his enlightened comments and observations along the way.

Introduction

The religion of Islam addresses all mankind, anywhere around the world, at any time. This universality derives from the belief that religion is not intended for a specific people or nation[1] and that all land is God's land, and thus it should be divided according to His will.[2] This principle was implemented during the Prophet Muhammad's mission when he called upon the leaders of the region to embrace Islam.[3] In this vein, religious scholars introduced the principle of *ʿālamiyyat al-Islām* (universality of Islam), which received in the modern era a broad interpretation regarding the relations of Muslims with the other peoples and nations of the world.[4]

According to *ʿālamiyyat al-Islām*, the Islamic religion applies to all people, everywhere and at any time. Therefore, every Muslim must uphold the religious decrees, abide by shariʿa laws, and practice them in both private and public life. Furthermore, every Muslim, anywhere and at any time, is under the obligation to call upon all people of the world to convert to Islam, and to disseminate it equally to all nationalities and lands without distinction.[5] In this sense, *ʿālamiyyat al-Islām* challenges Muslim minorities in non-Muslim countries to uphold the faith, especially in the context of the religious awakening and resurgence of Islamic identity prevalent among Muslim minorities in the West in recent decades.

Classic Islamic religious law is not equipped to deal with this shift and does not offer solutions to the challenges faced by Muslim minorities. Life under these newfound circumstances raises many fundamental questions; first and foremost is the mere settlement of Muslims in non-Muslim

[1] Qur'an verses 107:21, 28:34.
[2] Qur'an verses 128:7, 105:21.
[3] Muhammad Khalid ʿAbd al-Kadir. *Min Fiqh al-Aqalliyyat al-Muslima*. (Doha: The Qatari Office of Waqf and Islamic Affairs, 1997), 22–6.
[4] Mamduh al-Shaykh, "Hal Yatbalwar Mafhum Jadid li-ʿAlamiyyat al-Islam?" http://www.nashiri.net/articles/intellect-and-philosophy/2075–v15-2075.html 2008
[5] Yusuf al-Qaradawi, *Fi Fiqh al-Aqalliyyat al-Muslima: Hayat al-Muslimin Wasat al-Mujtamaʿat al-Akhra* (Cairo: Dar al-Shuruq, 1st edition, 2001), 13.

countries. Moreover, coping with an environment that differs significantly from the familiar surroundings of the Muslim world raises urgent religious quandaries in various fields: the public, private and personal spheres, and monetary interactions.

The questions that may arise in the public sphere include: are Muslims allowed to naturalize in non-Muslim countries, abide by their respective laws, and accept the obligations and rights that they entail? Are they allowed to serve in the armies of these countries, particularly if those are in a state of war against Islam? What are the rules for assuming political and public roles, and the appropriate conduct during elections? Can Muslims elect a candidate or be elected, form a political party and support it? Can they support a specific candidate or form a political party that is exclusively Muslim? And what are the rules regarding the establishment of Islamic institutions such as schools, clubs, and religious, cultural, social and economic institutions in non-Muslim countries?

In the private sphere, questions that may arise include: Can one eat from markets, especially where the meat is prepared by non-Muslims and is impossible to ascertain whether it was performed according to Muslim religious laws? Should one inquire about the nature of each food item purchased? Can one consume processed foods that are known to contain pork products? Can one eat at a restaurant that serves foods that are prohibited, such as pork or alcoholic beverages? Can they work in said restaurants? Can they trade these commodities with locals? Can one accept a colleague's invitation to dine at such establishments? Can Muslims send greetings cards to their acquaintances for a Christian or a national holiday? Can they invite locals to Muslim social events?

Questions that may arise in the personal sphere include: are marriages that are presided over by the church or a local official and not according to Muslim laws and traditions valid? Is it mandatory to formulate a new marriage contract at a mosque or an Islamic center where a Muslim cleric officiates the wedding? What is the validity of a divorce presided over by a civil judge for a Muslim couple, when the husband refuses to divorce the wife? What is the validity of a marriage that is not registered in accordance with the laws of that country (*'Urfi*)? What should a woman who seeks to get married without the consent of her guardian do? Is she allowed to turn to the Imam of the local mosque to serve as her guardian in the marriage? In such a case, who will guarantee her rights if she decides to divorce her husband? What is the rule for marrying a non-Muslim Western woman? Is she considered to have no religion and therefore should not be married, or does she belong to the 'People of the Book' who are suitable for marriage?

What is the rule regarding a woman who converts to Islam while her husband remains a non-Muslim? Should they be separated? Can a man who converted to Islam accept an inheritance from his non-Muslim father, which contradicts the hadith of the Prophet that prohibits the inheritance between a Muslim and a non-Muslim?

In the financial sphere, questions that may arise include: Can Muslims collaborate with banks and insurance companies that collect and pay interest to their clients? Can one deposit money that incurs interest? Can one have life insurance or homeowners insurance? What is the rule for profits garnered from interest on investments and compensations? When a Muslim is unable to buy a house, can he take out a mortgage with an interest rate?

Modern religious scholars remain divided on the manner in which Muslim minorities in the West should adapt to their surroundings and the different aspects of life; every religious faction offers a unique approach.[6] The *Salafi* School of thought rejects any *ijtihād* (independent reasoning) that is designed to amend religious laws to accommodate the living circumstances of Muslim minorities. It maintains that doing so constitutes a bidʿa, a new creation that is an abomination and utterly forbidden. Therefore, according to the *salafi* leaning, Muslims only mechanisms for coping are through the mere preservation of the religion and the faith of Islam while dissimilating from those surroundings, detaching themselves from the general public, and associating solely with Muslims.

Unlike the *salafis*, *wasaṭī* religious scholars argue that Muslim minorities require *fiqh khāṣ*, a special religious decree that originates from a true shariʿa *ijtihād* that takes into account their location, time, and particular circumstances and needs. According to these scholars, the conditions of the Muslim minorities in the West is direr than those of their brethren in Muslim countries due to the stressful environment they reside in, the plethora of temptations they face, and their inability to subjugate these societies to their religious laws. Therefore, Muslim minorities should deal with their adoptive societies according to their rules and regulations, even if those contradict to a certain degree the laws of Islam. Thus, according to the *ʿālamiyyat al-Islām*,[7] shariʿa laws should be altered in accordance with

6 On the various Islamic factions – *salafi*, *wasaṭī*, and liberal – see an extensive discussion in chapter one.

7 This does not concur with Middle East experts who interpret the "universality of Islam" in terms of Islamic expansion and world domination. In the book it is interpreted not as a political and cultural domination, but as a call to believe in the Islamic religion, accept its values, and follow its decrees anywhere around the word and at any time.

the circumstances, the times, and the place, so every Muslim will be able to uphold religious decrees without causing an unbearable burden.[8] This applies to Muslim minorities in non-Muslim countries that are unable to subjugate the majority of the population to shariʿa laws and at times are unable to perform religious obligations to the letter.

To cope with these newfound circumstances, Muslim minorities and religious scholars must search for religious solutions to allow them to continue to uphold the decrees and safeguard their religious identity. Meanwhile, they must avoid substantial, even irreversible, damage by preventing confrontation with the laws and accepted customs of their adoptive countries. Religious laws provide an infrastructure that alleviates some of the decrees, such as the religious obligation to hinder evil and wrongdoing, and the decree to assuage Muslim believers, free their burdens or remove obstacles from their path. Religious law assists in upholding the religion because it maintains that shariʿa laws can alter depending on the time, place and circumstance. Additionally, it provides the fundamental permission to deviate from the religious path in case of *ḍarūra* (necessity), which has encouraged the development of the doctrine of *fiqh al-aqalliyyāt al Muslima* (hereinafter: *fiqh al-aqalliyyāt*).[9]

Developed over the last two decades, *fiqh al-aqalliyyāt* is a jurisprudence designed to provide a religious solution for Muslim minorities, mainly in the West, taking into account their distinctive life predicaments. It aspires to incorporate the preservation of a religious Muslim identity and adherence to the laws of Islam with civil assimilation into a non-Muslim country. This is performed by altering shariʿa laws according to a religious methodology that is rooted in Islam and *uṣūl al-fiqh*, the principles of religion that stipulate the terms and conditions by which new decrees can be passed.

This book focuses on *fiqh al-aqalliyyāt* of the *wasaṭī* faction, a school of thought dominated by the Muslim Brotherhood that positions itself in the middle ground between conservative resistance to changing religious laws and the disintegration of the commitment to religious tradition. This work does not delve into the *salafi fiqh al-aqalliyyāt*, which serves only as a point of comparison, due to the fact that it possesses its own manner with which to resolve controversies and issues affecting Muslim minorities in the West; it does not offer a unique methodology for minority jurisprudence; and it is a proponent of returning to the traditions of the "righteous" ancestors, rejecting any *ijtihād* in the religious laws.

[8] Qaradawi, *Fi Fiqh al-Aqalliyyat al-Muslima*, 44–6.

[9] Ibid., 30–1.

This book examines the development of the *fiqh al-aqalliyyāt* doctrine, its position on the spectrum of Muslim religious law, and how various religious factions treat it. This is followed by a research analysis of the *fiqh al-aqalliyyāt* methodology and the religious tools, mechanisms and principles it utilizes to create religious decrees, an inquiry into whether those are applicable to all walks of life, and an examination of the consistent and systematic approach of the *fiqh al-aqalliyyāt* adjudicators in implementing its methodology among Muslim minorities. Finally, notwithstanding the disparity in life circumstances and conditions of different Muslim minorities, the applicability of *fiqh al-aqalliyyāt* is examined as it relates to all aspects of life for all Muslim minorities. The final goal is to consolidate conclusions on the validity of *fiqh al-aqalliyyāt* in the religious and judicial realms, and its standing as a sharīʿa policy whose scholars and philosophers aspire to apply it to Muslim minorities.

The personal sphere, which is seminal to Muslim religious law, is the test case. The rules of the personal realm regulate the basic relationships within the family, the nucleus and cornerstone of society, and determine everything in terms of family law, marital relations between husband and wife, childbirth, and child-rearing. These matters are so sensitive and inherent to Islam that it assigns God as the personal sphere's guarantor, in order to safeguard the purity of the family, the survival of its lineage, and the longevity of the Muslim nation. These matters are incorporated into the "rights of God" (*ḥuqūq Allah*), representing the public interest in the perpetuation of the nation of Islam. Therefore, within the doctrine of *fiqh al-aqalliyyāt*, the personal sphere attracts significant attention and study because Muslim minorities can be exposed to, and suffer from civil laws that contradict religious ones. Furthermore, a comparative study between Muslim minorities in various places is also possible due to the likeness of the topics in question: the validity of marriage or divorce, the religious affiliation of children, guardianship, custody and alimony.

Conclusions of the personal sphere discussion will provide an answer to the aforementioned questions on the role of the doctrine as an encompassing framework for religious jurisprudence. Moreover, it will assist in determining whether the methodology allows Muslim minorities to manage personal issues in their respective political-legal environments, particularly with civil arrangements enforced upon them by society in lieu of religious ones. If the methodology does allow for a religion-based solution to this sensitive subject, while also taking into account the unique circumstances of Muslims in non-Muslim countries and the possible contradictions between local civil courts and religious courts, it is a testimony that *fiqh al-aqalliyyāt* is indeed an all-encompassing, consistent and organized religious doctrine. However, if the methodology falls short of this, it would be reasonable to deduce that it was created to merely provide a limited solution for random issues Muslims encounter in the West. This research will make it possible to determine whether *fiqh al-aqalliyyāt* constitutes a novel approach to Muslim jurisprudence and not only a localized solution for Muslim minorities and whether it implements a fundamentally religious approach that transforms shariʿa laws, in accordance with the era, the situation, and the *maṣlaḥa* – the common good and interest of Muslims.

Tendencies in *Fiqh al-Aqalliyyāt* Research Literature

Researchers have been intrigued by Muslim minorities in the West, and research material abounds in regard to the diverse aspects of their lives: their position in society and social, political, and religious integration in the countries in which they settled. Several publications delve into the religious aspects of their lives, while others only skim the surface on the role of Muslim religious law in the life of the Muslim community and its influence on the formation of their identity and their relationship with their surroundings. Parts of the literature that describe the dangers Islam poses to Western culture are tainted by Islamophobia. Other segments of the research literature focus on the evolution of Muslim communities in the West, their integration, and predictions of what their futures entail.

Literature that researches Muslim minorities from the historical, sociological, geo-political and constitutional perspectives is not necessarily relevant to this book and will be discussed only at the point in which it intersects with the objectives of the book and complements them. This book does not refer to research conducted on Muslims in the West in general, or the various Islamist organizations in Europe and America. The focus is solely on the research on the development of the *fiqh al-aqalliyyāt* doctrine, its major trends and influence on Muslims residing in the West, and the manner in which they deal with the public and legal ramifications.

There is a body of work that has examined the general stature of the shariʿa, its position as part of civil jurisprudence in the West, and the degree to which civil courts have accepted Islamic law and implemented it.[10] These works do not deal with *fiqh al-aqalliyyāt* directly, rather with the approach of civil law to shariʿa, and not vice versa. Contrary to the aforementioned works that do not explore how the doctrine grapples

[10] Such researches include: Edge 2008, Rohe 2003; Rohe 2004; Rohe 2010; Yilmaz 2000.

with civil law, this study does so, while simultaneously exploring the treatment of civil law as a whole by *fiqh al-aqalliyyāt*, and the judicial norms that contradict religious law. The study further aspires to answer the following questions: does the doctrine promote mediation between civil and religious law or isolationism? Which religious apparatus can mitigate this issue?

Initially introduced as an organized doctrine on the writings of Yusuf al-Qaradawi and Taha Jabir al-ʿAlwani over a decade ago, *fiqh al-aqalliyyāt* is still marginally researched compared to the studies of Muslim minorities. Alexandre Caeiro examined the influence of the doctrine over the identity of Muslims in Europe and the call for the Islamization of the West.[11] Andrew March analyzed the doctrine's approach toward contemporary liberal theories such as freedom, religion and democracy.[12] Shammai Fishman explored the doctrine according to the teachings of al-Qaradawi and al-ʿAlwani.[13] Ralph Ghadban examined its place within Islamic religious law and whether it represented a conservative Islamist approach or whether it was influenced by modernization.[14] Uriya Shavit studied the functionality of theological concepts and religious decrees in general, and the *fiqh al-aqalliyyāt* methodology in particular, within the *wasaṭī* and *salafi* factions.[15]

These pioneering works on *fiqh al-aqalliyyāt* are indeed valuable, yet they lack certain topics. One such issue is the historical evolution of the doctrine of the *wasaṭiyya*, from which *fiqh al-aqalliyyāt* originated and upon which it is based. In addition, there is no sufficient in-depth discussion on the religious methods used in religious decrees according to the *fiqh al-aqalliyyāt* doctrine. Furthermore, the existing research refers to a small number of religious rulings in this field and does not examine the applicability of *fiqh al-aqalliyyāt* for diverse Muslim minorities.

[11] A. Caeiro, "The European Council for Fatwa and Research" (Paper presented at the Fourth Mediterranean Social and Political Research Meeting, European University Institute, Florence, Italy, March 19–23, 2003); A. Caeiro, "The Power of European Fatwas: The Minority Fiqh Project and the Making of an Islamic Counterpublic," *International Journal of Middle East Studies* 42/3 (2010): 435–49.

[12] A. F. March, "Sources of Moral Obligation to non-Muslims in the 'Jurisprudence of Muslim Minorities' (*Fiqh al-Aqalliyyat*) Discourse." *Islamic Law and Society* 16 (2009): 34–94.

[13] S. Fishman, "*Fiqh al-Aqalliyyat*: A Legal Theory for Muslim Minorities," *Research Monographs on the Muslim World*, Hudson Institute, Series 1 (Paper no.2, 2006).

[14] R. Ghadban, "*Fiqh al-Aqalliyyat* and its Place in Islamic Law," *Orient* 2 (2010): 56–63.

[15] U. Shavit, "The Wasati and Salafi Approaches to the Religious Law of Muslim Minorities," *Islamic Law and Society* 19/4 (2012): 416–57.

Discussion Objectives

This book has two chief objectives: (1) To complement the existing research on *fiqh al-aqalliyyāt* from the points of view and facets that have thus far been somewhat neglected, and for the first time present a comprehensive thesis for both the ideological aspect of religious law and the actual, practical implementation for Muslim minorities who differ from one another. (2) To examine the doctrine's implication on the development of Muslim religious law in the modern era. Despite their significant and noteworthy contribution in other fields, researchers of the *fiqh al-aqalliyyāt* doctrine have not answered a string of questions from which the aforementioned objectives derive: (1) What is the validity of *fiqh al-aqalliyyāt* in terms of religion and religious law, and what is the approach of the various factions of Islam to it? (2) Does the doctrine establish a broad, all-encompassing and organized religious framework for religious decrees on every subject that considers the special circumstances of Muslim minorities? Does it offer a comprehensive solution to the array of problems and challenges faced by the Muslim minorities? (3) What are the principles and pillars of the *fiqh al-aqalliyyāt* doctrine, and is its methodology systematically and consistently implemented by its adjudicators? (4) To what extent is the doctrine implemented from theory to practice? And to what extent is it accepted by Muslim minorities in the West?

In addition, the current study examines whether the doctrine applies to minorities with diverse geo-political characteristics, indigenous as well as immigrant. In this respect, it is important to examine the doctrine's approach to the distinction between immigrant and indigenous minorities. More often than not, the indigenous minority is also a national one, which may cause a rift with the state and the majority of the population that maintains a different nationality. As opposed to the immigrant minority, which is willing to adhere to the prevailing state of affairs in the adoptive country, the indigenous one usually claims civil and collective rights that relate to its distinctive identity. This triggers several questions: (1) Do the dissimilarities between those minorities affect the application of the doctrine in the case of the indigenous Muslim minority, and the manner in which it deals with its legal-political surroundings? (2) Does this divergence affect shariʿa laws, including matters of the personal sphere of each minority? (3) Is the doctrine legitimate and applicable to indigenous minorities in the same way it is for immigrant ones? (4) How does *fiqh al-aqalliyyāt* influence the development of Muslim religious law in the modern age?

Methodology

This book is based on qualitative research obtained through textual analysis[16] of publications and religious decrees by the *'ulama'* of Muslim minorities in the West, alongside field interviews of Muslim activists in Western countries. The work on this book consisted of the examination of hundreds of books, essays, bodies of research, and religious decrees by adjudicators and Islamic intellectuals since the late 1980s mainly, but not exclusively, from the *wasaṭī* faction. The majority of scholars serve as thinkers and adjudicators for Muslim minority communities in the West, while some of the writings are by Islamist thinkers who reside in Muslim countries. In addition, classical literature on religious law was also examined.

The book focuses on systematic content analysis of the fatwa (religious legal opinion), resolutions and research issued and conducted by the "European Council for Fatwa and Research" (ECFR), as published on its website and in its scientific journal – *al-Majallat al-ʿIlmiyya*. These essays provide an ideological framework for the religious rulings of the ECFR and guidance for adjudicators seeking to rely on the religious law principles and the methodology of *fiqh al-aqalliyyāt*. The book further analyzes essays and religious rulings by *wasaṭī* adjudicators based on the *fiqh al-aqalliyyāt* methodology, as well as fatwa by other *fiqh al-aqalliyyāt* scholars, mostly al-Qaradawi and al-ʿAlwani. In addition, essays, religious rulings and articles by scholars and thinkers from other factions regarding *fiqh al-aqalliyyāt* are also examined, including publications by British shariʿa councils.

Another pillar of this book is the in-depth interviews[17] conducted with prominent religious leaders in Islamic centers across the United States (New York, Washington, Virginia, Detroit, Texas, California, Utah, and Maryland), in Europe (London, Bradford, and Edinburgh in the United Kingdom, and Dublin in Ireland), as well as visits to and interviews with Muslims in France and Germany. These field interviews were designed to familiarize the author with the circumstances behind the aforementioned research and religious decrees. Moreover, these interviews were intended to explore the degree to which the *fiqh al-aqalliyyāt* doctrine is accepted by Muslim minorities in the West, their relationship with it, and the degree

[16] On textual content analysis, see Asher Shkedi, *Words of Meaning: Qualitative Research – Theory and Practice* (Tel Aviv: Tel Aviv University, 2007), 121–40.

[17] On in-depth interviews, see ibid., 69–80.

of its applicability in the West. In addition, the book explores the existing literature on *fiqh al-aqalliyyāt* and its applicability to Muslim minorities in the West. The book also surveys the literature that evolved from the doctrine, its roots, and its standing among religious scholars from different factions; scholars whose findings are then juxtaposed with the findings of this research.

The religious law methodology of *fiqh al-aqalliyyāt* and its founding principles and guidelines derive from the research and religious rulings of *fiqh al-aqalliyyāt* scholars. Also examined in this work is the adjudicators' systematic and consistent implementation of the methodology in their rulings in general, and in matters of the personal sphere in particular. In order to investigate the disparity between the religious law that evolved around *fiqh al-aqalliyyāt* and classical religious law, the book will compare rulings on similar subject matters by *fiqh al-aqalliyyāt* scholars and classical scholars. The book will also examine the *fiqh al-aqalliyyāt* doctrine from the point of view of the "legal pluralism" approach, developed for instances where the sovereign applies diverse legal systems on groups within the population, based on ethnic, religious, national or geographical criteria. This approach has already been utilized in research on Islamic societies. In the current study it was used to examine the behavior of Muslim minorities from the perspective of religious law and in comparison to state laws. Moreover, the current study investigates the effect of state law on the lives of Muslim minorities, and the relationship between religious courts and state laws, including the mutual influence of the two systems. In addition, it explores the behavior of *fiqh al-aqalliyyāt* in cases where shariʿa courts for Muslim minorities are established, such as in Israel, which allow the Muslim minority to litigate by means of religious and shariʿa laws.

1

Fiqh al-Aqalliyyāt: Theoretical Background and Evolution

Muslim Religious Law and Its Factions

Shariʿa (Religious Law) and *Fiqh* (Jurisprudence)

According to Muslim religious law scholars, shariʿa is everything that God decreed for believers – faith, ritual, morality, interactions between fellow men and ways of life. Shariʿa is designed to regulate the relations between God and mankind, but also among themselves, fulfilling their happiness in this world or the next. According to the Islamic perception, shariʿa originated from God, was heralded by his messengers, and all that was decreed by God through them constitutes the shariʿa.[1] Hence, it is a comprehensive set of rules that seeks to influence every facet of the believer's life.[2]

Fiqh is jurisprudence, the discourse by religious scholars regarding the divine law through which they portrayed and explored the shariʿa.[3] The literal meaning of *fiqh* is deep understanding, which in the Islamic religion means comprehension of the foundations of religion. Eventually, its denotation was extended to include an understanding of shariʿa laws, and what is permitted and prohibited according to the shariʿa sources. The legal methodology of *fiqh* relies on four main pillars: (1) the Qur'an, the living word of God "transferred" to the Prophet Muhammad; (2) the sunna, transcribed oral religious tradition that contains the Prophet's specific words, habits, practices, silent approvals and ratification; (3) *ijmāʿ*, the consensus of all religious law scholars regarding the law on a specific subject; (4) *qiyās*, the construction of new laws through the process of analogical reasoning derived from primary sources.[4]

The basis for *fiqh*'s legal methodology includes other secondary sources of religious rulings, such as *al-istiḥsān* (general directive of shariʿa ruling)

[1] Manna ʿal-Qatan, *Tarikh al-Tashriʿ al-Islami* (Cairo: Maktabat Wahba, 5th edition, 2001), 13–4.

[2] J. Schacht, *An Introduction to Islamic Law* (Oxford: Clarendon Press, 1964), 1.

[3] Ibid.

[4] Aharon Layish, "The Transforation of the Shariʿa from Jursits' Law to Statutory Law in the Contemporary Muslim World," *Die Welt des Islams* 44 (2004): 85–113.

or the construction of new religious laws through an analogy of the objective that lies at the heart of an existing law. That is to say, the construction of a new law is not based on an actual decree, rather on a realization of the core objective of an existing shariʿa law on the same subject. For example, *al-maṣāliḥ al-mursala* is legislation designed to fulfill the public interest (*maṣlaḥa*)in order to benefit the public and prevent it from incurring any harm or damage. This type of legislation relates to matters that have no precedence in the primary sources, or when primary sources refer to them generally, but not broaching their specific circumstances; *al-ʿurf* – the customs practiced by the public that are not prohibited by the primary sources; *al-istiṣḥāb* – the assertion that the prevailing verdict determines all future ones so long as the circumstances remain intact. These secondary sources, which may overrule laws extrapolated from the conventional ones, are used extensively in the revitalization and development of Muslim religious law, in order to modify it to the life circumstances of Muslim minorities.[5]

The Evolution of Islamic Courts and Religious Law

Mujtahidūn, or religious scholars, have developed Muslim religious law over the years by constructing laws based on conventional sources. According to the historical interpretation of Abd al-Karim Zidan,[6] shariʿa evolved differently during two major periods.[7] The first period was marked by the death of the Prophet Muhammad, the "descent" of the Qur'an to the Prophet, and the establishment of the sunna. This period is referred to as *ʿAṣr al-Tashrīʿ*, age of legislation, during which religious laws were crafted from the laws and decrees of the Qur'an and the sunna, and their divine authority stemming directly from God and his Prophet. Thus, the Qur'an and the sunna are the two primary and supreme sources of Muslim religious law; they can only be contradicted or deviated from in instances of *ḍarūra* (necessity) or *ḥājiya* (need).[8]

[5] Abd al-Karim Zidan, *Madkhal li-Dirasat al-Shariʿa al-Islamiyya* (Beirut: 16th edition, 1999), 55.

[6] Born in Iraq in 1917, he served as the Muslim Brotherhood's general secretary in Iraq, and is considered a leading Muslim religious scholar and an authority on the principles of Islamic jurisprudence (*uṣūl al-fiqh*).

[7] Researcher Wael Hallaq (1997) delineates the evolvement of Muslim law in a different manner. Nevertheless, since this research delves into the *fiqh al-aqalliyyāt* doctrine vis-à-vis Muslim religious law, I chose to focus on Zidan's delineation, which is widely accepted by various Islamic factions, in order to be able to ascertain its position and religious legitimacy from the point of view of those factions.

[8] Zidan, *Madkhal li-Dirasat al-Shariʿa al-Islamiyya*, 41.

The second period, spanning from the death of the Prophet until contemporary times, highlighted the evolution of the shariʿa through the *ijtihād* of authorized religious scholars based on explicit evidence from the Qur'an and the sunna. As mentioned, this creation is called *fiqh*, the science of law, and thus the second period is referred to as *ʿAṣr al-Fiqh fi al-Shariʿa*, the age of the science of religious law.[9]

Religious law in the latter period drew on four different sources:[10]

1. Laws originating from scriptures that are part and parcel of the Qur'an and the sunna and whose interpretation is beyond dispute;
2. Laws originating from scriptures that may or may not belong to the Qur'an and the sunna and are open to interpretation;
3. Laws originating from consensus among religious scholars (*ijmāʿ*) of a given moment in time;
4. Laws that do not have a written origin and were not ordained by the concord of religious scholars, but they were constructed from the *ijtihād* of religious scholars.

The laws originating in the scriptures of the Qur'an or the sunna and whose interpretation is beyond dispute are not eligible for *ijtihād*, and therefore should be unequivocally accepted and adhered to, regardless of the place and time. On the contrary, the rest of the aforementioned sources are eligible for *ijtihād* by authorized religious scholars if the matter in question is outside the scope of unanimous consensus.[11] The *ijtihād* has to be performed based on the following: the regulations and elements rooted in an understanding of the Arabic language and its governing principles; a deep knowledge of Muslim religious law and its origins; the comprehension of the significance and consequences of its origins; the command of written texts, their stature, and the objectives that are seminal to shariʿa law. This science, eventually termed *uṣūl al-fiqh*, or the principles of jurisprudence, is of utmost importance to the *mujtahid* (religious scholar) because it allows him to construct a ruling in the correct manner according to the shariʿa sources.

Modern scholars consider al-Shafiʿi as the founder of the legal doctrine *uṣūl al-fiqh*, as he was the first to write that it represents an independent skill required of every scholar when constructing new laws. Also, his book *Al-Risala* is regarded as the only work that delves into this subject. In fact, his theory is a synthesis of rationality and textual tradition, constituting

[9] Ibid., 183–4.
[10] Ibid., 230–1.
[11] Ibid., 231.

the initial attempt to exercise human logic within Muslim religious law and to position the Holy Scriptures as the pillars of Muslim law.

Traditional scholars (traditionalists) rejected *qiyās* (analogical reasoning) while the rational scholars (rationalists) hesitated to embrace al-Shafiʿi's theory. It was only in the 9th century that the two movements were integrated and *uṣūl al-fiqh* became the platform for *ijtihād*. The reconciliation between the rationalist and the traditionalist movements became apparent only due to al-Qadi abu Shurayh, recognized as al-Shafiʿi's successor. Shurayh created a bank of knowledge on rationality and tradition. Formulating a legal theory that is a synthesis of rationality and the textual tradition and thusly paving the way for his students to further promote and interpret that synthesis. During that period, the science flourished as a result of religious scholars such as al-Sayrafi and al-Qaffal, the emerging pertinence of the synthesis, and interpretations of al-Shafiʿi's *Al-Risala* that began to be published.[12]

The period following the death of the Prophet Muhammad, *ʿAṣr al-fiqh fi al-shariʿa* (the age of the science of religious law) is divided into four sub-periods:[13]

1. **ʿAṣr Ta'sīs al-Fiqh**– the age of the institution of the science of religious law, or the era of the "rightly-guided" Caliphs and the Umayyad state in the 7th and 8th centuries.
2. **ʿAṣr al-Nahḍa al-Fiqhiyya** – the age of revival of the science of religious law was also an incubator for various schools of thought and the codification of the hadith and the *fiqh*. The period is delineated by the establishment of the Abbasid state and the fall of Baghdad, the capitol of the Islamic empire in 1258, which symbolized the defeat of the Islamic state and the consequent marginalization of Islamic culture.
3. **ʿAṣr al-Taqlīd** – age of imitation, spanning from the fall of Baghdad until the late 18th century.
4. **ʿAṣr al-Yaqaẓa al-Fiqhiyya** – age of rejuvenation of jurisprudence lasting from the end of the 18th century until the modern era. During that period, movements aiming to reform religious laws were erected and the gates of *ijtihād* were reopened.

During the age of revival of the religious law science that commenced after the death of the Prophet, the *ṣaḥāba* substantially and comprehensively developed Muslim religious law. Initiated by the *ṣaḥāba*[14] and led by the

[12] W.B. Hallaq, *A History of Islamic Legal Theories* (Cambridge: Cambridge University Press, 1997), 30.

[13] Al-Qatan, *Tarikh al-Tashriʿ al-Islami*, 23–4.

[14] The term *ṣaḥābī* refers to every person who associated with the Prophet Muhammad and died a Muslim.

four Caliphs that succeeded the Prophet – Abu Bakr, ʿUmr ibn al-Khattab, ʿUthman ibn ʿAffan, ʿAli ibn abi Talib, and others – these scholars were well-versed in the Qur'an and its interpretation, and in the customs, humility, and sunna of the Prophet. The first rift in Islamic religious law also occurred during this period, driven by a political clash over leadership of the Islamic nation that later adopted religious-ethnic characteristics. Transpiring under the reign of Caliph ʿAli ibn Abi Talib when Muʿawiya ibn Abi Sufyan claimed his right to the throne, the two leaders agreed to resolve the dispute in arbitration rather than in war. Two arbitrators from each camp agreed to depose their respective leaders; while Abu Musa al-Ashʿari deposed of Ali, when it came time for Amru ibn al-ʿAas to do the same, he left Muʿawiya in power. Since then, Islam has been divided into three political factions that later on became religious factions: (1) *Jumhūr*, the general public (the sunna); (2) the Shiʿa, supporters of Ali who believe that his descendants are the true Caliphs and leaders of the Ummah; and (3) the *Khawārij*, those who opposed Ali and Muʿawiya alike.[15]

Unlike the *Jumhūr*, the assembly of all previous religious scholars, the *Khawārij fiqh* was characterized by meticulous conduct and the belief that the devotion of the Muslim is manifested in his behavior. At that time, extreme factions of the *Khawārij* developed, declaring that the Qur'an was the sole source of religious law and venturing to revoke the Prophet's sunna, because it is null and contradicts the decrees and instructions originating from the Qur'an.[16] On the other hand, the Shiʿites interpret the Qur'an in accordance with the perceptions of the Imams and Shiʿite religious scholars. In addition, they do not accept consensus of the scholars nor analogical reasoning (*qiyās*) as sources of religious law. According to their beliefs, religion does not derive from opinion, but rather from God, His messenger, and the Shiʿite Imams, the latter two of which are infallible due to the former (*al-Maʿṣūmūn*).[17]

Simultaneous to the rise of Abbasid rule, the *Khawārij* sect abated and currently is virtually non-existent.[18] At this moment in time, the Shiʿites represent about thirteen percent of the world's Muslim population and reside mainly in Iran, southeast Iraq, Azerbaijan, and southern Lebanon.[19] This research focuses on the Sunni world, which constitutes the majority

[15] Al-Qatan, *Tarikh al-Tashriʿ al-Islami*, 188.

[16] Ibid., 268.

[17] Ibid., 272.

[18] Ibid., 264.

[19] Pew Research Center, *The Future of the Global Muslim Population: Projections for 2010–2030* (The Pew Forum on Religion & Public Life, January 2011), 16. http://www.pewforum.org/The-Future-of-the-Global-Muslim-Population.aspx

of the Muslim world and differs from the Shiʿite faction on obligatory shariʿa laws and how the religious laws are constructed.

The Qurʾan, the sunna and the *ṣaḥāba* tradition of the first period, following the death of the Prophet, represented a fertile ground for religious law to grow and flourish, as numerous prominent religious scholars contributed to it during the second period – the age of revival of the *fiqh*. From the 8th century through the middle of the 10th century, the majority of these religious scholars were affiliated with one of the following four schools named after their founding father: the *Ḥanafī* School, the *Mālikī* School, the *Shāfiʿī* School, and the *Ḥanbalī* School. Some of the religious rulings were made by certain members of the *ṣaḥāba* and other religious scholars not belonging to one of these schools, and therefore might have been neglected and remained undeveloped.

During the aforementioned period, ideological movements began to propagate, vying over how Islam should be accepted and recognized and, in particular, over whether it should be accepted as it is written and followed blindly. These movements included *Madrasat Ahl al-Hadith wa-l-Athar*, the school of the people of the hadith and tradition, and the *Muʿtazila* movement, which believed that common sense and logic should be utilized in the acknowledgment and acceptance of the Islamic religion. The disparity between the two schools persevered until the Abbasid Caliph al-Mutawakil arbitrated it.[20]

During the third period, the age of imitation from the Mongol conquest of Baghdad in 1258 until the late 18th century, no significant advancements were achieved in Muslim religious law. The majority of scholars opted to imitate the predecessors from their respective schools, while only a handful chose a different path and called for a complete *ijtihād* from the primary sources that was independent of any school. Among these scholars were ibn Taymiyya[21] and his students Ibn al-Qayyim,[22] al-Imam al-Shatibi,[23] and al-Shawkani.[24]

20 *Siyāsāt al-salafiyya al-iḥyāʾiyya al-jadīda* (checked on May 19, 2011) http://www.alghad.com/?news=152823

21 Syrian religious scholar (1263–1328), among the most prominent religious scholars in the Middle Ages, referred to as "Shaykh al-Islam."

22 Syrian religious scholar (1292–1349), regarded as one of the greatest rejuvenators of Muslim religious law in the Middle Ages.

23 Religious scholar from Andalusia, Spain, renowned for establishing religious ruling according to the objectives of shariʿa (*maqāṣid al-shariʿa*).

24 Among the greatest Yemenite scholars (1759–1834), author of *Nayl al-Awtar fi al-Hadith* and *Fath al-Qadir fi al-Tafsir*.

Researchers dissent regarding the closure of the gates of *ijtihād* during that period. According to Joseph Schacht, religious adjudicators were allowed to rule based on direct personal study of the Holy Scriptures through the 10th century; yet after that time this practice was forbidden and they sufficed with basing their rulings on their predecessors, hence the age of imitation (*taqlīd*).[25] On the other hand, Wael Hallaq maintains that religious scholars were not unanimous about the closure of the gates of *ijtihād*, and that if such a closure did occur, it transpired in the 16th century (after the time of al-Suyyuti). This closure was not a mere rule of thumb, rather was instituted by the scholars themselves as they felt that there was no longer a religious scholar of such revere equipped to perform a complete *ijtihād* from the primary sources.[26]

Hallaq further argues that even after the 10th century, Muslim religious law continued to progress because scholars worked with the rulings and theories of their predecessors through the *tarjīḥ*, or favoring one decree over the other within the same school, and the *tasḥīḥ*, or the alignment of religious law. They based their arguments on the same religious principles utilized by their predecessors, on reasoning drawn from the pillars of religious law, *uṣūl al-fiqh*, and on the authenticity of the tradition and hadith of the Prophet. In the 11th century, Hallaq continues, religious scholars grappled with numerous legal issues, thus paving the way for an accurate religious interpretation of the subject matters pertaining to religious law. Furthermore, the surge of studies in this field has bred creative and ingenious legal theories such as aṣūliyyāt, which vastly influenced the development of *uṣūl al-fiqh*.[27]

During that period, a religious methodology was initiated that determined the strength of a text according to the degree of lingual clarity and the quality of their transfer from generation to generation. According to this methodology, the adjudicator would first examine the text for lingual classification and source verification and then provide his final interpretation and legal decree. Finally, the decree would be verified based on the *ijmāʿ* of similar cases, in order to ascertain whether those solutions are suitable to the new case brought before him.[28]

The works of ibn Taymiyya and al-Shatibi had far-reaching implications on the development of religious law. Ibn Taymiyya initiated a renewed

[25] This paragraph and comments rely on S. Fishman, "Ideological Islam in the United States: 'Ijtihad' in the thought of Dr. Taha Jabir al-Alwani," *Jamaa* 11 (2003): 13-end.

[26] Hallaq, *A History of Islamic Legal Theories*, 35.

[27] Ibid.

[28] Ibid.

examination of religious law that return to the ways of *al-salaf aṣ-ṣāliḥ*, an epithet for the ṣaḥāba, or the companions of the Prophet and the religious scholars that preceded them from the 10th century. He purified Muslim religious law from traces of *bidʿa*, a new creation that deviates from it, and his studies have innovated religious law. Al-Shatibi performed a renewed reading of Muslim religious law, seeking to restore and purify it from extremism through the creation of a new religious methodology called the goals of shariʿa (*maqāṣid al-sharīʿa*).

Coming into fruition in the late 18th century and prompted by Muslim interactions with European countries in the East, particularly after Napoleon's invasion of Egypt, the fourth period is the rejuvenation of *fiqh*, which is also referred to as the modern age. The period highlighted the supremacy of the West resulting from its culture and enlightenment, as opposed to the cultural bankruptcy, backwardness and ignorance demonstrated by Muslims. This cultural chasm has led to a counter reaction in the Muslim world that can be divided into two sections: (1) the liberals, who were proponents of interpreting Islam and religious law in accordance with the changing circumstances and spirit of modern times, without shackling religion and law to tradition; and (2) the *salafis*, who advocated for a return to the approaches of the gilded age of Islam and the pious ancestors (*al-salaf aṣ-ṣāliḥ*), namely the religious laws practiced through the 10th century.[29]

Sunni Muslim Factions in the Modern Age

The Salafi Faction

The *salafi* faction is an Islamic religious faction that seeks to preserve Muslim religious law and the tradition of Islam as forge during the time of the Prophet, the *ṣaḥāba* (his companions), and those who followed in their path (*al-tāʾibīn*) through the 10th century. It represents a purist Sunni approach to Islam that promotes a strict religious methodology with certain similarities to *Wahhabism*, which has ties to the religious establishment in Saudi Arabia. Contemporary *salafis* boast a very demanding interpretation of monotheism that leaves very little room for the absence of faith. In addition, as extremely suspicious toward sources of religious knowledge and influences external to the Holy Scriptures, they maintain

[29] Emmanuel Sivan, *The Clash Within Islam* (Tel Aviv: Am Oved, 2005), 30–1.

a broad definition of *bid'a* (a new creation) that limits the scope of acceptable Muslim religious law.[30]

The *salafis* believe that in the golden days of early Islam, religion could evolve and progress based on resilience and attentiveness to shifting conditions, while also preserving its spirit. In their point of view, Islam had lost this capacity by the end of the third century,[31] thus religious law sources are solely the Qur'an, the sunna of the Prophet, and the *ijmāʿ* of *al-salaf aṣ-ṣāliḥ*.[32] They renounce any new *ijtihād*, unless it derives directly from the Qur'an, the sunna or the *ijmāʿ* of the righteous forefathers. Any innovation constitutes a *bid'a*, or a new creation, and any new creation constitutes a ḍalāla, or a deviation from the path of religion, which will result in eternal damnation. Therefore, religion must be accepted as it developed until the tenth century and common sense should not be utilized in constructing new shariʿa rulings, including the use of analogy (*qiyās*).[33]

In academic research, a dissonance exists regarding the creation and evolution of the *salafi* faction. Henri Lauziere claims that the term salafism has been used in academic research haphazardly due to a lack of acknowledgement of the term's historical authenticity; many research works argue that *salafism* existed in the Middle Ages, even though the evidence of its existence is meager at best. According to Lauziere, *salafiyya* only began to thrive as a concept during the twentieth century, and thus perceptions of *salafiyya* as common to the 'ulama' during the Middle Ages are unsubstantiated. At best, the *salafiyya* served as a solely theological perception. This careless management of secondary sources has also perpetuated the

30 H. Lauzi`ere, "The Construction of Salafiyya: Reconsidering Salafism from the Perspective of Conceptual History," *ijmes* 42 (2010): 369–72.

31 Muhammad 'Imara, "Khamsun 'Am 'ala Istishhad Hasan al-Banna, Mashruʿ Islami li-l-Nahda al-Hadariyya," *Al-Mujtamʿ* 1337(1999): 22; Sivan, *The Clash Within Islam*, 31.

32 Ibn Taymiyya believes that *ijmāʿ* spells the consensus of all living religious scholars on the topic in question, and that anything less would not suffice. Due to the expansion of the Islamic world and the difficulty to obtain the consensus of all religious scholars, Muslim religious law only observed *ijmāʿ* during the period of the *ṣaḥāba*, the Prophet's companions. Thus, any claim of the existence of *ijmāʿ* is nullified if met by opposition. Nevertheless, religious law can be constructed based on *ijmāʿ* in any generation. For further discussion see: Muhammad Abu Zuhra, *Ibn Taymiyya, Hayatuh wa-'Asrutuh-Araw'uh wa-Fiqhuh* (Beirut: Dar al-Fikr al-'Arabi, 1991), 390–2; and Saleh Bin Fawzan, *Sharh al-'Aqida al-Wasatiyya li-Shaykh al-Islam Ahmad bin Taymiyya* (Riyadh: Maktabat Dar al-Islam,1994), 150–70. Contrary to Ibn Taymiyya, Ibn Hazm al-Zahiri and Ibn Habban argue that *ijmāʿ* could only exist during the time of the *ṣaḥāba*. See Ibn Hazm, 506–9. Without a date.

33 Rabee bin Hadi Al-Madkhali, *Sharh Usul al-Sunna li-l-Imam Ahmad bin Hanbal* (Cairo: Dar al-Minhaj, 2007), 5–15.

notion that every age has a different version of the *salafiyya*. Therefore, the academic claim that Jamal ad-Din al-Afghani[34] and Muhammad ʿAbduh[35] created or led a reformist movement advocating enlightened Islamic reform with a slogan of "*salafiyya*" is erroneous, similarly to the modern claim in contemporary Muslim communities that *salafiyya* began as an enlightened reform movement geared toward the progress and revival of Islam.[36]

Lauziere maintains that the research of Louis Massignon was responsible for integrating this fallacy into the academic canon. Through a bookstore and publishing house named "al-Maktaba wa-l-Maṭbaʿa as-Salafiyya" which published the writings of modernistic religious scholars in the early twentieth century, Massignon incorporated the term in the works of a few modernist religious scholars, such as al-Afghani, Muhammad ʿAbduh, and Rashid Rida. Thus, the term *salaf* was coined from the name of the bookstore and publishing house that played a considerable role in the appearance of *salafism* and catapulted the term *salafiyya* to unprecedented acclaim. Through its choices of books and editorial decisions, the store and publishing house have inadvertently determined the bounds of what was considered *salafism*, causing some to believe that the term represented a widespread movement of Islamic modernism, albeit still insufficiently substantiated. The development of the publishing house demonstrates that the commercialization of different inflections of *salafiyya* has fueled the confusion that caused the conceptual infusion of *salafism* and Wahhabism in the early 1920s.

The fall of the Ottoman Empire, the establishment of the French and British mandates in the Middle East and the annulment of the Caliphates rendered the fragility of the Muslim nation abundantly evident. Under these circumstances, influential reformists, among whom was Rashid Rida, turned to religious conservatism and shifted their support to the young Saudi state – paragon of hope for social and political revitalization in the Middle East. Concurrently, the Wahhabi faction, named after its founder Shaykh Muhammad ibn Abd al Wahhab,[37] spread across the Arabian Peninsula. The founders of the aforementioned publishing house

[34] Born in Afghanistan (1838–1897), among the pioneering religious thinkers who called for religious reform in the modern age.

[35] Born in Egypt (1849–1905), the most prominent reformist Muslim religious scholar in the modern age, served as the Mufti of Egypt and the Grand Imam of al-Azhar.

[36] Lauzi`ere, "The Construction of Salafiyya," 369–72.

[37] Islamic theologist (1703–1792), founder of the Wahhabi movement designed to "purify Islam from the superstitions it had contracted since the ninth century."

highly venerated the Wahhabi faction, becoming avid supporters of the Saudi state.[38]

Many in the Wahhabi faction adopted the term *salaf* and aspired to clarify that the roots of the Wahhabi movement ran deeper than its founder Shaykh Muhammad ibn Abd al Wahhab, but rather represented a return to the righteous of path predecessors. By embracing Wahhab's School of thought, they demonstrated their loyalty to the faith, thinking, comprehension and implementation of Islam by the righteous of path. Thus, the term *salaf* became synonymous with the Wahhabi faction, whose proponents believed they alone walked in the footsteps of the righteous of path predecessors.[39]

The Liberal Faction

The Liberal faction is an Islamic faction that proclaimsits loyalty to the founding father of *salafism*, while subscribing to international culture. It accepts Muslim religious tradition and also allows for a modernistic-driven interpretation that relies on human logic. It is not comprised of thinkers who call for the abandonment of the shari'a and the construction of new decrees that defy *uṣūl al-fiqh*, the principles of jurisprudence.

The Liberal faction aspires to promote a social-political and cultural agenda based on human logic and freedom of thought while still conforming to religion. Its supporters believe that in the modern world Islamic tradition should play a diminished role in the guidance of the individual and of society, and therefore, they encourage other manmade cultural products.[40] Their discourse consists of novel notions such as legal equality for women and non-Muslim minorities. Despite their elitist nature and, unlike the Muslim Brotherhood movement, lack of a broad social base, the liberals have influenced intellectual life and cultural agents, such as teachers and journalists.[41] Similar to the *salafi* faction, the Liberal faction also developed in the nineteenth century. Among its founders are thinkers, jurists, writers and religious scholars such as Rifa'a Rafi' al-Tahtawi,[42] Muhammad

[38] Lauzi`ere, "The Construction of Salafiyya," 380–3.

[39] Muhammad Sa'id al-Buti, *Al-Salafiyya Marhala Zamaniyya Mubaraka La Madhhab Islami* (Damascus: Dar al-Fikr, 1998), 231–6.

[40] S. Polka, "Between liberalism and Fundamentalism: The Political Thought of Mainstream Islam (Wasatiyya) in Contemporary Egypt" (PhD Diss., Ramat Gan: Bar Ilan University, 2000), 18–9.

[41] Sivan, *The Clash Within Islam*, 30–1.

[42] Egyptian thinker (1801–1873), considered the leader of enlightened thinking in the modern age.

ʿAbduh[43] and his successor Rashid Rida,[44] Ahmad Lutfi as-Sayid,[45] Taha Hussein,[46] Ali Abd al-Raziq,[47] Muhammad Husayn Haykal,[48] Abd al-Rizaq al-Sanhuri,[49] and later on, Faraj Fuda[50] and Husayn Ahmad Amin.[51]

In his research, Wael Hallaq examined the direction of some of Muhammad ʿAbduh's successors during the twentieth century and identified tendencies that led him to advocate for a change in Islamic religious law, in order to adjust it to the challenges of the period. Based on his research, Hallaq argued that ʿAbduh did not offer a new legal methodology but devised a theology that promotes the rehabilitation of legal notions and their reconstruction. ʿAbduh sought to remain in the main Sunni faction by emphasizing the importance of human logic alongside the revelation.[52] Hallaq further argued that the Liberals ignore the principles set by traditional religious scholars and seek to create a new legal methodology. Simultaneously, he continues, they adopt the rationalist side of ʿAbduh's doctrine, unlike the utilitarians[53] who attempt to extend the

[43] Egyptian scholar (1849–1905), among the greatest innovators in Muslim religious law in the modern age, he called for a reform and revival of the Islamic world.

[44] Religious scholar, born in modern-day Lebanon and lived his life in Egypt, religious scholar, head of al-Azhar in the 1930s, and among the greatest modern reformers.

[45] Egyptian thinker and philosopher (1872–1963), considered to have spearheaded the Egyptian revival and enlightenment movement.

[46] Egyptian writer (1889–1973), among the leaders of the Arab cultural movement in modern times.

[47] Abd al-Raziq (1888–1996), al-Azhar graduate who served as Waqf and Religious Affairs Minister in Egypt. Known for his book, *Al-Islam wa-Usul al-Hukm*, in which he advocated the separation of religion and state.

[48] Prominent Egyptian jurist, author, poet and politician (1888–1956).

[49] Prominent Egyptian jurist (1895–1971), served as Transportation Minister and head of the State's Council under King Farouk. A voice for new civil legislation.

[50] Egyptian thinker and writer (1945–1992), known for his position on separation of religion and state and the establishment of a civil state. Harshly condemned by al-Azhar scholars, he was labeled a heretic and murdered by assassins.

[51] Egyptian thinker, writer and historian (1878–1954), utilized a rationalistic, innovative methodology to write the history of Islam.

[52] Hallaq, *A History of Islamic Legal Theories*, 212–3.

[53] The thinkers situated between the two ends of the spectrum – the traditionalists and the secular – are referred to by Hallaq as Utilitarians. By extending the boundaries of common legal methodology, they successfully merge basic religious values of Islam to create substantive law that meets the needs of transitioning modern society. Guided by the principles of benefit, interest, need and necessity, Utilitarians subject Muslim law to these principles. Among the Utilitarians, Hallaq includes Rashid Rida (born in modern-day Lebanon, resided in Egypt, died in 1935), ʿAbd al-Wahhab Khallaf (born in Egypt, died in 1956), ʿAlal al-Fasi (born in Morocco, died in 1973), and Hassan al-Turabi (born in Sudan). Hallaq demonstrates how these religious scholars, each in their own way, base

boundaries of the existing legal methodology.[54] The Liberals refuse to follow the utilitarians, who they view as subjugating Muslim law to issues of their interest and benefit. Hallaq believes that both factions have a common goal: to reform the jurisprudence in order to generate a harmonious union between the basic religious values of Islam, thus creating a substantive legal system befitting the needs of an ever-changing modern society.[55]

The Liberals include people like Abd al-Raziq who raised the issue of separation of religion and state, and jurist al-Sanhouri who meticulously strived to change laws in Egypt while employing creative thinking and logical reasoning. In this group Hallaq also includes Mohammad Shahrour, a Syrian engineering professor that successfully redrafted a reform in the Muslim legal theory. Among the many reasons he managed to achieve this feat include his ability to make the theory socially accessible, his ingenuity and his intellectual integrity.[56] Liberals such as Mohammad Shahrour and others faced fierce Islamist opposition, which to Hallaq is ironic because those Liberals not only offer a new legal theory, but their theory also conforms to the set of Islamic laws and thought. They strive to analyze the original texts of Islam so that it coincides with the values of humanistic law not necessarily dictated by divine decree.

Contrary to religious scholars who view *ijtihād* as a revelation of god's commands and will, Liberals do not regard *fiqh* writings as ordained by god, but rather as manmade, and as such they can be replaced by more updated laws that are also created by men. Furthermore, they oppose the attempts to extract liberal concepts out of the religious law books of the various schools, instead calling for a comprehensive, modern and progressive perception of religious law.[57] Among Liberal intellectuals there were some who radicalized their opinion and sought to detach the laws from the sources by applying interpretations that coincide with the spirit of the modern age, thus creating a new progressive Islamic law.[58]

their theory on the public interest of Muslims- maṣlaḥa, which they expand and transform into an essential component of judicial methodology and theory, in the process manipulating the guiding principles of Middle Age jurists. The main deficiency in their method, according to Hallaq, is their perception that religious law is subjective and determined by the individual opinion which dictates the public interest. See also, Hallaq, *A History of Islamic Legal Theories*, 215–31.

54 Ibid., 214.

55 Ibid., 213.

56 Ibid.

57 S. Fishman, "The Fiqh al-Aqalliyyat Doctrine in the Writings of Taha Jabir al-Alwani and Yusuf al-Qaradawi" (Master's Thesis, Jerusalem: Hebrew University of Jerusalem, 2006), 16.

58 Ali, 2003.

The Wasaṭī *Faction*

A new faction called *wasaṭī*, or the middle, developed in the last two decades of the twentieth century amidst two aforementioned factions. The founders of the *wasaṭī* faction perceive their main role to be in the *tarshīd* (guidance) of the modern Islamic revival, as they invest intellectual efforts in the formalization of the Islamic option as a cultural alternative, and as a framework for the inception of an Islamic nation. The *wasaṭīyya* relies on the perspectives of Hassan al-Banna (1906–1949), which he had strived to adapt to the challenges of the modern age. The *wasaṭī* faction is led by Islamic intellectuals such as Ahmad Kamal Abu al-Majd (1930–), Muhammad ʿImara (1931–), Fahmi Huwaydi (1936–), and Mohamed Selim el-Awa (1942–). The most famous and prominent among the thinkers and intellectuals of the *wasaṭī* faction is Shaykh Yusuf al-Qaradawi (1926–).[59]

Ahmad Kamal Abu al-Magd drafted a general manifesto of the *wasaṭī* faction in 1991 in a pamphlet entitled "Ruwʾya Islamiyya Muʿasira – Iʿlan mabadiaʾ" ("Modern Islamic Vision – Declaration of Principles).[60] Similar to the *salafi* faction, *wasaṭī* is among the political factions that deem Islam as a religion and a state, thusly supporting perceptions of the Islamists (Islāmiyyūn)such as implications of the shariʿa and *ḥākimiyyat allah* (the sovereignty of god); however, it simultaneously aspires to be perceived as liberal, and so favors compromise with regard to Islamic principles. It considers itself as moderate, truly understanding the intentions of Islam and its primary sources (the Qurʾan and the sunna), and an embodiment of Islamic traits of leniency and compromise. In their opinion, they represent a mediator between the sects that favor rational consideration over the text, and those that give the text precedence over rational consideration. In addition, it attempts to purify Islam of *fiqh* perceptions and terms referring to non-Muslims that have caused Islam great harm in the modern age.[61]

Al-Qaradawi mentioned the *wasaṭī* faction as early as 1960, in his book *al-Halal wa-l-Haram fi al-Islam* (*The Lawful and the Prohibited in Islam*).He did not claim to be forming a new religious faction and did not refer to his work as *wasaṭīyya*. In the preamble to the book al-Qaradawi wrote that the

[59] Dr. Yusuf al-Qaradawi (born in 1926), a religious scholar of Egyptian descent, graduate of al-Azhar. Considered the most prominent religious scholar in the Islamic world, heading many Islamic organizations including the International Union of Muslim Scholars and the ECFR. Residing in Qatar, he regularly appear on "Al-Jazeera."

[60] Polka, "Between liberalism and Fundamentalism," 1.

[61] Ibid., 1A.

majority of modern thinkers in Islam belong to two groups: the Liberals, who are enamored with the charms of Western culture, and co-opt its principles and traditions, steering the interpretation in the latter's direction when they collide with the principles of Islam; and the *salafis*, who entrenched themselves in beliefs that originate in the texts or in ancient religious law literature. Until the 10th century, this group has not budged from these views, and has not endeavored to compare them with other views in order to reconcile the latter with Islamic religious law. The *wasaṭī* approach rejects both of these worldviews and did not tie themselves to a specific school or teachings by an ancient religious scholar. In order to explain the issues at hand and balance the views surrounding them, they acted according to the evidence present within the shari'a and relied on science and modern ideas.[62]

Al-Qaradawi emphasizes the superiority of the *wasaṭīyya* way through the exaggeration (*ifrāṭ*) of the conservatives on the one hand, and the negligence (*tafrīṭ*) of the Liberals on the other. Finally, he presents the middle way, the way of the *wasaṭīyya*, adhering to the true compromise of the gilded path. This logical reasoning echoes the writings of Rashid Rida in *Yusr al-Islam wa-Usul al-Taysir al-ʿAm* (*The Accommodating Spirit of Islam and the Sources of General Jurisprudence*), which makes the distinction between *ḥumāt al-taqlīd* (guardians of the imitation), *duʿāt al-ḥaḍāra al-ʿaṣriyya* (those who call to modernize civilization), and the gilded path represented by *duʿāt al-iṣlāḥ al-Islāmī al-muʿtadilīn* (the moderates who call for Islamic reform).[63]

In his book, *Kalimat fi al-Wasatiyya al-Islamiyya wa-Maʿalimuha* (*Words in the Islamic Mainstream and its Characteristics*), al-Qaradawi details his *wasaṭī* doctrine, which he admits to adopting many years prior. He refers to his preamble to *The Lawful and the Prohibited in Islam* from 1960, where he explicated a methodology that well-represented Islam. He argues that during the time of the Islamic awakening in the 1970's, the *wasaṭī* inclination grew stronger, touting it as the savior of Islam vis-a-vis the devastation and extinction caused by the practices of both the extremists and the lenient. In his book, al-Qaradawi outlines the principles and guidelines for proponents of the *wasaṭīyya* with three clauses. The main clause was a call to integrate factual, ideological, scientific and moral realities and adherence to the Islamic identity. This adherence is extremely

[62] Yusuf al-Qaradawi, *Al-Halal wa-l-Haram fi al-Islam* (Cairo: Maktabat Wahba, 22nd edition, 1997), introduction.

[63] Rida, 1956, 7.

important in light of the existence of Muslim minorities around the world. Hence, adapting the Muslim religion to the needs of these minorities is one of the most essential aspects with which this faction deals.[64] Sagi Polka lists several key characteristics of the *wasaṭīyya* principles:[65]

1. Balance between the notion of *salafiyya*, a return to the origins, and the concept of renewal, or *tajdīd*, based on the hadith and its claim that every one hundred years God sends the Muslim nation a man to renew the religion;
2. An all-encompassing understanding of Islam, *shumūl al-Islām*: Islam is all-encompassing and touches on every aspect of life;
3. Balance between constant aspects in religion, *thawābit*, and the flexible aspects, *mutaghayyirāt*, and a call to avoid exaggeration in religious law, *a'lu*;
4. A distinction between divine law and manmade law;
5. A belief that there is no contradiction between *ʿaql* (rational faculty of the mind and *naql* (the written sources);
6. A gradual implementation of shariʿa;
7. Openness to learn from other schools and religions.

The *salafis* poignantly criticized the *wasaṭīyya*. Hassan Mallat,[66] a *salafi* supporter, wrote in an article[67] that the nation of Islam need not have waited until 2002 to discover it was a "*wasaṭ*" (middle) nation, since God referred to it as such in the Qurʾan.[68] Therefore, those who garner support for the *wasaṭī* faction in fact call to defy the Qurʾan. He claimed that the *wasaṭīyya* supports (*muwālīn*) colonialism and idle and depraved tyrants, and distorts the values of Islam to placate the West. According to Mallet, the Saudi King initiated this faction and also supervised it, in order to defuse the outrage of Muslims reacting to the Palestinian plight, and the realities in Iraq and Lebanon. He ends his article with a call to preserve the values and culture of Islam, and to not relinquish to the permissive and subversive that call themselves *wasaṭīs*.

[64] Yusuf al-Qaradawi, *Kalimat fi al-Wasatiyya* (Kuwait: Al-Markaz Al-ʿAlami li-l-Wasatiyya, 2007).

[65] Polka, "Between liberalism and Fundamentalism," 42–4.

[66] Islamic Syrian researcher affiliated with the *salafi* faction, published numerous books on Islam in the modern age.

[67] Hassan Mallat, "Tayyar al-Wasatiyya," Mokarabat website, 2009 http://www.mokarabat.com/s5938.htm

[68] In Qurʾan verse 143:2.

In this vein, Tariq Abdelhaleem[69] maintains that none of the *wasaṭī* thinkers are eligible to be a *mujtahid, wasaṭīyya* distorts the true understanding of Islam, and the *wasaṭī* faction modifies the permanent foundations of Islam, not the religious matters in question. To Abdelhaleem, it is apparent that Western culture and the personal inclinations of the factions' proponents influenced the innovations; these factors are also erroneous in their perception of the concept of jihad, which they believe should be achieved through persuasion, while fighting is designed for defensive purposes. If that was indeed the case, he ponders, why did the first Caliphs wage war outside the Arabian Peninsula? He further argues that despite the claim that Islam acknowledges other religions, it is still God's religion and the Muslims should strive to unite mankind under its banner. In addition, he also attacks their interpretation on the notions of citizenship and minority rights.[70]

Muʿtaz al-Khatib[71] also wrote an acute and lucid criticism against the *wasaṭīyya* faction, claiming that the argumentations of its thinkers are superficial, ideologically and philosophically ungrounded, and that they do not constitute an established scientific-research discipline. He continues: *wasaṭīyya* supporters assert that it integrates two poles in the *salaf* tradition (the tradition of the predecessors, righteous of path) and the *tajdīd* (innovation), yet the connection it makes between the originality and modernism is superficial and compromising, and their logic is political rather than scientific. Therefore, al-Khatib regards these notions as declaratory and devoid of meaning, arguing that the main achievement of this faction is borrowing notions and principles from Western culture and shrouding them in Islamic garb in a simplistic and unscientific manner.[72]

Despite the harsh *salafi* criticism of it, the *wasaṭīyya* faction enjoys a sympathetic ear both among the general public and Islamic intellectuals and religious scholars. Its leaders and views have become vastly more popular than the *salafis* or the Liberals. This is apparent in blockbuster al-Jazeera programs that more often than not host Shaykh al-Qaradawi or

[69] Islamic researcher of Egyptian descent residing in Canada. Lectures on Muslim shariʿa for the American Open University. Published numerous books on Muslim religious law and theology as well as the periodical "Ummat al-Islam."

[70] Tariq Abdelhaleem, "Al-Wasatiyya al-Muhaditha wa-Athruha al-Dar ʿala Din al-Ama," Mawqʿ al-Maqreze, 2010: http://www.muslm.net/vb/showthread.php?t=411667.

[71] Islamic researcher of Syrian descent residing in Qatar, published numerous books on Islamic thought, and edits religious programming on "Al-Jazeera."

[72] Muʿtaz al-Khatib, "Fi Naqd al-Qawl bi-l-Wasatiyya wa-l-Aʿtidal," Islamonline, without a date: http://www.islamonline.net/servlet/Satellite?c=ArticleA_C&cid=12093gename=Zone-Arabic-MDarik%2FMDALayout 59452088&pa

other *wasaṭī* scholars, and the wide exposure received by internet websites that preach in favor of *wasaṭīyya*. For example, "Islam-online" (islamonline.net), considered one of the most popular Islamic websites, registers more than 80,000 hits daily.[73] Furthermore, many religious institutions and Islamic research centers that promote the *wasaṭī* doctrine have been founded around the world, such as "al-Muntada al-ʿAlami li-l-Wasatiyya" (Al-Wasatiyya International Center of Kuwait).

Alongside the emergence of the *wasaṭīyya* and coinciding with the same principle religious methodology, a doctrine of religious law that aspires to guide Muslim minorities around the world, particularly in the West, gradually developed. *Fiqh al-aqalliyyat*, modified to the *wasaṭī* principles of religious law and methodology, is based on the *maqāṣid al-sharīʿa* (the goals of shariʿa), *ʿālamiyyat al-Islām* (the universality of Islam), and the combination of *ʾaṣāla* and *muʿāṣira* (originality and modernity). Together, they are designed to allow Muslim minorities to honorably subsist and integrate into their new countries while preserving their Islamic identity. Moreover, *fiqh al-aqalliyyat* doctrine dictates that Muslim minorities should serve as a shining example to the general public, in order to bring it closer to Islam.[74] Despite several of the doctrine's thinkers and founders, such as al-ʿAlwani, declaring that they do not belong to the *wasaṭī* faction, the doctrine is an ideological derivative of it and of al-ʿAlwani's religious law doctrine, and is a continuation of the *wasaṭī* methodology.

The Legitimacy of Muslim Resettlement in Non-Muslim Countries

Over the ages, religious scholars have diverged over the question of the treatment of non-Muslim others and their countries. Dissonance also existed over the implications the nature of the country, Muslim or non-Muslim, might have on the decrees and shariʿa laws. For instance, the decree to disseminate the Islamic religion, the law on settling on another man's land, the dynamics of the interactions between people for purposes of commerce or study, the influence of the balance of power between Muslims and non-Muslims over their relationship, to name a few. This issue crucially impacts religious laws for Muslim minorities in non-Muslim countries, *fiqh al-aqalliyyat* and the religious legitimacy of its doctrine.

[73] Data obtained from: http://www.alexa.com/siteinfo/islamonline.net

[74] Fishman, "The Fiqh al-Aqalliyyat Doctrine in the Writings of Taha Jabir al-Alwani and Yusuf al-Qaradawi," 23–8.

Dividing the World: Islamic Country vs. Other Countries

The first religious scholars divided the world into two countries, based on the faith of the residents and the type of rule: the land of Islam, *dār al-Islām* and the land of infidelity, *dār al-Kufr*. A country governed by the laws of Islam is considered an Islamic land, while a country controlled by non-Muslims, in which infidelity is practiced and the laws of Islam cannot be upheld, is a land of disbelief.[75] The land of disbelief was divided by religious scholars into two types: *dār al-ḥarb*, land of war, and *dār al-ʿahd*, land of treaty. A land of war is considered any country that is in a state of war or preparing to wage war on an Islamic country, and does not have a treaty with it or maintains a state of conciliation (*ṣulḥ*). Nonetheless, in a country that has a temporary cessation of hostilities agreement with an Islamic country and both follow the terms of *dār al-ʿahd*,[76] its residents are referred to either as *ahl-al-ʿahd* (men of the treaty), *ahl al-ṣulḥ*, or *ahl al-hudna* (men of the ceasefire). Religious scholars believe that when the terms of the treaty are met, the Islamic country is obligated to fulfill its commitments to that country, as decreed in the Qurʾan verse (7:9).[77]

It is noteworthy to mention that during its inception, Islam regarded a non-Muslim country not as a *dār al-ḥarb*, rather as al-Ḥabasha, or modern-day Ethiopia, which accepted the first migration of Muslims. Therefore, the Prophet commanded believers to avoid violence with Ethiopia as long as it reciprocated the peace, which was eventually interpreted as a decree to recognize Ethiopia's right to exist as a state, despite its Christianity. As a result, Ethiopia became *dār al-ḥiyād*, land of neutrality that lay beyond the bounds of jihad, as long as it does not attack Islam or Muslims.[78] Among the prominent figures in *al-Azhar*, Ahmad al Hafni al-Kiwani published in 1902–3 a comprehensive essay on Ethiopia that was adopted by *al-Azhar* leadership. In it, he claims that the aforementioned

[75] Shams al-DinAl-Sarakhsi, *Kitab al-Mabsut li-l-Surakhsi* (Beirut: Dar al-maʿrifa, 1910), 9, 126–44. For a broader discussion on this point see, TSulaiman Tubuliyak, *Al-Ahkam al-Siyasa li-l-Aqalliyyat al-Muslima fi al-Fiqh al-Islami* (Jordan: Dar al-Nafaʾis, 1997), 1–25.

[76] Al-Sayyid Muhammad Shata al-Dumyati, *Iʿana al-Talibin ʿala Hal al-Faz Fath al-Muʿin li-l-ʿAlama Zayn al-Din al-Malibari* (Beirut: Dar al-Fikr li-l-Tibaʿa wa-l-Nashr wa-l-Tawziʿ, 1997), 3, 206–7.

[77] Ibn Qayyam al-Jawziyya, *Ahkam Ahl al-Dhimma* (Beirut: Dar al-ʿIlm li-l-Malayin, 1983), 2, 476–7.

[78] M. Khadduri, *War and Peace in the Law of Islam* (Baltimore: Johns Hopkins Press, 1955), ch.12.

decree by the Prophet explicates Ethiopia's survival, independence, and freedom from the inception of Islam through modern day.[79]

The approach toward the "other" country has been a controversy among religious scholars through the modern age. In his book, *Fi Fiqh al-Aqalliyyat al-Muslima* (*Muslim Minority Jurisprudence*), al-Qaradawi divides the world into *dār al-Islam*, land of Islam, and *khārij dār al-Islām*, external to the land of Islam. Nevertheless, in the show broadcasted on al-Jazeera *"al-Shariʿa wa-l-Hayat"* ("Religious Law and Life"), al-Qaradawi adopts both modern and original religious scholars' terminology.[80] According to al-Qaradawi, Imam Abu Hanifa divides the world into *dār al-Islām* and *dār al-ḥarb*, the latter of which he perceives as every country that does not belong to the nation of Islam, even if it is not in a state of war with Islam. Contrary to Abu Hanifa, al-Qaradawi states that other religious scholars divide the world into three: *dār al-Islām, dār al-ḥarb* and *dār al-ʿahd* (land of treaty) or *dār al-daʿwa* (land of invitation to the Islamic religion). At times, al-Qaradawi classifies the world into *dār al-daʿwa* and *dār al-ijāba*, the land of acceptance, meaning the countries whose citizens and rulers became Muslims after answering the call of Allah.[81] Al-Qaradawi adds that currently the world can be divided into three lands: lands of Islam, controlled by Muslims; lands of the treaty, lands that have international treaties and conduct diplomatic relations with Islamic states, and therefore do not constitute lands of war; and lands of war, which are in a state of war with Islamic states, such as Israel and Serbia.[82]

Taha Jabir al-ʿAlwani does not accept the dichotomous distinction between the land of Islam and the land of disbelief. He renounces the mere use of territorial terminology and argues that the Qurʾan does not include the basis for any such division and terms, and that in the modern age these concepts are inapplicable to international relations.[83] In his opinion, this terminology is noxious and limits the horizons of the Islamic mission around the world.[84] He maintains that Islam does not have geographical borders and a land of Islam constitutes every land in which Muslims can safely uphold the religious decrees, even if the majority of the population is not Muslim. Therefore, the land of disbelief is every land where

[79] Ahmad Hanafi al-Qinawi, *Al-Jawahir al-Hasan fi Tarikh al-Habshan* (Cairo: 1902–3), 13–14.
[80] Minutes of the show are found on Qaradawi's website: http://www.qaradawi.net/new
[81] Qaradawi, *Fi Fiqh al-Aqalliyyat al-Muslima*, 16–17.
[82] Minutes of the show are found on Qaradawi's website: http://www.qaradawi.net/new
[83] Taha Jabir al-ʿAlwani, "Mudkhal Ila Fiqh al-Aqalliyat (long)," *Majallat al-ʿIlmiyya li-l-Majlis al-Urubi li-l-Iftaʾ li-l-Buhuth* 4–5 (June, 2004): 19–21.
[84] Ibid., 47.

a Muslim cannot safely practice his religion, even if he lives amongst a Muslim majority.[85]

As previously mentioned, al-ʿAlwani rejects this dichotomous division, yet accepts the alternative division presented by Imam Fakhr al-Din al-Razi[86] in the "great commentary"[87] by Qaffal al-Shashi.[88] In his interpretation of the Qur'an verse 110:3 that Muslims should "decree the good and deny the obscene," al-ʿAlwani refers to the term *ammat al-daʿwa* (the nation of the invitation to Islam). According to this approach, the world is divided between *dār al-daʿwa*, the land whose citizens are not Muslim and should be invited to the religion of Islam, and *dār al-ijāba*, the land of acceptance, whose citizens became Muslim.[89] Al-ʿAlwani substantiates this division in the classical Muslim literature,[90] which he believes coincides with the Qur'an's view of geography that all the land is god's, and every land is the land of Islam, whether now or in the future, and the citizens of each country are either Muslim or people that should be approached so it assumes the religion of Islam.[91]

Tariq Ramadan[92] calls to reconsider the predecessors' classification of *dār al-Islām, dār al-ḥarb, and dār al-ʿahd*, since this division, in the current reality, eliminates the religious meaning out of these concepts. Thus, he offers a different division to the land of Isalm, and *dār al-shahāda*, land of testimony, based on the Qur'an verse 143:2.[93] According to the verse, Muslims residing in a non-Muslim country are a testimony, which corresponds with the Islamic theme of serving as an example for the non-Muslims.[94]

85 Ibid., 111.

86 Muslim theologist and philosopher (1148–1209), composed numerous essays on diverse subjects such as: *uṣūl al-fiqh*, theology, interpretation and philosophy.

87 Fakhr al-Din al-Razi. *Al-Tafsir al-Kabir aw Mafatih al-Ghayb* (Beirut: Dar al-Kutub al-ʿIlmiyya, 1990), section 8, 156.

88 Prominent *Shāfiʿī* religious scholar, born in what is known today as Tashkent, Uzbekistan (904–976), composed noteworthy, original religious literature.

89 Al-ʿAlwani, "Mudkhal Ila Fiqh al-Aqalliyat (long)," 112.

90 See example in al-Razi, *Al-Tafsir al-Kabir aw Mafatih al-Ghayb*.

91 Al-ʿAlwani, "Mudkhal Ila Fiqh al-Aqalliyat (long)," 98, 112.

92 Swiss philosopher of Egyptian descent, born in 1962. Completed his studies in al-Azhar, he specializes in the field of Muslim minorities in the West. The grandson of Hassan al-Banna, founder of the Muslim Brotherhood.

93 T. Ramadan, *Western Muslims and the Future of Islam* (Oxford: Oxford University Press, 2004), 73.

94 Interview with Tariq Ramadan, "Islamonline," September 10, 2003, http://site.matariaonline.com/dindetail.asp?id=29

The Legitimacy of Muslim Resettlement in Non-Muslim Countries According to Classical Religious Law

The basic premise in religious law is that a Muslim should settle in the land of Islam in order to fulfill his destiny – worshiping god. Thus, his settlement in a non-Muslim country is allowed only for a motive acknowledged by Muslim law and in condition he is planning on forsaking the non-Muslim country when this motive expires. This law derives from the fact that permanent settlement in a non-Muslim country is prohibited in the absence of an acknowledged reason.[95] Moreover, the classical religious scholars maintain that immigrating to the land of Islam is the obligation of every man in a land of disbelief who converted to Islam and there is fear for his religious practices, so long as he is able to leave that land.[96] This is based on two hadiths by the Prophet Muhammad prohibiting settlement among infidels.[97] A Muslim that does not emigrate under these conditions is in violation of the religious decree and is removed from the congregation of believers.[98]

The aforementioned premise makes the stipulation that a Muslim is allowed to settle in a non-Muslim country only if he can practice the Islamic religious and its decrees without fear that he or his family will be tempted to deviate from them. Only if he is unable to carry the word of god or his religion is in jeopardy he should return to the land of Islam.[99] Nevertheless, the majority of the religious scholars (*Jumhūr*) prefer that the Muslim would emigrate from the land of disbelief even if he is able to practice his religion in public, which is preferable so the land of disbelief does not grow and he will not stray after its customs and influences.[100] However, this conviction by the scholars is altered when the Muslims in question are a group that can defend itself and its religion, and safeguard itself from outside influences. In this case, the group is forbidden to leave that country, and its place of residence becomes land of Islam. If they were to emigrate from it, then it would become a land of war. In such an

95 Al-Kadir, *Min Fiqh al-Aqalliyyat al-Muslima*, 66. He quotes Dr. Al-Zuhayli, an important Syrian religious scholar.

96 Shaykh Imam al-ʿAllama Muwafaq al-Din Abi Muhammad ʿAbdullah ibn Ahmad bin Mahmud bin Qudama et al. (Beirut: Dar al-Kutub al-ʿIlmiyya, without a date), 10, 514–15.

97 Al-Imam Abi Sulayman al-Bist, *Maʿalim al-Sunan wa-huwa Sharh Sunan al-Imam Abi Daud* (Beirut: al-Maktaba al-ʿIlmiyya, 2nd edition, 1981), 2, 272–3.

98 Al-Sarakhsi, *Kitab al-Mabsut li-l-Surakhsi*, 10, 74. See also, supra note 113, 510–4.

99 Bin Muhammad bin Qasim, *Majmuʿ Fatawa Shaykh al-Islam Ahmad ibn Taymiyya* (Saudi Arabia: Majmaʿ al-Malik Fahid li-Tibaʿa al-Mushaf al-Sharif, 2004), 28, 204–5.

100 Al-Sarakhsi, *Kitab al-Mabsut li-l-Surakhsi*, 9, 126–44.

instance, Muslims must fight the non-Muslims or call on them to convert to Islam, if they have the power to do so.[101]

American professor Khaled Abou El Fadl has researched this issue extensively. In an article he published in 1994 dealing with the history of Muslim minorities in territories occupied by Christians,[102] he writes that indeed Islam divides the worlds to two: *dār al-Islām* and *dār al-ḥarb*, this binary division overlooks a far more complex historical reality. Abou El Fadl argues that a meticulous examination of the history of Muslim minorities in *dār al-ḥarb* enables a deeper and clearer understanding of the religious scholars' discourse on the subject. The latter attributed a great importance to the legal and ethic obligations to the shariʿa and to political entity that hosts the Muslim minorities. Indeed, the religious law discourse shows that attempts have been made throughout history to reconcile religion's theoretical demands with the challenges of reality.

Abou El Fadl surveys the historical progression of Muslim settlement in non-Muslim countries, and depicts the discourse between the religious scholars of the different schools and factions. According to El Fadl, the first Muslim immigration to a country with a non-Muslim sovereign was to Habesha, a Christian country, which served as a precedent for immigration out of the need to avoid persecution and disseminate the religion of Islam. It was permitted even though the immigrants settled in a non-Muslim country, in this instance a Christian one, to find a place they will not be persecuted in.[103]

The first four hundred of Islam lacked a systematic discourse on Muslim minorities.[104] In the 12th century large groups of Muslims moved to live under a different role after non-Muslim entities, mainly Crusaders, conquered lands that were part of the nation of Islam. Therefore several hundred years passed until the madhāhib developed their position in this matter, and only after the 12th century did a systematic position begin to formulize.[105]

The most central position in the 12th century came from the *Shāfiʿī* School. Imam al-Mawardi[106] determined that if a Muslim can uphold his

101 Shamsu al-Din al-Ansari, *Nihayat al-Muhtaj ila Sharh al-Minhaj* (Beirut: Dar Ihyaʾ al-Turath al-ʿArabi, 3rd edition, 1992), 8, 78.

102 Abou El Fadl, "Islamic Law and Muslim Minorities: The Juristic Discourse on Muslim Minorities from the Second/Eighth to the Eleventh/Seventeenth Centuries," *Islamic Law and Society* 1/2 (1994): 141–87.

103 Ibid., 143–4.

104 Ibid., 148.

105 Ibid., 142.

106 *Shāfiʿī* religious scholar, died in 1058.

religious practices in an infidel country, the place will be considered *dār al-Islām*, with the hope that other inhabitants will follow suit and convert to Islam. Ibn Hazm al-Zahiri,[107] did not look favorably on Muslims entering a region where shariʿa did not reign. al-Sarakhsi[108] of the *Ḥanafī* School prohibited Muslim from immigrating to non-Muslim countries and procreate there. In the 12th century the *Malaki* position was that a Muslim can reside temporarily in such a place so long as his safety is secured, and if there is hope that he will persevere against the infidels.[109]

It would seem that in the beginning, the various scholars, when voicing their position on the issue, first referred to different situations and scenarios. In this sense, it is noteworthy to mention Ibn Rushd's (the grandfather)[110] response to the Christian conquer of the Iberian Peninsula. Ibn Rushd published a fatwa quoting Malik Ibn Anas, and determining that a Muslim is absolutely forbidden to enter or live in *dār al-ḥarb*, including or purposes of commerce. Commerce with a land of disbelief is only allowed when a non-Muslim comes to *dār al-Islām*. In case Muslims break this law, their credibility is questioned, and the Muslim court would not accept their testimony. Another *Malaki* scholar, al-Mazari[111] argued that these Muslims do not lose their credibility and in terms of practicality, Muslim communities under foreign rule still must have qādis to officiate in inner disputes. The fact that the qādis are nominated by a foreign power is regretful, yet nonetheless essential.[112]

12th century Shiʿite and *Shāfiʿī* scholars maintained that Muslims are allowed to reside in regions under foreign rule, albeit obligated to emigrate from them in case of fear of losing their religion. There are some religions scholars who deviated from the dichotomous division into *dār al-Islām* and *dār al-ḥarb*. *Al-Muʿtazila*, *al-Zaydiyya* and *Khawārij*, developed doctrines that demanded immigration even from Muslim countries that went under a foreign rule.[113] In the 13th century, following the great conquests by the Mongols, the Crusaders and the Spanish in West, the situation for the Muslim minorities under foreign role became direr. Among the various newfound dilemmas, *Fiqh* scholars

[107] Andalusian religious scholar (994–1064), considered among the greatest Muslim religious scholars.

[108] *Ḥanafī* religious scholar, died in 1090.

[109] Fadl, "Islamic Law and Muslim Minorities," 149.

[110] Andalusian religious scholar (1126–1198).

[111] *Mālikī* religious scholar, resided in Sicily (1061–1141).

[112] Fadl, "Islamic Law and Muslim Minorities," 150–1.

[113] Ibid., 152.

discussed whether foreigners, who converted to Islam while living in a non-Muslim territory, should immigrate to *dār al-Islām*. Abou elFadl believes that they were reserved with regard to immigration, and did not issue a sweeping demand to do so.[114] The historical developments and the discourse between the various religious scholars originated the formulation of established religious standpoints, particularly from the 12th century onward. The *Mālikī* School rejects settling in a non-Muslim territory since the prevailing law there is not a shari'a one. This approach is manifested in two religious decrees by al-Wansharisi.[115] To him, the official bond with Islam is of a supreme moral value that trounces any emotional argument or self-serviceable justification. He further rejects the differentiation between a conquered territory that was once controlled by Muslims, and a territory that was never ruled by them.[116] In another *fatwa* it is argued that a Christian sovereign known for its wickedness can never be trusted, and thus life under its yoke would lead to assimilation and the obliteration of Islamic characteristics.[117]

The *Mālikī* School, highly influential in Andalusia and Sicily, reached conclusions that were based on its experiences with such situations. Al-'Adawi,[118] as well as Al-Sawi,[119] permitted immigration only in case the Muslim had to comply with the laws of the infidels. Nevertheless, it seems that there are certain approaches within the *Mālikī* School, substantiated by other *Mālikī* religious decrees, guiding Muslims how to keep their religion covertly while under foreign rule.[120] Other schools would not automatically assume that a Muslim cannot uphold his religion when he lives in a territory under foreign rule, and therefore believe it should be decided on a case to case basis. The *Ḥanbalī* and *Ja'farī* Schools claimed that so long as a Muslim can live securely without a fear for his religion he is under no obligation to emigrate. According to Bernard Lewis, *fiqh* scholars referred to a situation similar to the "patronage" (*dhimma*), in Islamic states, a community autonomy that comprises of control over personal status and religious affairs. Other scholars, mainly *Ḥanafī*, require the existence of Muslim judges, and even a Muslim governor, in implementing the shari'a.

[114] Ibid., 145.
[115] North African *Mālikī* religious scholar (1430–1510).
[116] Fadl, "Islamic Law and Muslim Minorities," 153.
[117] Ibid., 155.
[118] Egyptian *Mālikī* religious scholar (1715–1786).
[119] Egyptian *Mālikī* religious scholar (1761–1825).
[120] Fadl, "Islamic Law and Muslim Minorities," 156.

Shāfiʿī's and *Ḥanbalīs* stipulate life under foreign rule in the ability to perform *ʿibādāt* – ritual, and not *muʿāmalāt* – civil transactions. Therefore, there is not consent over the degree of religious freedom required to label a place as worthy of Muslim life.[121]

Al-Ramli and other *Shāfiʿī* scholars offer a slightly different approach.[122] In his *fatwa*, he prohibits any Muslim from migrating from a country that is accommodating for leading Muslim life, since the Muslim is a conduit that spreads Islam, and the country is considered *dār al-Islām*.[123] The two aforementioned al-Wansharisi decrees supply a vague definition of *dār al-Islām*. According to the *Ḥanafī* School, which maintains a position of significant legal importance on this topic, a place even under foreign rule can be considered *dār al-Islām*. A conquered Muslim territory will cease to be Muslim only if the following three conditions are met: (1) infidel rules prevail in it; (2) the occupied territory is isolated from *dār al-Islām*; (3) the Muslims and the *dhimmas* do not enjoy the protection of the previous Muslim regime. According to this point of view, territories captured by the Christians and the Mongols are still considered *dār al-Islām* while praying is permitted and they have Muslim qādis. *Shāfiʿī* scholars took another step and determined that occupied territories never become *dār al-kufr* in theory, rather perhaps only in practice. The fatwas and religious decrees encourage emigration out of fear of oppression, yet there is no religious obligation to do so. If the inhabitants feel that they are able to disseminate Islam and enjoy a level of religious autonomy and independence, they are required to stay.[124]

To conclude, the earlier religious scholars presented three approaches to the question of legitimacy of Muslim immigration to non-Muslim countries: (1) The *Ḥanafī* School rejected the permanent settlement of Muslims in non-Muslim territories, while permitting temporary stay for commerce and similar purposes; (2) The *Mālikī* School prohibited Muslims from settling in an area suffering from moral deficiency;[125] (3) The *Shāfiʿī* School examined every case by its merit and permitted Muslim converts outside of the land of Islam to remain in their countries, provided that they are not coerced to renege on their religion.[126]

[121] Ibid., 157.
[122] *Shāfiʿī* religious scholar, died in 1596.
[123] Fadl, "Islamic Law and Muslim Minorities," 153–6.
[124] Ibid., 159.
[125] Ibid., 146.
[126] Ibid., 147.

The Legitimacy of Muslim Resettlement in Contemporary Non-Muslim Countries

Dissent also existed among modern religious scholars on the legitimacy of settlement in non-Muslim countries. Several scholars mainly from the *salafi* faction cite Qur'anic verse 72:8, which dictates that every Muslim who cannot exercise his religion in public, nor safeguard his honor and possessions, is required to emigrate to a country where he is granted those freedoms and securities, they maintain that Muslims should return to Islamic lands to precisely and literally fulfill the decrees and rituals of the Qur'an.[127] Regarding the West as an inhabitable swamp,[128] the *salafi* faction therefore adopted this position, discounting the possibility that the West would convert to Islam.

Nevertheless, some *salafi* scholars believe that presently this position is unfeasible for two reasons: (a) as Islamic countries are not equipped to receive millions of oppressed Muslims from all over the world, it is uncertain whether they would accept them at all;[129] (b) in the modern age, most immigration to the West was motivated by economic-materialistic reasons, while only a handful immigrated due to governmental and dictatorial oppression. Therefore, *salafi* scholars assume the latter will not eagerly return to Islamic countries,[130] and believe that Muslims should work to safeguard their identity, uniqueness, and customs. As the locality of the next Islamic triumph is not yet evident, and could perhaps even occur in Western countries, they are commanded to encourage all of mankind to believe in Islam. In the *Jāhiliyya* period the feeble, scattered and militarily-weak Arab tribes ushered in the victory, and subsequently, the nomadic Turks helped Islam to prevail, reinstated the nation of Islam and expanded it to Europe.[131]

Contrary to the *salafis* and stemming mainly from the moderate *wasaṭī* faction, other modern religious scholars, such as Abdallah bin Bayyah,[132] believe that a Muslim who can perform the religious decrees and rituals in a non-Muslim country does not have to immigrate to the land of Islam.

127 Shaykh ʿAbd al-ʿAziz bin Baz, speech at the sixteenth International Conference of Young Muslims, *Majallat al-Buhuth al-Islamiyya*, no.6, 346.

128 Kamal Kamal ʿAbd al-Hamid Nimr, *Majallat al-Buhuth al-Islamiyya*, no.22, 250.

129 Al-Kadir, *Min Fiqh al-Aqalliyyat al-Muslima*, 69–70.

130 ʿAbd al-Rahmanal-Khaliq, *Awlwiyat al-ʿAmal al-Islami fi al-Gharb*, Kuwait, 1993, 7, http://d1.islamhouse.com/data/ar/ih_books/single5/ar_awlawiat_amal.pdf

131 Ibid., 10.

132 Religious scholar from Mauritania (born. 1935), served as the Minister of Religion and Waqf. A prolific writer on Muslim minorities he resides today in Saudi Arabia.

This claim is justified by the Prophet's hadith that commands one to avoid evil and uphold the decrees wherever one is located. Based on the teachings of the *Shāfiʿī* School, and particularly al-Mawardi, bin Bayyah further argues that a Muslim residing in a non-Muslim country should not abandon it due to the fear that it will be devoid of Islam. Therefore, he believes that in the modern age it is permissible to settle in a non-Muslim country.[133]

Yusuf al-Qaradawi maintains that Muslims are not only allowed to settle in the West, but in fact are obliged to, despite the potential influences of their surroundings on their religious identity. This obligation is derived from the *maṣlaḥa*, or the common good for Muslims and Islam, and the shifting historical and geo-political circumstances. The stark power differentials between the ancient and modern worlds necessitate al-Qaradawi's view; today Western countries hold the power and control the world's policies, economy and culture. Al-Qaradawi also opines that had Muslim's never immigrated to the West Muslims should have created it, in order to protect Muslim residents of these countries and assist Islamic converts that resides there. Moreover, Muslims must spread their religion by resettling in those countries because Islam brings mercy unto the world; had this not been the case, the Islamic religion would never have traversed the Arabian Peninsula.[134]

In a later essay nevertheless, al-Qaradawi determined that the legitimacy of a Muslim settling in a certain country is dependent on its citizens and their perspective on Muslims and Islam. Insofar as a country grants freedoms of rite and religion, no impediment exists against a Muslim to immigrate to that country; however, if the country is hostile toward religion, it is forbidden to immigrate to it, unless it was formerly a Muslim country. In the latter case, one should persevere despite the hardships and adhere to the decrees, without regard to the government's constraints; Qaradawi bases this position on the Muslim immigration to Ethiopia.[135]

Muhammad al-Ghazali[136] maintains that Muslim immigration to non-Muslim countries represents an extraordinary detriment to Islam, although they can serve as a vanguard in proselytizing and as a conduit of Islam to non-Muslim countries. Simultaneously, al-Ghazali hopes that

[133] Abdallah bin Bayyah, "Al-Hadana fi al-Sharʿ," *Al-Majallat al-ʿIlmiyya li-l-Majlis al-Urubi li-l-Ifta' li-l-Buhuth* 8–9 (June 2006): 273–86.

[134] Qaradawi, *Fi Fiqh al-Aqalliyyat al-Muslima*, 33.

[135] Yusuf al-Qaradawi, "Al-Watan wa-l-Muwatana fi Dawʾ al-Usul al-ʿAqadiyya wa-l-Maqasid al-Sharʿiyya," *Al-Majallat al-ʿIlmiyya li-l-Majlis al-Urubi li-l-Ifta'* 12–13 (July 2008): 72–7.

[136] Egyptian religious scholar (1917–1996).

idyllic Muslim communities will be erected on every continent, through which Islam can spread. Nonetheless, every Muslim residing outside the land of Islam should immediately return to it if he senses that his religion and his sons' religion is in jeopardy; failing to do so calls for extrication from the Islamic religion. According to al-Ghazali, the Prophet Muhammad referred to such instances in the hadith that addresses a Muslim who settles among infidels.[137]

Al-ʿAlwani asserts that the relevant issue is not about a Muslim settling in a non-Muslim country because, he argues, all of the land is God's that he bequeathed to certain men. Muslims are commanded to spread Islam in order to liberate themselves from the enslavement of men and to worship God. Concepts such as the "land of Islam," the "land of war" and geographical division are futile as Islam has no boundaries. Any country that guarantees a Muslim's safety is an Islamic country, even if the majority of its inhabitants are non-Muslims. He quotes Imam al-Mawardi, who prefers settling in a land of disbelief where Muslims can publicly uphold the religion over residing in a Muslim country because in the former one can attract people to Islam through direct interactions with them.[138] Tariq Ramadan went further than others in claiming that the Muslims who immigrated to Europe or America have become European-Muslims or American-Muslims, akin to African-Muslims. These Muslims serve as a testimony to the spirit of verse 143:2 in the Qurʾan: a shining example and role model for these countries' population, representing the Islamic model and contributing to the dissemination of Islam.[139]

Dissonance also exists between modern religious scholars and the early scholars even on the issue of permanent settlement in a non-Muslim country. The predecessors believed that it is permitted on the condition that the Muslim will emigrate as soon as the shariʿa-acknowledged reason to settle there in the first place, expires or becomes irrelevant.[140] Alternatively, modern religious scholars do not regard settlement in non-Muslim countries, particularly in the West, as a provisional settlement deriving from unique circumstances, rather as a continuous and prosperous permanent resettlement.[141] They further call for the populating of Islam in the West,

[137] Muhammad al-Ghazali, *Mustaqbil al-Islam Kharij Ardih Kayf Nufakr fih* (Cairo: Dar al-Shuruq, 1997), 78.

[138] Al-ʿAlwani, "Mudkhal Ila Fiqh al-Aqalliyat (long)," 111.

[139] Ramadan, *Western Muslims and the Future of Islam*. See also his interview on "Islamonline," September 10, 2003, http://site.matariaonline.com/dindetail.asp?id=29

[140] Al-Kadir, *Min Fiqh al-Aqalliyyat al-Muslima*.

[141] Al-ʿAlwani, "Mudkhal Ila Fiqh al-Aqalliyat (long)," 116.

tawṭīn al-Islām fī al-gharb, arguing that Muslims in the West should disengage from the nations of Islam's circle of influence.[142] Religious scholars from al-Azhar[143] and the ECFR have issued two decisive modern religious decrees about the issue,[144] according to which, a Muslim can settle in a non-Muslim country as long as he maintains freedoms or practicing rituals and religion.

The Contemporary Relevance of the Discourse and Legitimacy of Muslim Settlement in Non-Muslim Countries

It is an irreversible contemporary reality that Muslim minority communities exist in non-Muslim countries. As a result, discussions of the religious legitimacy of such communities have lost all relevance. Any call by religious scholars for Muslims to leave their respective countries for the land of Islam would be ineffectual for the very same reasons these communities were formed in the first place. Indigenous Muslim minorities whose country was once part of the Muslim nation, but whose territory was annexed by a non-Muslim country, will not relinquish their homeland and emigrate from it. While those who immigrated to non-Muslim countries for personal or financial progress – e.g. to work, study or seek asylum – will be unlikely to return to their countries of origin because the majority of conditions that motivated them to emigrate will not have changed sufficiently to justify a return to the lands of Islam.

This reality has lured religious scholars from various factions to revisit the discussion on the legitimacy of settling in modern non-Muslim countries, but instead focusing on the behavior required of a Muslim in this context. Scholars are divided on the Muslim's duties in this reality, both in the personal realm and in regards to proselytization. The issue of permitting settlement in non-Muslim countries is pivotal to the *fiqh al-aqalliyyat* research that seeks to regulate the personal life of Muslim minorities in terms of religious law. By sanctioning Muslim settlement in non-Muslim countries, scholars must consider the demands, constraints, and specialized needs created by the public, political, legal and social considerations

142 S. Fishman, "Some Notes on Arabic Terminology as a link between Tariq Ramadan and Shaykh Dr. Taha Jabir al-Alwani, Founder of the Doctrine of 'Muslim Minority Jurisprudence' (*Fiqh al-Aqalliyyat al-Muslima*)," December, 2003, 3, www.e-prism.org/images/tariqfinal291203.doc

143 Jad al-Haq, "Fatwa fi Ba'd Ahkam Tat'alliq bi-l-Aqalliyyat al-Muslima fi Ghayr Diyar al-Muslimin." *Majallat al-Azhar* 6, year 63 (December–January 1991): 618.

144 Decisions and Fatwas issued by the European Council for Fatwa and Research, 2002, 29.

in those countries. Herein lies the need to reexamine religious law so that it adequately addresses these circumstances.

Muslim Assimilation in Non-Muslim Countries

"Minority" is a modern political term coined after the establishment of Europe's nation-states. The usage of this term is based on the constitutional and legal interpretations found in the state and international literature. The common definition follows: "a non-dominant group of people outnumbered by the general population, whose members have ethnic, religious, or lingual characteristics that distinguish them from the rest of the population, and harbor a sense of solidarity, at least from the majority of the population, aimed at preserving their culture, traditions, religion or tongue."[145] Will Kymlicka claims that a group of citizens that share history, community, territory, language and/or religion is entitled to the status of a nation, people or culture. He defines minority groups in cultural terms, asserting that in order to preserve their cultures they should be defined as separate and distinct. A "minority" is most commonly defined according to its position within the state, but it may also be defined by its relation to a vast geographical region, such as a country, or by its relation to a smaller geographic area, such as a settlement.[146]

Citizens voluntarily or involuntarily adopt minority status, depending on the circumstances. Often groups of citizens voluntarily become minorities either due to immigration or consenting to unite with one or more of the nations, people or cultures in a same-state entity. Sometimes a minority position is involuntarily imposed through occupation, settlement (colonialism) and/or other countries' expansionist policies. The main characteristic of the minority group is its lack of agency, or the lack of power to make decisions that impact their own lives. Thus, according to international law, the members of the minority groups are entitled to protection by both the local legal and international systems. A stark discrepancy exists between this sociological-political approach and the philosophy underpinning citizenship in the United States, which is based on the assumptions that a citizen's connection to the state is individual by

[145] F. Capotorti, "Minorities", in: R. Bernhardt, ed., 8 *Encyclopedia of Public International Law* (1985): 385–95.

[146] W. Kymlicka, *Multicultural Citizenship: A Liberal Theory of Minority Rights* (Oxford: Oxford University Press, 1995), 34–48.

nature and unrelated to religion, race or origin, and that the arrangement of individuals into groups is interest-driven.[147]

Modern religious scholars differ on the definition of "minority." Mainly due to immigration, the assimilation of populations, and the intersection of different cultures, Abdul-Majeed Al-Najjar believes that the term "minority" (*aqalliyya*) embodies political, social and legal significance. Al-Najjar bases his definition on two components: (1) a smaller group vis-à-vis to the majority group; (2) racial, ethnic, religious or cultural differences between the two.[148] British Shaykh Zaki Badawi (deceased, 2006) maintained that the term "minority" indicates a small number in relation to a large number; however, when it is used to describe Muslims in the West, it does not relate to quantity but rather to might or strength.[149] The community that controls legislation, even if smaller in size, is considered the majority by definition, while the converse is also true; a larger community devoid of legislative power is the minority.[150] Tariq Ramadan rejects the usage of "minority" in relation to Muslims because they possess universal and comprehensive Islamic values, which render Muslims perpetually a majority in terms of values. The term "minority" connotes weakness and marginality, which in turn excludes Muslims, and harms their position and that of Islam.[151]

A survey of the positions of various scholars reveals a common definition of a "Muslim minority": "a group of Muslims living outside the lands of Islam, and is unable to compel the society it lives within to abide by shariʿa laws, and therefore is forced to cope with the society's regulations and laws that contradict Muslim religious law."[152] Therefore, in the Islamic perception, "minority" (*aqalliyya*) does not represent only inferiority in numbers but also weakness and the inability to uphold God's decrees and the laws of the shariʿa. Islamic history is rife with examples of a minority

[147] Taha Jabir al-ʿAlwani, "Mudkhal Ila Fiqh al-Aqalliyat (short)." In *Maqasid al-Shariʿa* (Beirut: Dar al-Hadi, 1st edition, 2001), 70–2; Qaradawi, *Fi Fiqh al-Aqalliyyat al-Muslima*, 15.

[148] Abdul-Majeed al-Najjar, "Nahwa Taʾsil Fiqh li-l-Aqalliyyat al-Muslima fi al-Gharb," January 14, 2004, http://www.islam-online.net/Arabic/contemporary/2004/01/article02.shtml

[149] Taha Jabir al-ʿAlwani, *Toward a Fiqh for Minorities: Some Basic Reflections*, with an introduction by Shaykh Zaki Badawi (London & Washington: The International Institute of Islamic Thought, 2003).

[150] Al-ʿAlwani, *Toward a Fiqh for Minorities*, viii.

[151] See interview of Tariq Ramadan in "Islamonline," September 10, 2003, http://site.matariaonline.com/dindetail.asp?id=29

[152] Qaradawi, *Fi Fiqh al-Aqalliyyat al-Muslima*, 30–1.

that overcame the majority, yet a minority that is unable to subjugate society to Islam and to lead the majority to abide by its laws and decrees, necessitates a specialized approach.[153]

International law distinguishes between indigenous and immigrant minorities and the rights to which they are entitled. An indigenous minority, native to the land, may enjoy collective rights, such as the right to self-governance or special representational rights. Nevertheless, international law determines that these collective rights should be applied on a case-by-case basis. When national minorities demand recognition as cultures or peoples, Kymlicka attributes greater significance to permanent collective rights that are inherent to the national minority. Often the best solution for these minority groups is to disconnect themselves from the majority; yet, in other instances, their collective rights can be adjusted through a combination of special representational rights and self-governance.[154]

The Terminology on Immigration and Citizenship

Through a series of political developments and religious wars, secular, democratic nation states replaced Europe's defeated empires. The Peace of Westphalia (1648) ended the religious wars in Europe and signified the rise of the modern nation states. The French Revolution and the American War of Independence marked the establishment of the first two states of the modern era that regarded their citizens as sovereign. These developments formalized the notion of citizenship, or *muwāṭana*, which captivated the hearts and minds of the masses.[155] The notion of citizenship conveys the political and legal relationship between the individual and the state, of which he is a member and to which he belongs. Accompanying this belonging are both obligations toward the state and also rights granted from the state.[156] According to political theory and international law, citizenship is interpreted as binding to all citizens, regardless of nationality, sex or race, because equal rights and obligations stem from sharing a territory and not from a religious belief.[157]

153 ʻAbd al-Kadir, *Min Fiqh al-Aqalliyyat al-Muslima*, 16–22.

154 W. Kymlicka, "Multicultural States and Intercultural Citizens" *Theory and Research in Education* 1/2 (2003): 138–49.

155 E Kedourie, *Nationalism* (London: Hutchinson University Library, 1966), 9–11.

156 Badr al-Dinal-Shashuki, *Al-Mujaz fi al-Qanun al-Dawali al-Khas* (Jedda: Maktab al-Khadmat al-Haditha, 1973), 1, 65.

157 Rached al-Ghannouchi, "Al-Islam wa-l-Muwatana," Al-Jazeera, http://www.aljazeera.net/NR/exeres/81878E28-53C4-4638-9F9B-008B572B7197.htm 2010

The View of Religious Scholars on Muslim Assimilation in Non-Muslim States

The assimilation of Muslims in non-Muslim countries has been profoundly discussed in the doctrines of religious scholars from all factions, with significant dissension and controversy. One of the first scholars to grapple with this idea was Hassan al-Banna; he prohibited Muslims from assimilating into non-Muslim countries, labeling one who has done so a sinner.[158]

Tunisian Rached al-Ghannouchi[159] also believes that despite the values of equality and solidarity that the notion of citizenship entails, a Muslim is required to reject citizenship of a non-Muslim country because *al-muwāṭana* (citizenship) is a secular notion that contradicts the pillars of religion and faith in god and because the benefits associated with citizenship do not justify the concessions on religious matters. For these reasons, al-Ghannushi calls to adhere to Islam and abandon assimilation of Muslims in Western countries that are hostile to Islam.[160] The Saudi Arabian Islamic Fiqh Academy, *Majmaʿ al Fiqh al-Islami*, determined that accepting citizenship from a non-Muslim country implies allegiance to it (*walāʾ*), and willing loyalty to non-Muslims is heresy. Therefore, the Academy's religious scholars argued that accepting such citizenship without coercion is prohibited.[161]

Other modern religious scholars, mainly from the *wasaṭī* faction, developed a pragmatic religious approach toward Muslim assimilation in the West and their transformation into de jure citizens in their respective countries of residence. They favorably view the stature that grants immigrants personal and political rights, through which they attain personal and religious freedoms and improved personal, social and financial conditions. As citizens they can also help other Muslims by influencing the other citizens of the state. Therefore, they claim that a Muslim should become a citizen of the non-Muslim state he has settled in, notwithstanding the

158 Polka, "Constructing Muslim Identity in Western Society: The Rulings (Fatawa) of Shaykh Yusuf Al-Qaradawi for Muslims in the West," in *Muslim Minorities in Non-Muslim Majority Countries: The Islamic Movement in Israel as a Test Case*, Elie Rekhess and Arik Rudnitzky eds. (Tel Aviv: Tel University, and The Konrad Adenauer Program for Jewish-Arab Cooperation, 2011), 51.

159 Islamic politician and intellectual, born in 1941. Member of the International Guidance Bureau of the Muslim Brotherhood, and leader of the Tunisian al-Nahda.

160 Al-Ghannouchi, "Al-Islam wa-l-Muwatana."

161 *Majallat Majmaʿ al-Fiqh al-Islami*, sixteenth conference, 3, 1987, 2, 1152.

consequences that contradict the principles of the religion (i.e. sporadic obstacles in upholding rituals and religious decrees).[162]

The ECFR discussed this topic in 2007 at its seventeenth session. As a result, its journal *al-Majallat al-ʿIlmiyya* published in the twelfth and thirteenth issues in July 2008 researches on assimilation into non-Muslim countries. The most prominent research, al-Qaradawi's "Al-Watan wa-l-Muwatana fi Dawʾ al-Usul al-ʿAqadiyya wa-l-Maqasid al-Sharʿiyya" (Homeland and Citizenship Based on the Foundations of Faith and Objectives of the Shariʿa),[163] addressed the notion of citizenship based on the values of freedom and equality, the privilege to partake in the management of the country, and civil responsibility. To al-Qaradawi, citizenship necessitates equality among citizens in terms of rights and obligations, without exceptions for religion, sex, race, social strata, or ideological stance. He further argues that this notion is not secular nor contradictory to religion, but rather impartial to it. He cites *al-Umma*, the Covenant of the Nation, as a type of constitution to the developing Islamic nation and evidence to Islam's impartiality on the subject; signed by the Prophet Muhammad when he immigrated to the city of al-Medina and established the nation of Islam, the concept of "citizens," *ahl al-dār* (people of the land), has existed in Islam through the covenant since its inception. It grants the Muslim and Jewish citizens of al-Medina responsibility over their respective finances, yet commits them defend the city as a single entity, thus acknowledging two religious groups as part of one political nation. According to al-Qaradawi, for this reason all schools of Islamic thought recognized non-Muslim citizens and considered them citizens of the nation of Islam.[164]

Despite the differences in religion, common citizenship creates camaraderie among all of the state's inhabitants, and necessitates solidarity, love and equality between them. Adversity arises when there is a clash between Islamic and civic requirements; in which case, al-Qaradawi determines that religious affiliation is paramount because unlike citizenship, it has no

162 Al-ʿAlwani, "Mudkhal Ila Fiqh al-Aqalliyat (long)," 83–4.

163 See also Salah al-Din Sultan, "Al-Muwatana fi Ghayr Diyar al-Islam bayn al-Nafin wa-l-Muthabitin," *Al-Majallat al-ʿIlmiyya li-l-Majlis al-Urubi li-l-Iftaʾ* 12–13 (July 2008): 135–72. In this article, Sultan presents the positions for and against the naturalization of Muslims in non-Muslim countries, depicting both sides of the argument. Much like the position of Qaradawi and bin-Bayyah discussed in this chapter, he infers that Muslims are allowed to naturalize in said countries.

164 Qaradawi, "Al-Watan wa-l-Muwatana fi Dawʾ al-Usul al-ʿAqadiyya wa-l-Maqasid al-Sharʿiyya," 34–9.

alternative, as demonstrated by the Prophet Muhammad when he adopted a new citizenship by immigrating from his hometown of Mecca to Medina.

According to the al-Qaradawi interpretation, the prophetic hadith that prohibits co-habitation with non-Muslims is only applicable at times of war or when obtaining citizenship will perpetuate foreign rule over a Muslim country. In other instances, he determines that a Muslim is permitted to become a citizen as it requires him to receive all of the rights that pertain to citizenship and undertake the obligations that it entails. He should be loyal to that state and its citizens, as long as there is no contradiction between the Islamic faith and assimilation in that country.[165]

Abdallah bin Bayyah also reaches the same conclusion after discussing issues of *al-walāʾ*. He defines citizenship as a mutual relationship between an individual and a group that settled in a country whose citizens have not necessarily originated from one founding father, one historical narrative or one religion. This mutual relationship is based on a binding set of laws which determines the rights and obligation of every individual in the group. Belonging to the group is voluntary and all of the individuals are equal regardless of their tenure in the group. In this sense, assimilating into a state through naturalization does not contradict loyalty to religion, which is paramount to all other loyalties. Naturalization does not annul the loyalty to religion, as long as it does not cause the individual to violate the foundations of the Islamic religion.[166]

Following the discussion of these two works, the ECFR reached decision 17/1 (that reiterated decision 16/3) that permits Muslims to naturalize in non-Muslim countries. The decision also communicated that assimilation does not contradict devotion to Islam, and there is no objection to it in terms of the shariʿa because the opposing evidence to this claim does not prohibit a Muslim from naturalizing, or that evidence is based on vague interpretations of hadiths that are not reliable for binding religious decrees.[167]

Andrew March claims that even though Islamic law prohibits loyalty to and alliance (*muwālā*) with a non-Muslim, *wasaṭī* scholars have permitted, based on diverse religious sources and a number of justifications, settlement and assimilation of Muslims in non-Muslim countries.[168] One

165 Ibid., 89.

166 Abdallah Bin Bayyah, "Al-Walaʾ bayn al-Din wa-l-Dawla," *Al-Majallat al-ʿIlmiyya li-l-Majlis al-Urubi li-l-Iftaʾ* 12–13 (July 2008): 101–13.

167 *Al-Majlis al-Urubi li-l-Iftaʾ wa-l-Buhuth*, ECFR ruling 17/1, 2008 *in Al-Majallat al-ʿIlmiyya li-l-Majlis al-Urubi li-l-Iftaʾ* 12–13 (July 2008): 498–9.

168 March, "Sources of Moral Obligation to non-Muslims in the 'Jurisprudence of Muslim Minorities,'' 45.

approach is based on the Qur'an and the hadith, which call to protect people that are not Muslims, and especially the *Kitābiyyūn*, or People of the Book, and treat them according to the laws of justice (*'adāla*) and decency (*qisṭ*). Another approach is rooted in the perception that in actuality a formidable security (*amān*) contract has been signed between the Muslim and the state in which he settled. A third approach is justified by the benefit derived from settling and naturalizing in those countries, which surpasses the damage it incurs. The fourth approach cites the religious imperative to promote the call to Islam (*da'wa*).

Muslim Minorities in Western Countries: Approach to the Public Sphere

The Muslim communities in the West are not cut from the same cloth, as the individuals that comprise them differ in their origin, their level of devoutness, the religious faction they belong to – *salafi*, *wasaṭī* or liberal – and their perception of the public sphere. These differences, alongside their distinctive life circumstances and conditions in various Western countries, have bred numerous diverse approaches toward the public sphere in non-Muslim countries.

Dilwar Hussain found several approaches that prevail in Britain, which may be applicable to Muslims anywhere in the West.[169] Supported by a segment of the Muslim public in the West, one approach calls for isolation from the public sphere. Dilwar Hussain refers to this approach as "working from outside the system" and as the "race for the caliphate;" it is also the approach of Hizb al-Tahrir.[170] Utterly rejecting the democratic system and aspiring to establish a Muslim caliphate, this approach encourages Muslims to pursue the latter goal by strengthening Muslim elements and undermining common Western conventions. A second approach calls Muslims to action via establishing parallel institutions and mechanisms to society's existing ones, and is referred to as "action for alternative institutions." This approach was adopted by Kalim Siddiqi, founder of the "Muslim Institute" in London.[171] In 1989, he called for the establishment

169 H. Dilwar, "Muslim Political Participation in Britain and the 'Europeanisation' of Fiqh," *Die Welt Des Islams*, 44/3 (2004): 387–95.

170 An Islamic party established in Jerusalem in 1953 with branches in various countries. The party calls for the establishment of an Islamic Caliphate and uniting Muslims under the rule of a Muslim caliph.

171 Pakistani thinker who immigrated to London and died in 1996. Published the "*Al-Hilal*" journal for the development of ideology for a global Islamic movement. Maintaining that Islamic sovereignty is worldly and without borders, he refused to acknowledge the modern

of a Muslim Parliament to enable Muslims to debate various high profile topics and formalize policies, while also being accessible to the general Muslim community. A third approach calls for the establishment of a Muslim party. This party participated in the 1989 general elections in Great Britain, yet failed decisively even in Muslim-populated areas due to the lack of credibility in the eyes of the voters, the absence of community involvement in its inception, and its narrow political platform. The failure was also due to the fact that Pakistani and Bangladeshi Muslims do not approve of the involvement of religious figures in politics, in addition to parties that are perceived as too religious. A fourth approach adopts lobbying for the following: the promotion of cooperation and consensus among Muslims and the well-being of the Muslim community, the improved perceptions and acceptance of Muslims among the general population, equal rights for the Muslim community, the removal of all symbols of discrimination from the general population, the encouragement of inner-faith relationships, and the attainment of a fair society. Lately, interest groups have developed on the internet, encouraging Muslim political involvement through activity in the public sphere and contact with the public officials. A fifth approach calls for Muslim participation in local activities within civil society, in order to promote their agenda and familiarize themselves with the non-Muslim population. A sixth approach promotes integration into the general society. Developing since the 1960's, this approach calls for Muslims to integrate into local political establishments, parties, municipalities, civil service and so forth, in order to influence the public sphere from within the system. Many Muslim activists operate within British political parties, but this activity is performed by individuals and not by groups that promote candidates. Some believe that Muslims have immersed well into British political life. Historically, Muslims voted mainly for the Labor party, yet a shift in this tendency has been detected. In the 2010 elections, eight Muslims were elected to the British Parliament out of 650 MPs, compared to four in 2005, two in 2001, and one in 1997. Previously, no Muslim had ever been elected to Parliament. In the House of Lords twenty Muslims serve out of eight hundred members, in addition to Muslim ministers who have served in government.[172]

nation states. In 1989, he initiated the establishment of the Muslim Parliament of Great Britain which he believed held the authority to discuss, decree and act in matters pertaining to Muslims across the lands of Islam.

[172] Amin, Mohammed. Interview by author. London, October 16th, 2011. Amin is a British Muslim of Pakistani descent, graduate of the Faculty of Mathematics at Cambridge University, and a member of the board of the Muslim Council of Britain that was founded in 1997.

Muslim Minorities' Religious Laws

As classical Muslim religious law discussed a state governed by Islam, its religious scholars did not address a situation in which Muslims are the minority, limiting their influence on the lives of those Muslims. Outside the land of Islam, the sovereign dictates the way of living that the minority has to cope with in both their private and the public sphere. Muslim minorities were faced with, and continue to be faced with, an array of pressures and needs foreign to the classical Islamic state. The religious law grappled with three questions on this subject: (1) whether the Muslim living under foreign rule is part of the Muslim nation? (2) if so, does the Muslim nation assure his life and property and therefore, compelled to defend them? (3) if so, by what virtue?[173] In answering the first question, most *fiqh* scholars claim that every Muslim, wherever he may be physically, belongs to one nation – the nation of Islam. The opinions on the second question are divided. The scholars of the *Ḥanafī* School claim that the religious obligation to protect the life and property of Muslims is contingent on the territory. A Muslim residing outside of the land of Islam has the moral right to protection granted by the Muslims of the world, yet it is not mandatory. Therefore, any injury he suffers is immoral, yet the injuring party is not liable for reparations according to Muslim law. The belongings of a Muslim in an occupied territory are considered his by the law of possession, but his lands and non-Muslim family members are not protected under Muslim law, and other Muslims are not obliged to defend them. The *Shāfiʿī* School maintains that a Muslim's belongings, non-Muslim family members and land are treated as his and to be protected, even if he resides outside the land of Islam. The *Zaydī* and *Jaʿfarī* Schools argue that the origin of the protection clause is religious rather than territorial, although it does not apply to non-Muslim family members nor lands outside the land of Islam. Nevertheless, a Muslim injuring another is charged similarly to all other Muslims, even if the offender or the victim reside outside the land of Islam. The *Mālikī* School concurs with the *Ḥanafī* School on the origin of the defense rights of the Muslim; however, Ibn Rushd (the grandson)[174] claims that Malik intended that only a Muslim body, not his property, is protected outside the land of Islam. On the issue of burial, there is disagreement over the protocol for an unidentified body in a non-Muslim territory.[175]

[173] Abu El Fadl, "Islamic Law and Muslim Minorities," 164.
[174] Andalusian *Mālikī* religious scholar (1198–1273).
[175] Fadl, "Islamic Law and Muslim Minorities," 166.

According to al-Shafiʿi, the obligation to adhere to the laws of Islam is not dependent on the religious status of a territory; therefore, Muslims must uphold the laws and decrees of Islam wherever they are located. This view is shared by the majority of religious scholars from the other schools – *Ḥanbalī*, *Mālikī* and *Shāfiʿī*. Nonetheless, the *Shāfiʿī* School maintains that a Muslim can be exempt from performing the laws of Islam if he claims to be ignorant of them from within a non-Muslim territory. On the other hand, the *Ḥanafī* School believes that in the majority of cases it is mandatory for the Muslim to uphold the decrees everywhere; yet, from a legal standpoint, a Muslim who committed a felony outside of *dār-al Islam* is not under the jurisdiction of shariʿa courts. This declaration is important due to the fact that some religious prohibitions do not apply to Muslims living outside the land of Islam. *Ḥanafī* scholars argue that Muslims residing in non-Muslim countries are allowed to collect interest from non-Muslims, trade in non-halal foods, and participate in businesses that are considered prohibited in Islam, as long as they act in accordance with the rules of the territory. They argue this is true because the application of Muslim law is dependent on the land, so territories that are outside the land of Islam are not subjugated to it. These claims are rejected by the other schools; however, even as *fiqh* scholars demand the comprehensive fulfillment of religious life and vast application of the shariʿa everywhere, they accept that under certain circumstances adherence to shariʿa law outside the land of Islam is impossible.[176]

This discussion breeds two questions: (1) what is the commitment of the Muslim to the governing body where he resides? (2) how would a Muslim act if there is no place for him to totally fulfill his Muslim duties and life? The religious scholars assume that a Muslim in a non-Muslim territory is implicitly under an unwritten contract of *amān* (security). According to this agreement, the Muslim's safety is guaranteed in exchange for adherence to the laws and norms of the prevailing political authority, and he cannot unilaterally breach this agreement. The *Shāfiʿī* scholar al-ʿAsqalani[177] decreed that a Muslim residing in a foreign country has to abide by the *amān* and is forbidden from defrauding or cheating the local inhabitants. He further declared that a Muslim that violates this fatwa will be sentenced by a Muslim court outside of his place of residence and will be required to compensate the individual he defrauded or cheated.[178] Classical religious

[176] Ibid., 173.

[177] Religious scholar born in Egypt to a Palestinian family (773–850 according to the *hijri* calendar).

[178] Fadl, "Islamic Law and Muslim Minorities," 15–176.

law does not provide an answer on how to act when the *amān* and state laws do not concur with the shariʿa. One can assume that since settling in non-Muslim territories is permitted, religious scholars were cognizant of the possibility of forging compromises and that any attempt to fully control these populations is destined to fail.

Classical religious scholars' central pillar on the discourse of the applicability of the shariʿa for Muslim minorities is that Muslims residing outside the land of Islam should maintain an isolated identity. Nevertheless, when upholding the laws of Islam is not feasible, shariʿa laws can be modified and religious obligations can be somewhat relaxed if immigration to the land of Islam is not a viable solution.[179] For instance, when common business practices are ridden with corruption, to the degree that negotiations and transactions are only possible through dubious dealings, Muslims are allowed to act in accordance to local customs.

Religious Laws for Muslim Minorities in the Modern Age

In the modern age Muslim minorities have become a permanent reality. Nevertheless, controversy exists among modern religious scholars on the manner in which these minorities should react to their surroundings and living circumstances in the West. Every religious faction purports its own way to cope with the evolving times and the circumstances of Muslim minorities. The *salafis* prohibit immigration to infidel countries in the West, except for pre-defined instances. They believe that Muslims should dissimilate in terms of conduct, dress and society, and should erect their own segregated schools, Islamic cultural centers and mosques. They should learn Arabic as the language of the Qur'an, through which they can maintain their distinctiveness, religion and faith. As the infidel faith negates Islam, Muslims should not consort with the infidels, imitate them, learn from them nor accept anything from them, detaching themselves totally (*al-baraa'*). They are allowed to marry Christian or Jewish women (*kitabiyat*) only according to Muslim religious law.[180] Under no circumstance are they permitted to abide by a sovereign or law that contradicts the shariʿa. They are discouraged from supporting (*muwālā*) or trusting an infidel as only Muslims can be trusted and supported; Muslims should strengthen the bond between themselves (*al-walā'*).

[179] Ibid., 178.

[180] ʿAbd al-Khaliq, *Awlwiyat al-ʿAmal al-Islami fi al-Gharb*, 1993.

Nonetheless, Muslims residing within the lands of Islam should support Muslim minorities in the West and supply them with means to establish their institutions. They must send preachers to the West to teach them the religion, and to assist them in preserving their Muslim identity and structuring their personal and public lives based on the decrees of Islam.

The *salafis* oppose renovating or moderating religious law and accepting local non-Muslim laws in order to obtain the *daʿwa* because it can only be attained through adherence to religious decrees. On the other hand, the *wasaṭī* will alter religious law to realize the *daʿwa*. The *salafis* reject any *ijtihād* designed to renew religious laws and adapt them to the life circumstances of Muslim minorities. They perceive these actions as *bidʿa*, an obscene new creation which is utterly forbidden. The challenge of every Muslim is to observe religious laws and religion to the letter, dissimilate from his surroundings, detach from the general public and withdraw to the company of Muslims solely. Uriya Shavit writes that based on the *salafi* perception of religious law, its scholars developed a doctrine of *fiqh al-aqalliyyāt* that differs from the *wasaṭī fiqh al-aqalliyyāt*.[181]

Muhammad al-Ghazali harshly criticized the religious approach of the *salafis*, claiming it led to the stagnation of the Islamic religion and dealt a crucial blow to the call to Islam in the West. In his essays on Islam in the West, he discussed a necessary alteration in the Islamic, in order to promote the call to Islam; religious law should be distinct from tradition and customs. The foundations of the shariʿa are the Qurʾan and the sunna of the Prophet, so shariʿa laws must be drawn from them. The religious law tradition is not a religiously binding authority and can be changed due to variations in time and place. Moreover, religious laws should be less restrictive in order to attract people to Islam; they should be held accountable to modernity and scientific developments and should not discriminate against woman because in al-Ghazali view, Islam advocates for equality between the sexes. He further believes that grappling with theoretical religious questions is futile, and instead, one should address the contemporary issues that affect Muslims and the call to Islam.[182]

Wasaṭī religious scholars believe that Muslim minorities in non-Muslim countries require *fiqh khāṣ* – a specialized religious law based on an authentic shariʿa *ijtihād* that accounts for their surroundings, modern life, needs and particular circumstances. Contrary to al-Ghazali, they maintain that in comparison to other Muslims, Muslim minorities are disadvantaged

[181] Ibid., 198.
[182] Al-Ghazali, *Mustaqbil al-Islam Kharij Ardih Kayf Nufakr fih*, 78.

due to the pressured surroundings and the various temptations they face. In their opinion, Muslim minorities are unable to subjugate the societies they live in to their religious laws, and so they must adjust to the society's laws and regulations, some of which may contradict Muslim religious law. These perceptions of religious law have bred the doctrine of *fiqh al-aqalliyyāt al-Muslima.*[183]

The Development of *Fiqh al-Aqalliyyāt al-Muslima*

The newfound presence of Muslim communities in non-Muslim countries, particularly in the West, and the emergence of a Muslim religious identity among them have elevated the public discourse around the issue of maintaining a religious Islamic lifestyle under a non-Muslim sovereign and civil state laws to the forefront. These challenges to religious law have been identified and answered by the various religious factions. Yusuf al-Qaradawi and al-ʿAlwani were among the first scholars to directly discuss the difficulties faced by Muslim minorities in non-Muslim countries, coining the term *fiqh al-aqalliyyāt al-Muslima*, religious laws for Muslim minorities (and hereinafter *fiqh al-aqalliyyāt*). Both scholars concurrently developed the doctrine and promoted it as a religious law methodology for Muslim minorities, mainly in the West.

In the preface to his book *Fi Fiqh al-Aqalliyyat al-Muslima*,[184] al-Qaradawi states that, as early as the 1970s, following lectures to audiences of Muslim minorities in the West and East,[185] the organization of "Rabitat al-'Alam al-Islami," (The Muslim World League) located in the city of Jeddah in Saudi Arabia, requested that he write a comprehensive book on the subject. A decade prior to the publication of his book, two conferences organized by the "Union of Islamic Organizations of France" were held in France and hosted several of the scholars intrigued by the subject of Muslim minorities and their lives. The meaningful discussions among the participants led to several religious decrees and important decisions regarding the issues challenging Muslim minorities. To al-Qaradawi's dismay, these conclusions were not published.[186]

To develop the doctrine of religious laws for Muslim minorities, al-Qaradawi gave lectures, wrote books and participated in television

[183] Qaradawi, *Fi Fiqh al-Aqalliyyat al-Muslima*, 30–1.
[184] Ibid., 5.
[185] Ibid., 7.
[186] Ibid., 6.

broadcasts, mainly by Al-Jazeera and the Abu Dhabi TV Network. He also published religious decrees and essays on his website and on "Islamonline," and leverage his position as the head of the ECFR to distribute his doctrine.[187]

In an article by Caeiro and Mahmud al-Saify[188] published as part of a collection of research essays about al-Qaradawi, the authors claim that his work positions him as the central figure on the topic of Muslims in Europe. Furthermore, they claim that after the deaths of Mustafa al-Zarqa,[189] Abu-Ida,[190] and Muhammad al-Ghazali,[191] al-Qaradawi is the most prominent Sunni religious scholar. In their opinion, his widespread presence in Europe, manifested through personal visits, translated publications, religious decrees and television appearances, is indicative that Muslims residing in Europe have a uniform religious authority. Al-Qaradawi is increasingly becoming a household name for European Muslims, particularly due to his pan-European approach that does not focus on any specific country.[192] While the majority of al-Qaradawi's followers are affiliated with the "Muslim Brotherhood," he also appeals to the general Muslim population in Europe.[193]

Contrary to al-Qaradawi's critics, who brand him as the leader of modern fundamentalism and anti-Westernism, Caeiro and al-Saify would argue that he is striving to promote peace between Islam and Europe. They also maintain that *fiqh al-aqalliyyāt* marks the transition of Islamic revival (*al-sahwah al-Islamiyyah*)[194] from a discussion on the identity of the state to focusing on social issues.[195] Al-Qaradawi's book *Al-Halal wa-l-Haram fi al-Islam* (*The Lawful and the Prohibited in Islam*) was first published in 1960 and signifies the beginning of his interest in Muslims in the West. In the third volume of his autobiography, he described a pivotal meeting in Lugano, Switzerland in 1977 with Muslims in the West in which

187 Ibid., 7.

188 A. Caeiro and M. al-Saify, "Qaradawi in Europe, Europe in Qaradawi? The Global Mufti's European Politics," in *Global Mufti: The Phenomenon of Yusuf al-Qaradawi*, ed. Bettina Graf et al. (London: Hurst & Company, 2009), 109–48.

189 Syrian religious scholar (1904–1999).

190 Syrian religious scholar (1917–1997).

191 Caeiro and al-Saify, "Qaradawi in Europe, Europe in Qaradawi?," 113.

192 Ibid., 109.

193 Ibid., 119.

194 A name coined for the popular revival movement in the Muslim world in the early 1970s, promoting a return to Islamic values and identity. Led to the global fortification of the various factions of political Islam, to broad Islamic awakening, and revival of Islamic tradition as a counter culture to the propagation of Western culture into Muslim societies.

195 Caeiro and al-Saify, "Qaradawi in Europe, Europe in Qaradawi?," 111.

he discussed the applicability of shariʿa laws on their lives.[196] In his book, *Awlawiyyat al-Haraka al-Islamiyya fi al-Marhala al-Qadima* (*Priorities of the Islamic Movement in the Coming Phase*), he writes about the need for the public in Islamic states to support Muslim minorities and send them religious authorities.[197]

Their article further argued that although al-Qaradawi does not live in Europe, he frequently visits European Muslim communities and is considerate of their worries, anxieties, condition and situation in life. The ECFR aspires to receive its decisions by general consent, yet those echo al-Qaradawi's positions.[198] According to Caeiro and al-Saify, al-Qaradawi regards the West as *dār al-ʿahd* (land of the treaty),[199] and believes *fiqh al-aqalliyyāt* is comprised of efforts to construct religious laws (*ijtihād*) borne out of necessity (*ḍarūra*), in order to alleviate the upholding of religious decrees (*taysīr*). He opposes assimilation and is a proponent of integration. One should differentiate between integration, which he defines as accepting the laws of the land where the minority resides, and assimilation, accepting the culture of the place. He allows taking mortgages that incur interest and eating meat butchered by Jews and Christians.[200]

Another religious scholar who shaped the doctrine of *fiqh al-aqalliyyāt*, and according to Muhammad Khalid Masud even coined the term *fiqh al-aqalliyyāt*[201] is al-ʿAlwani, head of the "Fiqh Council of North America" (*Al-Majles al-Fiqhi l'America al-Shamaliya*).[202] Al-ʿAlwani's first religious decree on *fiqh al-aqalliyyāt* was published in the *Asharq al-Awsat* newspaper on November 13, 1999. Later, he published his book *Fi Fiqh al-Aqalliyyat al-Muslima*,[203] as well as the essay "*Madkhal ila Fiqh al-Aqalliyyat: Nathrat Th'siasiya*" (Establishing Glances: Introduction to Minority Jurisprudence). The latter was published as a chapter in his 2001 book *Maqasid al-Shariʿa* (*Goals of the Shariʿa*),[204] the same year al-Qaradawi published his book *Fi Fiqh al-Aqalliyyat*. This chapter was

196 Ibid., 174–7.
197 Ibid., 112.
198 Ibid., 114.
199 Ibid., 116.
200 Ibid., 117.
201 Fishman, "The Fiqh al-Aqalliyyat Doctrine in the Writings of Taha Jabir al-Alwani and Yusuf al-Qaradawi," 8.
202 A.F. Masud, "Islamic Law and Muslim Minorities," ISIM Newsletter vol. 11, December 2002, 17, http://www.isim.nl/files/newsl_11.pdf 2002
203 Al-ʿAlwani, *Fi Fiqh al-Aqalliyyat al-Muslima*.
204 Al-ʿAlwani, *Mudkhal Ila Fiqh al-Aqalliyyat* (short).

also published as an independent article on "Islamonline."[205] In this book, however, the discussion will be based on another longer and more comprehensive article with a similar title that was published in June 2004 in *Al-Majallat Al-'Ilmiyya-l-Majlis al-Urubi li-l-Ifta'* by the ECFR.[206]

In his writing, al-ʿAlwani established the doctrine as a new branch of Muslim religious law addressing the adaptation of the shariʿa to Muslim minorities, mainly in the West. Al-ʿAlwani emphasizes that he had envisioned the notion of *fiqh al-aqalliyyāt* well before he immigrated to and settled in the United States. It originated in the interest generated by the "International Conference of Young Muslims," in which the Muslim world converged in Mecca at the Al-Imam Muhammad Ibn Saud Muslim University, which was training Saudi emissaries to the United States. In 1976, the Muslim Students Union commissioned al-ʿAlwani to write an essay on religious law for minorities. Commencing the essay in 1985, he included the paramount questions raised by the Muslim minority communities and presented it to the International Islamic Fiqh Academy (*Mujama' al Fiqh al Duli*), which postponed the discussion of the essay for three years. Claiming that the association provided evasive responses to the delays and at times, did not respond at all, al-ʿAlwani was determined to spearhead an effort to establish religious laws for Muslim minorities.[207]

When consenting to head the "Fiqh Council of North America" in 1986, al-ʿAlwani called upon the member scholars to join hands in the creation of minority jurisprudence. When his call was met with relative silence, al-ʿAlwani began composing essays and lecturing on the subject. By 1993–4, when he established the Graduate School of Islamic and Social Sciences in Herndon, Virginia, the subject of minority religious law became a staple of its core studies and the *madkhal*, introduction to the *fiqh al-aqalliyyāt* doctrine. In an article in *Asharq al-Awsat* titled "Tawtin al-Islam baʿd Istitan al-Muslimin fi al-Gharb" ("Assimilation of Islam after Muslim settlement in the West"), al-ʿAlwani declared his hope that Muslim communities in the West remain untainted by outside influences from Muslim countries. According to al-ʿAlwani, this was seconded by Saudi King Fahd, who wished that inner-Arab feuds would not hinder the praiseworthy endeavors of spreading Islam to the West. Al-ʿAlwani believes that this has promoted *tawṭīn al-daʿwa* (assimilation and acceptance of the call

[205] Al-ʿAlwani, "Nazrat Ta'sisiyya, Mudkhal Ila Fiqh al-Aqalliyyat." http://www.onislam.net/arabic/madarik/politics/89619-2001-02-11%2014-50-15.html

[206] Al-ʿAlwani, "Mudkhal Ila Fiqh al-Aqalliyat (long)."

[207] Ibid., 64.

to Islam) in non-Muslim countries, and that *fiqh al-aqalliyyāt* fulfills an urgent need, due to the importance of building "identity institutions," such as schools and mosques.[208]

The endeavors of al-ʿAlwani and al-Qaradawi are sustained and enriched by the writings of other members of fiqh councils in Europe and the United States, as well as by religious scholars and thinkers, such as Abdallah bin Bayyah, Dr. Ajeel Al-Nashmi,[209] Dr. Abdul-Majeed Al-Najjar,[210] and Dr. Muhammad al-Hawari.[211] These and other shaykhs have continued to develop the doctrine by writing books and publishing religious pronouncements. A useful tool for publication of the latest updates to the doctrine is *Al-Majallat Al-ʿIlmiyya*, the scientific journal of the ECFR.

With regard to the origins of *fiqh al-aqalliyyāt*, Dr. Maher Hathout[212] claims that an Egyptian physician residing in the United States, Doctor Muhsin Fathi was the first to coin the term during debates on the religious tendencies and unique problems of Muslims in the US in 1974. Following the inception of *fiqh al-aqalliyyāt*, Egyptian thinker Fahmi Huwaydi published an article about it in the *Al Ahram* newspaper, which was poignantly criticized by the Saudi religious establishment. Subsequently, the formulation and development of *fiqh al-aqalliyyāt* was halted, only to be revived with vigor several years later, spearheaded by the same Saudi religious establishment.[213]

Researchers are divided over the objective of the development of *fiqh al-aqalliyyāt*. Caeiro believes that the presence and assimilation of Muslim minorities in Europe necessitated recognition of its legitimacy and a reorganization by the religious authorities and adjudicators to accommodate the challenges faced by Muslim minorities. This is based on Caeiro's claim that the doctrine was designed to fulfill the needs of Muslims in

[208] Article published in *Asharq al-Awsat* on January 18, 2000.

[209] Born in Kuwait in 1946, he holds a PhD in Islamic Studies from al-Azhar University, and serves as Dean of the Faculty of Islamic Studies in Kuwait University.

[210] Tunisian religious scholars, born in 1945, holds a PhD in Islamic Studies from al-Azhar University. Among the founders of the al-Nahda movement, and a member of the International Union of Muslim Scholars.

[211] Syrian, born in 1931. Expert member of the International Union of Muslim Scholars, and the Organization of Islamic Cooperation in Jeddah.

[212] Egyptian doctor who resides in the United States, serves as an imam of the South California Islamic center mosque. Author of the book, *In Pursuit of Justice: The Jurisprudence of Human Rights in Islam*, Los Angeles: The Muslim Public Affairs Council, 2006.

[213] The position of Dr. Maher Hathout in response to my question regarding their position on *fiqh al-aqalliyyāt*. The discussion took place at an international meeting with a group of leaders on April 1, 2011, at the Islamic Center in Los Angeles.

Europe, solve their problems and conduct reciprocal relationships with their European surroundings, while taking into account necessities, obligations, life circumstances and living conditions. Contrary to this approach, Shavit and Fishman argue that the purpose of *fiqh al-aqalliyyāt* is to promote the *da'wa*. Shavit claims that the *wasaṭī* approach was designed to allow Muslim minorities in the West a more comfortable life that enables the preservation of their Islamic identity and the support for the Islamization of the West (*al-taysīr fī al-fatwā wa'l-tabshīr fī al-da'wa*).[214] Fishman reaches the same conclusion, (that the development of the doctrine was intended to promote the *da'wa* and the Islamization of the West.) He also argues that the tendency of *fiqh al-aqalliyyāt* scholars to alleviate religious constraints in terms of integration into politics and the army is designed to assist in the dissemination of Islam around the world.[215]

The European Council for Fatwa and Research – Origins and Methodology

Following the progress in religious law for Muslim minorities, the Federation of Islamic Organizations in Europe (FIOE), alongside other Islamic institutions and with the support of the Maktoum Family Fund from Dubai, established the European Council for Fatwa and Research (ECFR). Aspiring to position itself as the utmost religious authority for Muslims in Europe, the ECFR represents a wide array of groups, such as Hindi-Pakistani Muslims from Great Britain or Turks from Germany, although the pre-eminent ethnicity is still Arab.[216] The ECFR has pledged to explore those facets of religious law that pertain to minorities and their shari'a-driven difficulties and needs. In 1999, a conference was held in the United State, in which shari'a scholars discussed the issues that are relevant to Muslim minorities.[217] Through religious decrees, the ECFR seeks to guide Muslims in Europe, to assuage their problems, to ameliorate their living conditions, and to regulate their mutual relationship with European societies, while simultaneously upholding the laws of the shari'a and the objectives of the religion. The council strives for a symbiosis between life in the West and shari'a law, which will assist Muslims in their integration

214 Shavit, "The Wasati and Salafi Approaches to the Religious Law of Muslim Minorities," 416–57.

215 S. Fishman, "Fiqh al-Aqalliyyat: A Legal Theory for Muslim Minorities," *Research Monographs on the Muslim World*, Hudson Institute, Series 1 (Paper no.2, 2006).

216 Caeiro, "The European Council for Fatwa and Research," 6–8.

217 Ibid., 9.

and allow them to develop and prosper. Thus, their private and collective lives will serve as a paragon of Islam – the religion that brought mercy to the world.[218]

The directive for ECFR scholars is the unification of the *fiqh*, dispensing collective decrees designed to solve the problems of the Muslims in Europe. This is achieved through arduous work in publishing research on the shariʿa pertaining to Islam in Europe, and the provision of guidance to the Muslim population and its religious clerics.[219] In fact, the Council is the champion of the *fiqh al-aqalliyyāt* doctrine and its executive branch. It develops and disseminates the doctrine among the general public via the research it commissions and the publication of its decisions and religious decrees.[220]

The founders wanted the Council to become a focal point for questions and petitions from the Muslim population in Europe, as well as a tool for spreading Islam to the West. To achieve these goals, the council chooses religious scholars with stature to enhance public support, relies on credible sources and evidence, utilizes research and materials produced by other organizations, attains recognition by the authorities of European countries in order to become the authority on Muslim minorities, holds courses for religious and *daʿwa* clerics, and organizes seminars on religious law.[221]

Every Muslim with an academic education and ordained in the shariʿa and Arab language by an acknowledged institution of religious studies or an organization publishing writings on religious law that is recognized by the religious scholar community, can become a member of the Council. He must conduct himself appropriately, be up-to-date on current affairs, and approved by the majority of Council members. An elected member will continue to serve without the need for re-election. The members must reside in Europe, albeit some do not reside there.[222] As mentioned, the President of the council is al-Qaradawi, with two vice presidents: one

[218] Abdul-Majeed Al-Najjar, "Takdim," *Majallat al-ʿIlmiyya li-l-Majlis al-Urubi li-l-Iftaʾ li-l-Buhuth* 18 (July 2011): 67–102.

[219] Caeiro, "The European Council for Fatwa and Research," 5.

[220] The visit to the ECFR headquarters on February 12–13, 2012 shows that the council is not an established organization that operates year round. It does not have permanent work teams, organized archives and libraries, and even committees to prepare the annual meeting. It is fully voluntary, including the council's staff and president. The location of the headquarters is determined by its general secretary's place of residence. Thus, following the election of Shaykh Hussein Halawa, the offices moved from London, where former general secretary Abdulla al-Judai resided, to Dublin, where Halawa lives.

[221] *Decisions and Fatwas issued by the European Council for Fatwa and Research*, 6–10.

[222] Ibid., 9.

European, Abdulla al-Judai from the UK,[223] and one outside of Europe, Ali Qaradaghi.[224] The current General Secretary is Hussein Mohammed Halawa.

Questions referred to the council pertain mostly to the issue of *ibadat* (or ritual), such as the times of prayers in the summer and the commencement of Ramadan, but also to *muʿāmalāt* (civil transactions, such as finances, food products, elections and interest on money.) Other questions may include: Can a funeral take place in the West for a person who died in the state of origin? Can a marriage agreement be constructed for a couple who has been married for a significant time not under an Islamic agreement? Is it permissible to collect and hand out zakat? The questions are received via email and regular mail by three regionally affiliated committees in Germany, France and the UK that collect and answer the questions. Questions from formal establishments, such as governments, are referred to the Council for discussion and verdict. They start in the sub-committee of the Council located in the General Secretary's office. The research committee assigns members to research the subject at hand and submit their findings. The research paper is accepted only if it adheres to the scientific standards set by the council. Most of the researches are published as religious decrees by the ECFR, but only by the consent of a majority of the members. Any member is free to adjudicate according to his personal convictions, but not in the name of the council.[225] Halawa explicated that in its earliest stages, the Council only held debates on principles, theology and religion. Only after those were resolved did it move on to current affairs. The council also plans to focus on *fiqh al-mālāt*, considerations of the ramifications of the religious decree on the Muslim public. Independent and not belonging to the ECFR, Islamic centers like the Federation of Muslim Organizations in Europe grapple with public matters rather than with questions of religion and religious laws because the ECFR is considered the religious authority of the federation. For Muslims, the Council has become a religious authority, *marjaʿiyya*, which provides them with religious decrees that take into account their unique circumstances and reality, that are in accordance with the age and the place, *al-ʿaṣr wa-l-maṣr*, and that are based upon *marjaʿiyya Islamiyya taṣḥiyḥiyya*, a true Islamic authority. Halawa emphasizes that the Council decrees only for the

223 British of Iraqi descent, born in 1959, graduate of the Islamic Institute in Basra, Iraq.

224 Born in Kurdistan in Iraq in 1949, holds a PhD from the al-Azhar University, served in various capacities in religious law unions.

225 Halawa, Hussein Mohammed. Interview by author. ECFR offices in Dublin, Ireland, February 12–13, 2012.

circumstances and the everyday reality of Muslims in Europe. By Europe it means both East and West, as every place has its own circumstances to take into consideration. According to him, most Muslims in Europe accept the approach and decrees of the council, including a majority of the Turkish Muslims. Halawa infers that the majority of questions have been referred by non-Arabs since they were written in English rather than in Arabic.

During its initial period, the Council met twice a year; yet four years ago, they began meeting once a year in June. According to Halawa, the change was made so that the members could delve into their research work. Before the meeting, the members receive the topics on the agenda and study former religious decrees by religious law institutions in Mecca, Al-Jahar and Jeddah. However, they do not automatically adopt decrees from the Islamic world, and try to employ a lenient approach. Every member is entitled to voice his opinion in a democratic manner, but achieving consensus is preferable. Driven by a strong desire to spread the religious decrees and educate the Muslim population in the West, the release of every religious decree entails an arduous process of writing and editing.

2

Fiqh al-Aqalliyyāt: Methodology and Implementation in the Field of Personal Standing

The *Fiqh al-Aqalliyyāt* Methodology

Fiqh al-aqalliyyāt originates from the principle of the universality of Islam (*ʿālamiyyat al-Islām*), according to which Islam is an international religion that appeals to all of humanity, universally and across time. Thus, contrary to classic religious law, the doctrine permits and even encourages Muslims to settle and naturalize in non-Muslim countries. Nevertheless, this doctrine is concerned with the fragility of Muslim communities, especially as they exist in relation to non-Muslim majorities, and in comparison to Muslims residing within the lands of Islam. Acknowledging that religious law must adapt to shifting circumstances, *fiqh al-aqalliyyāt* recognizes that the condition of Muslims in the West may preclude adherence to certain decrees and laws of the shariʿa. This is especially relevant with regard to the traditional obligation of Muslims in non-Muslim countries to serve as role models and call upon the majority to join Islam. Therefore, according to *fiqh al-aqalliyyāt*, the circumstances of Muslim minorities have shaped the decrees and laws by which they must abide.[1]

According to Qaradawi, Muslim minorities require specialized religious law that is not a direct corollary of *al-fiqh al-ʿām* (general religious law). Over time, as religious scholars became more familiar with the circumstances of minorities in non-Muslim countries, they began developing specialized law based on general religious law. In the same way that medical law and politics are rooted in classical Muslim religious law, *fiqh al-aqalliyyāt* is a defined branch of religious law designed to address the issues that pertain to the lives of Muslim minorities. Generally speaking, Muslim religious law is unorganized – vague rather than particular, incomplete rather than whole, and adapted to time and place. Thus, Qaradawi argues, the laws of one generation do not necessary address the

[1] Yusuf al-Qaradawi, *Fi Fiqh al-Aqalliyyat al-Muslima: Hayat al-Muslimin Wasat al-Mujtamaʿat al-Akhra* (Cairo: Dar al-Shuruq, 1st ed., 2001), 40–60.

concerns of another, whose reality could not have been imagined by previous generations.[2]

It is impossible for Muslim minorities to subjugate the societies they live in to their own religious laws; within non-Muslim society, Muslims are bound to abide by rules and regulations that, at times, might contradict Muslim religious law.[3] Therefore, *fiqh* scholars believe Muslim minorities living outside of the lands of Islam require specialized religious law (*fiqh khāṣ*), which takes their particular circumstances into consideration while remaining rooted in true shariʿa *ijtihād*. Qaradawi surmises that *fiqh al-aqalliyyāt* originates from general religious law, specifically the Qurʾan, which dictates rules and principles, and the sunna, which contains binding content and legislation. Qaradawi argues that because it includes that word of the Prophet, the leader of the nation of Islam and the messenger of God, the sunna should be interpreted according to the Qurʾan.

Another source for minority religious law is the *ijmāʿ*, the consensus of the religious scholars. Laws originating from the *ijmāʿ* may be modified according to the prevailing conditions and norms of the contemporary period in which they are enacted. Despite the conflicting opinions with regard to its source, *qiyās* (analogy) also assists in formulating these decrees. Additional bases of religious law include secondary sources that do not rely directly on the scriptures, such as *maṣlaḥa*, a ruling in accordance with the public good.[4]

To Qaradawi, *fiqh al-aqalliyyāt* takes into account the tradition of Muslim religious law, while also considering the recognized factions, problems and conditions specific to each generation. It is designed to link the universality of Islam to its lived reality in the realm of the mundane; to establish a balance between the scriptures and the general goals of religious laws; and to preside over the pressing issues of Muslims residing in non-Muslim countries in a way that prioritizes the principles of the religion while still taking into account mitigating circumstances. This is done in order to preserve an Islamic identity – on the level of the individual and of the group – within the surrounding societies.[5]

The basic premise of the religious decrees from which Qaradawi derives his *fiqh al-aqalliyyāt* ruling is very much influenced by the writing of al-Imam al-Ghazali, the approaches of Ibn al-Qayyim al-Jawziyya (the

[2] Ibid., 32.
[3] Ibid., 30–1.
[4] Ibid., 37–9.
[5] Ibid., 35–6.

disciple of Ibn Taymiyyah), and by Imam al-Shatibi, who formulated *fiqh al-maṣlaḥa* and *fiqh al-maqāṣid*. According to *fiqh al-maqāṣid*, shariʿa has five objectives: (1) the preservation of religion; (2) the preservation of the soul; (3) the preservation of mental capacities; (4) the preservation of the lineage; and (5) the preservation of property. Adjudicators must thus fulfill these objectives in their rulings. Rashid Rida also utilized the tool of *maṣlaḥa* for innovation in religious law. Qaradawi, influenced by the writing of al-Ghazali, expanded the application of *maṣlaḥa* to other objectives: preservation of honor; preservation of peace; preservation of rights; and preservation of freedom. These objectives have given birth to the institutionalization of justice, the abolishment of exploitation, the integrity of man, and alleviation of religious decrees and practices in everyday life. Furthermore, they allow a greater margin for individual *ijtihād*. The *wasaṭī* approach encourages integration in, and reciprocal relations with, non-Muslim society, thus advocating for modifications to shariʿa law according to circumstances. Employing this methodology attests to the potential impact of *maṣlaḥa* on shariʿa law.[6]

Qaradawi adopted the more lenient approach toward religious law, *al-taysīr bi-l-fiqh*, which takes into consideration one's context and other extenuating circumstances. In light of the *maṣlaḥa* that represents the five objectives of the shariʿa (*maqāṣid al-sharīʿa*), Qaradawi supports the religious principle that necessity can provide significant grounds to revoke a prohibition (*al-ḍarūrāt tubīḥ al-maḥẓūrāt*).[7] Shariʿa was formulated in order to accomplish the aforementioned objectives through decrees, prohibitions, and permissions. *Al-maṣlaḥa* and *maqāṣid al-sharīʿa* provide the rationale behind the existence of Muslim communities in non-Muslim countries. Taking into account a communities' circumstances and needs, these principles allow for modifications to religious law according to predetermined methodologies, which enable the minorities to continue to prosper in their environment.[8] Qaradawi elaborates upon this religious approach as it is found in the writings of the first religious scholars attempting to promote the interest of Muslims. These early scholars formulated the *maṣlaḥa* through innovative religious interpretation that is

[6] Ibid., 35-6.

[7] S. Polka, "Constructing Muslim Identity in Western Society: The Rulings (Fatawa) of Shaykh Yusuf Al-Qaradawi for Muslims in the West," in *Muslim Minorities in Non-Muslim Majority Countries: The Islamic Movement in Israel as a Test Case*, eds. Elie Rekhess and Arik Rudnitzky (Tel Aviv: Tel Aviv University and The Konrad Adenauer Program for Jewish-Arab Cooperation, 2011), 46–7.

[8] Ibid., 45.

predisposed to consider the unique circumstances of Muslims, rather than promote a strict and inflexibly literal interpretation of the Holy Scriptures. This approach can be found in Caliph ʿUmr ibn al-Khattab's abolishment of the poll tax (*jizya*) for Christians in the Tughlib tribe, replacing it with *ṣadaqa* and zakat (a religious decree to pay two and a half percent annually for any yearly income over a certain amount).[9]

According to Qaradawi, these principles have resulted in *fiqh al-awlawiyāt* (priorities in jurisprudence) and *fiqh al-muwāzanāt* (balance in jurisprudence). Because religious decrees are not uniform in their severity, one decree will necessarily be prioritized over another, in the same way that one religious interpretation or attitude will be preferred over others; these decisions are made with an eye toward the circumstances, needs, and benefits of the Muslim, in order to attain the goals of the shariʿa. To Qaradawi, attaining these goals is paramount to textual interpretation, and *ijtihād* is preferable to imitation of other religious scholars. Moreover, a lenient approach to shariʿa laws is preferable to a strict one; the rights of mankind should be favored over divine rights, and collective rights over private ones.[10] In *fiqh al-muwāzanāt*, Qaradawi seeks to balance the interests (*al-maṣāliḥ*): the certain interest should be promoted over the possible interest; the vast interest over the minute; the group interest over the private; and the vital interest over the marginal. Furthermore, the *fiqh al-muwāzanāt* takes into account the benefits and damages resulting from the actions of a Muslim, as well as differentiating between minor damage and potentially grave damage. Therefore, when there is a conflict of interest or a contradiction between potential damage and the preservation of an interest, acting according to *fiqh al-awlawiyāt* and *fiqh al-muwāzanāt* will minimize the damage and safeguard Muslim interests.[11]

From the aforementioned principles of religious law, Qaradawi has created nine pillars for Muslim minorities' jurisprudence; these seek to address particular predicaments while making accommodations for Muslims living in non-Muslim countries:

1. A modern *ijtihād* showcases the depth and relevance of the shariʿa for any time and place. A portion of the *ijtihād* in particular (*intiqāʾī*) turns to religious tradition in order to extract laws that, under the

[9] Yusuf al-Qaradawi, *Al-Siyasa al-Sharʿiyya fi Dawʾ Nusus al-Shariʿa wa-Maqasidha* (Cairo: Maktabat Wahba, 1998), 216.

[10] Yusuf al-Qaradawi, *Taysir al-Fiqh li-l-Muslim al-Muʿasir fi Dawʾ al-Qurʾan wa-l-Sunna* (Beirut: Muasisatur-Risalah, 2000), 47–end.

[11] Ibid., 425–61.

circumstances, fulfill the goals of the sharīʿa and promote the well-being of the people. For instance, in a non-Muslim country, a woman's conversion to Islam while her husband does not convert does not constitute sufficient grounds to nullify the marriage.[12] The other portion is creative *ijtihād* (*ijtihād inshāʾī*), which, in cases lacking any relevant religious decrees, grapples with innovation and modernity.[13]

2. The *mujtahid* – the religious scholar who constructs a new decree – must study the circumstances and reality of the concerned party in the most objective manner, properly taking each into account.[14]
3. As prescribed by the Qurʾan and practiced by the Prophet and his followers, a lenient approach must be adopted (*al-yusur*),[15] which lightens the burden of religious decrees for the sake of the believer; this lies in contrast to the self-imposed excessive shackling to the Qurʾan and the sunna exhibited by the generations that followed the Prophet.[16]
4. The ruling must acknowledge that Muslim minorities outside the lands of Islam are inherently less powerful than Muslims residing within them, and that their respective life circumstances differ greatly. Therefore, decrees issued for Muslim minorities can deviate from decrees issued in the lands of Islam, as the former should embody alleviation of religious practices and recognition of the customs of those countries (*ʿurf*).[17] Based on the public interest (*maṣlaḥa*) that Muslims should necessarily be able to live in any city in the West, Qaradawi deduces that a Muslim can be buried in a Christian cemetery if a Muslim one is not available in that area.
5. One should acknowledge necessity (*ḍarūra*) and human needs in order to rescind prohibitions on food, drink, clothing, contracts, and debts. The life circumstances of Muslim minorities may make necessary what is otherwise prohibited, and thus it becomes essential to alleviate the burden of observance.[18] For instance, this principle has brought forth permission for a Muslim residing in the West to purchase a house using

[12] Qaradawi, *Fi Fiqh al-Aqalliyyat al-Muslima*, 40.

[13] On the meaning of *ijtihād* see Yusuf al-Qaradawi, *Al-ijtihad fi al-Shariʿa al-Islamiyya Maʿ Nazareth Tahliliyya fi al-ijtihad wa-l-al-Muʿasir* (Cairo: Dar al-Qalam, 1999), 11–3.

[14] Yusuf al-Qaradawi, *Fi Fiqh al-Aqalliyyat al-Muslima: Hayat al-Muslimin Wasat al-Mujtamaʿat al-Akhra* (Cairo: Dar al-Shuruq, 1st ed., 2001), 45.

[15] On the methodology of alleviation (*taysīr*) see Qaradawi, *Taysir al-Fiqh li-l-Muslim al-Muʿasir fi Dawʾ al-Qurʾan wa-l-Sunna* (Cairo: Maktabat Wahba, 1999), 24–37.

[16] Qaradawi, *Fi Fiqh al-Aqalliyyat al-Muslima*, 50.

[17] Ibid., 83–4.

[18] Ibid., 55.

a bank mortgage that incurs interest. The permission was granted because ownership of a house is considered a necessity.

6. One should liberate oneself from the age-old Muslim religious tradition of adhering to a specific school (*al-iltizām al-madhabī*), that is Hanafi, Hanbali, and so on. Muslims in the West originate from countries with different prevailing schools of thought and consequently their customs may differ. Because each school will have its own approach (lenient or exacting) to each issue, and because the life of a minority community should be homogenous, any religious law by any given school pertaining to Muslim minorities should be adopted by the community at large, regardless of personal affiliation. Thus, an individual in a Muslim minority community should renounce adherence to any specific school, and accept relevant laws for Muslim minorities from other schools. This principle has enabled a Muslim woman of consensual age to marry without a proper guardian.[19]
7. One must take into consideration the guidelines of the general *fiqh*, which permits opting for the less harmful path.
8. Religious laws that benefit the public should be favored over laws benefitting the individual at the public's expense.
9. There is an obligation to uphold laws and prioritize decrees according to importance.

On the position of minority religious law in relation to Muslim religious law, the majority of *fiqh al-aqalliyyāt* scholars and thinkers, including Abdul-Majeed al-Najjar[20] and Abdallah bin Bayyah,[21] followed Qaradawi's understanding. The two maintained that this doctrine was part of *fiqh al-furūʿ*, the branch of religious law pertaining to the details of the law and not part of a legal theory (*uṣūl*). Bin Bayyah maintained that *fiqh al-aqalliyyāt* is a branch of religious law that refers to the two primary sources – the Qur'an and the sunna – and relies on necessity (*al-ḍarūrāt*) and on the needs that become necessities (*al-ḥājiyāt al-munazila manzila al-ḍarūrāt*).[22]

Contrary to the abovementioned scholars, al-ʿAlwani argues that *fiqh al-aqalliyyāt* is not a branch of religious law (*fiqh al-furūʿ*) but, rather,

[19] Ibid., 57–60.

[20] Abdul-Majeed al-Najjar, "Nahwa Ta'sil Fiqh li-l-Aqalliyyat al-Muslima fi al-Gharb," January 14, 2004, http://www.islam-online.net/Arabic/contemporary/2004/01/article02.shtml

[21] Bin Bayyah, "Wa-Madha ʿan Fiqh al-Aqalliyyat al-Muslima," 2006, http://www.binbayyah.net/portal/artciles/274

[22] Bin Bayyah, "Al-Farq bin al-Drura wa-l-Haja Tatbiqa ʿala Baʿd Ahwal al-Aqalliyyat al-Muslima," *Al-Majallat al-ʿIlmiyya li-l-Majlis al-Urubi li-l-Ifta'* 4–5 (July 2004): 95–145.

general religious law (*al-fiqh al-ʿām*) and great religious law (*fiqh akbar*). Religious questions are approached comprehensively in accordance with general shariʿa laws, the principles of the Qurʾan, the binding supreme values, and basic objectives of religious law. At the same time, consideration is given to the long-term Islamic goals of expansion and strengthening. According to al-ʿAlwani, the purpose of *fiqh al-aqalliyyāt* is not to seek the permissible within classic religious law, but to give a different interpretation – a positive outlook through which the minority can surmount the challenges of its surroundings.[23]

Al-ʿAlwani repudiates the claim that *fiqh al-aqalliyyāt* is based on needs and necessities. He calls for an overall examination of religious law tradition and for its reevaluation in light of the creating source, the Qurʾan, and the interpreting source, the sunna (with the former overriding the latter). Therefore, al-ʿAlwani believes that religious tradition should not be accepted at face value, nor is it sufficient to amend laws originating from it according to *uṣūl al-fiqh*. After all, not all religious laws are equal: some were passed from God to the Prophet, whereas others were codified by human beings.[24]

In his essay "Nazrat Taʾsisiyya, Mudkhal ila Fiqh al-Aqalliyyat" ("Foundational Views: Introduction to Minority Jurisprudence"), al-ʿAlwani writes that *fiqh al-aqalliyyāt* should not be included in the common *fiqh al-furūʿ* but in a more general *fiqh* encompassing all facets of the law. Alluding to the Prophet's words that "If God desires good for a person, He provides him with understanding of His religion" (*tafqahatu fi al-dīn*), al-ʿAlwani believes *fiqh akbar* is required. To him, *fiqh al-aqalliyyāt* is a qualitative *fiqh* bridging the gap between the shariʿa and the group it is meant to serve – a group that is unique and privileged compared to other groups. Therefore, in order to comprehend Muslim minorities' religious law, one must study economics, sociology, political science, international relations, and the social sciences.[25] In fact, al-ʿAlwani indicates that the size of the group is not necessarily a testament to its magnitude. This point of view is shared by Tariq Ramadan who claims that even when Muslims are a numerical minority, they are still a majority in terms of values and principles; in other words, the quality outweighs the quantity.[26]

[23] Al-ʿAlwani, "Mudkhal Ila Fiqh al-Aqalliyat (long)," *Majallat al-ʿIlmiyya li-l-Majlis al-Urubi li-l-Iftaʾ li-l-Buhuth* 4–5 (June, 2004): 74–6.

[24] Ibid., 67–78.

[25] Ibid., 4.

[26] Ibid., 67–78.

It is worthwhile to note a way in which al-ʿAlwani diverges from the aforementioned thinkers regarding his approach to *fiqh al-aqalliyyāt* and its development. Al-ʿAlwani wishes to formulate new religious law that draws on the primary sources and will serve as a paragon of Muslim religious law in the modern age. Al-ʿAlwani, who does not regard himself as part of the *wasaṭī* faction,[27] also differs from thinkers and scholars such as Qaradawi, who attempt to mitigate and bridge between religious law, as manifested in religious tradition, and the realities of Muslim minorities in the modern age. Nevertheless, both approaches produce similar religious laws, as the disparity in the final outcome is inconsequential and only apparent on the level of principle. Similar to al-ʿAlwani, Dr. Abu Bakir al-Shanqiti believes that religious law is based on general principles (*kulliyyāt*) and not on specific cases (*juzʾiyyāt*). Ruling according to the text is considered insufficient in that it does not offer an interpretation in relation to other texts, nor indeed to reality. Qaradawi's perception connects the *salafi* generation with a younger generation, and those who are more traditional with those who are more innovative. Al-Shanqiti criticizes Qaradawi's religious perception, labeling it traditional rather than creative. Thus, compared to al-ʿAlwani's reformist (*iṣlāḥiyya*) approach, within his religious doctrine, Qaradawi represented both factions, a middle ground capable of popular appeal.

Al-ʿAlwani's approach was harshly criticized by those members of factions within *fiqh al-aqalliyyāt* who were proponents of Qaradawi. Al-ʿAlwani's partner and colleague in the doctrine, Ajeel Jasem Al-Nashmi, claimed that religious law is formulated by proof obtained from shariʿa, and thus al-ʿAlwani's argument that *fiqh al-aqalliyyāt* is comprehensive and total has no religious significance whatsoever. It is not defined by whether Muslims are a majority or a minority but, rather, according to the circumstances. Al-Nashmi believes that there is no fault in founding *fiqh al-aqalliyyāt* on necessity and need, as those priorities were decreed by God. Hence, there is no place for creating a new, comprehensive religious law to serve as a template, as suggested by al-ʿAlwani.[28]

In an attempt to reconcile these positions, Hussein Mohammed Halawa[29] clarifies that an *ijtihād* should be performed on every issue,

[27] S. Fishman, "The Fiqh al-Aqalliyyat Doctrine in the Writings of Taha Jabir al-Alwani and Yusuf al-Qaradawi" (Master's thesis, Jerusalem: Hebrew University of Jerusalem, 2006), 25.

[28] Al-Nashmi, 2005, 26–8, 47–50.

[29] Halawa, Hussein Mohammed. Interview by author. ECFR offices in Dublin, Ireland, February 13, 2012. In the interview, Halawa, the general secretary of the ECFR, emphasized that the council is more than Shaykh Qaradawi who heads the council's meetings and

even those substantiated by religious traditions. The exception to this, he claims, are for issues of *qaṭʿī al-dalāla wa-qaṭʿī al-thabūt*, or texts whose meaning and authenticity are uncontroversial. That is to say, they were obtained from primary sources – the Qurʾan and the sunna – from which there should be no deviation. Any other decree is open to *ijtihād*. In this respect, he concurs with al-ʿAlwani whom he regarded to be at the forefront of the revolution against the abolishment of *ijtihād*. Al-ʿAlwani himself does not call for the abandonment of a religious law tradition, but rather a renewed approach based on contemporary circumstances; this is based on an understanding that earlier religious scholars ruled according to their own circumstances, and thus their rulings may lose relevance over time. Therefore, Muslims are not obliged to adhere by previous rulings, and instead should perform an *ijtihād* in order that the religious law will address their contemporary circumstances.[30] Like Qaradawi, Halawa believes that alleviation for Muslims in Europe stems from a similar position to that of *fiqh al-ḍaʿīf*, religious law for the frail. In this sense, the relief does not derive from a particularized religious law for minorities, but rather from a general religious law that seeks to alleviate the burdens of the weak; this may be compared to the ways in which a sick person is entitled to unique laws due to his condition.

Ralph Ghadban does not accept the distinction between Qaradawi and al-ʿAlwani in terms of their approaches to *fiqh al-aqalliyyāt*. On the question of whether this doctrine was designed to Islamicize the West or to herald the modernization of Islam, Ghadban asserts that *fiqh al-aqalliyyāt* can be understood as reaction to Muslim modernization in general, but is relevant specifically in non-Muslim countries.[31] Despite al-ʿAlwani's view that the doctrine represents universal religious law, Ghadban argues that it is solely designed for, and applicable to, Muslim minorities in non-Muslim countries. Hence, al-ʿAlwani's approach – albeit the most progressive in terms of modernization of Islam vis-à-vis *fiqh al-aqalliyyāt* – is largely similar to that of Qaradawi. Nonetheless, al-ʿAlwani's position displays the boundaries of this legal experiment, which, if conducted appropriately, might lead to an inevitable shift from *fiqh* to theology.[32]

sessions, but cannot publish religious decrees in its name or rule in its stead. Admittedly, he holds sway over the council, but he cannot force his position, and he can be overruled by the council. Halawa demonstrates this with the case regarding the right of a Muslim woman to remain with her non-Muslim husband, on which Qaradawi changed his original stance following discussions in the council.

30 Halawa, Hussein Mohammed. Interview by author. Dublin, February 13, 2012.

31 R. Ghadban, "Fiqh al-Aqalliyyat and its Place in Islamic Law," *Orient* 2 (2010): 57.

32 Ibid., 62.

Ghadban further argues that Tariq Ramadan opposes the employment of Muslim religious theology in the construction of minority religious law. This opposition is rooted in an understanding of Muslim religious law as singular and universal – indivisible into laws intended for the lands of Islam and laws for Muslim minorities. Ramadan calls for an intellectual revolution that would enable Muslims to acknowledge their religion's universality, manifested in its ability to incorporate all societies. This will be achieved not through global conquest, but rather through the assimilation of the West into the world of Islam. Ghadban claims that Ramadan regards rational thought as misguided and opposes freethinking that draws from the primary Islamic sources. Rather, the only valid thought is found in *ijtihād* and *al-istinbāṭ*: constructing new religious laws from existing ones based on the principles of religious law.[33] Contrary to Ghadban, Caeiro believes that Islamic *fiqh* is based on the dialectic relationship between Holy Scripture and context, which according to *fiqh al-aqalliyyāt* scholars serves as the basis for *ijtihād*. Responding to the specific circumstances of Muslim minorities, the scholarly amalgamation of classic religious law and its initiated norms provides *fiqh* its strength.[34] Therefore, Caeiro argues that *fiqh al-aqalliyyāt* religious decrees transgress classic religious law, as the status of *fiqh* is transformed from holy law to rational, individual law.[35]

Uriya Shavit concurs with Caeiro, yet goes further by claiming that the *wasaṭī* approach employs theological notions that enable alleviation and facilitation of shariʿa laws. It is through a liberal application of religious law principles that the *wasaṭiyya* doctrine allows for such alleviation and mitigation.[36] The prominence of the approach stems from the amalgamation of classic religious law and the norms initiated by the *wasaṭī* scholars in order to cope with the unique circumstances of Muslim minorities. Nonetheless, Shavit argues that some theological views can serve various functions and thus lead to different and even contradictory conclusions.[37] While Fishman agrees with Caeiro's conclusion, he also claims that *fiqh al-aqalliyyāt* merges al-ʿAlwani's concept of the universality of Islam (*ʿālamiyyat al-Islām*) with the notion of ruling based on the goals of the shariʿa (*maqāṣid al-sharīʿa*), which he affixes to the foundations of classic

33 Ibid.

34 U. Shavit, "The Wasati and Salafi Approaches to the Religious Law of Muslim Minorities," *Islamic Law and Society* 19/4 (2012): 416–57.

35 S. Fishman, "Fiqh al-Aqalliyyat: A Legal Theory for Muslim Minorities," *Research Monographs on the Muslim World*, Hudson Institute, Series 1 (Paper no. 2, 2006).

36 Shavit, "The Wasati and Salafi Approaches to the Religious Law of Muslim Minorities."

37 Shavit, "The Wasati and Salafi Approaches to the Religious Law of Muslim Minorities."

religious law (*uṣūl al-fiqh*). He thusly produces the religious precedent for Muslims to settle anywhere in the world and promote the dissemination of Islam.[38] However, those researchers are not convinced that modern religious law processes (i.e., ones that take into account the unique circumstances of Muslim minorities) actively contribute to the preservation of Islamic ideas, nor to the advancement and adaptation of Muslim law. For that purpose, Muslim thinkers must reexamine the origins of classic decrees, striving to redefine legal and social norms in light of the shifting reality. Therefore, it is paramount to redefine the laws of Islam as part of minority jurisprudence in order to adapt Islam to life in the West, and ensure that Muslims may be successfully absorbed into those societies without forfeiting their religious identity.[39]

Sources and Methodology behind the Religious Decrees of the European Council of Fatwa and Research

In its rulings, the ECFR relies on the Qur'an, the sunna, *qiyas*, and *ijmāʿ*. Other sources include *istiḥsān*, *maṣlaḥa*, *istiṣḥāb*, *ʿurf*, and *mudhhab ṣaḥābī*. The council has adopted the *wasaṭiyya* ideology and its members regard their work as a continuation of Rashid Rida's philosophy. For instance, they have decided that religious law should not be formulated based on one *mudhhab*, but by choosing suitable religious law from the entire corpus of *madhāhib*. In addition, the council accepts religious decrees based on the public interest (*maṣlaḥa*), the objectives of the shariʿa (*maqāṣid* al-shariʿa), and custom (*ʿurf*). The ECFR's religious methodology was founded on three principles: (1) religious law studied and obtained from the four *madhāhib* is permissible; (2) alongside the considerations, every fatwa should include the source upon which it is based; (3) a ruling should be straightforward and rely on the shariʿa. As for alleviation or easement (*taysīr*), Qaradawi prefers the EFCR religious decrees to be more lenient. In the twelfth session held in December 2003, Qaradawi presented the council's guiding objectives:[40]

1. Congruence between the unalterable principles of the shariʿa and the transformation of time.

[38] Fishman, "Fiqh al-Aqalliyyat: A Legal Theory for Muslim Minorities."
[39] Kristine Sinclair, "Muslim Organizations in Denmark – Five Years after the Cartoon Controversy," Syddansk Universitet, 2011, http://static.sdu.dk/mediafiles//8/0/9/{80922C6E-1D2B-455D-9A98-7BC29829098D}1106KS.pdf
[40] Polka, "Constructing Muslim Identity in Western Society," 44–5.

2. Understanding the texts of the Qur'an and the sunna by their general objectives.
3. A more lenient religious approach to warm the hearts of the public toward Islam through pleasantries.
4. A harsher line in terms of the pillars of Islam (*arkān al-Islām*), alongside alleviation in its various branches.
5. Firm objectives with flexible means.
6. Preferring essence over appearance, and the deeper layer over the outer one.
7. A comprehensive understanding of Islam (*shumūliyya al-Islām*).
8. Preaching and calling to Islam with a pleasant manner and a thoughtful discourse.
9. Converging the ECFR's devotion to believers and tolerance toward unbelievers.
10. A war effort (jihad) against aggressors, and peaceful relations with Islam's sympathizers.
11. Cooperation, harmony, and tolerance among Muslim groups on controversial issues.
12. Consideration of the time and the place in passing a decree, preaching, teaching, and in court.
13. Adopting a wise, measured approach.
14. Integration of knowledge and faith, materialism and spirituality, economic fortitude and moral fortitude.
15. Focusing on human values and principles such as freedom and human rights.
16. Liberating women from the binds of tradition, from sinful customs, and promiscuous Western culture.
17. A call to rejuvenate religion from within through *ijtihād* by those who are worthy of it.
18. Insistence on building rather than destroying, uniting rather than dividing.
19. Adopting the good within the traditions of religion and religious law.
20. To take inspiration from the past, live in the moment, and look toward the future.

Implementation of the *Fiqh al-Aqalliyyāt* Methodology

Implementation of *fiqh al-aqalliyyāt* methodology has allowed for religious decrees that view shariʿa laws in context and generate new religious laws for Muslims in the West. These decrees differ both from classic religious law and from decrees for Muslims residing within the lands of Islam. To Halawa, the council's greatest achievement has been enabling Muslims to reside in the West without plight (*ḥarj*), as decreed in the Qur'an (verse 78:22): "*Wa-ma ja'ala 'alaykum fi al-dīn ḥarj*."[41] The council addressed the following topics: participation in political life, civil marriage and divorce, preeminence of the lunar calendar, zakat, women's rights and obligations, medicine, interfaith dialogue, and affiliation with a school of thought (*mudhhab*). For example, the council decreed that a woman needs her husband's permission to get a haircut if it would notably alter her appearance, and that a woman can participate in Islamic conferences.

Halawa deems revolutionary the decrees that a woman who converted to Islam may remain with her non-Muslim husband, and that mortgage is permissible, as these decrees negate prevailing religious laws. The council deliberated on the former case for eighteen months and, in my opinion, it is indeed revolutionary; relating to marriage, divorce, and the child's affiliation, which fall under the category of divine rights, these are extremely sensitive issues in terms of Islam. Halawa is somewhat apologetic when defending the decree on mortgages, pointing to its caveat that interest is forbidden (*haram*) and that Muslims in Europe should find other ways to finance a house. He emphasizes that the solution offered by the decree is temporary and should only be employed if no religiously acceptable alternative is available. *Fiqh al-aqalliyyāt* scholars have adopted the approach, advocating for integration into society and calling upon Muslims in the West to establish mutual relations with local citizens. These measures seek to rectify the negative prejudices against Muslims and demonstrate that they can assimilate in all facets of Western life: economy, manufacturing, local administration, and the political arena. In order to harmoniously and cooperatively coexist, *fiqh al-aqalliyyāt* advocates for intensive participation in all political spheres – governmental and otherwise.

To Dr. Tahir Mahdi,[42] this involvement assists Muslims in breaking down the walls of isolation in a world that has become a global village. Nonetheless, integration also requires safeguarding the Muslim identity and respect for the religious, cultural and social distinctiveness of the Muslim minority.[43] Based on the Islamic decree to command the good and prohibit the bad (*al-amr bi-l-ma'rūf wa-l-nahī 'an al-munkar*), Qaradawi claims Islam and democracy are harmonious; Muslims, he asserts, should partake in politics,

[41] Halawa, Hussein Mohammed. Interview by author. Dublin, February 12–13, 2012.
[42] Dr. Tahir Mahdi, member of the European Council for Fatwa and Research.
[43] Mahdi, 2006, 53–6.

joining existing political parties in their countries of residence. Caeiro maintains that Qaradawi's position begets decrees that encourage participation in elections in order to thwart the wickedness and tyranny characteristic of *fiqh al-muwāzanāt*, the jurisprudence of priorities and balances.[44]

The ECFR has ruled that participation in an election or running as part of a non-Muslim political party falls under the discretion of the local Islamic institution. If Muslims might benefit from the election, as their interests are only attainable through cooperation with a non-Muslim party, then they are allowed to do so, so long as they do not surrender a more significant interest than that they wish to achieve though participation.[45] Dilwar Hussain – a member of the Islamic center in Leicester, England, and associated with the *wasaṭiyya* faction – is a proponent of Muslim political involvement at the national level. Much like Joseph who was Pharaoh's protégé (albeit the ruler in that case was a non-believer), Muslims may involve themselves in politics and government in a Christian country.[46] This position is based on the famous fatwa by al-ʿAlwani, permitting Muslim participation in the political arena.[47]

Indeed, this chapter focuses on the implementation of *fiqh al-aqalliyyāt* methodology on issues of personal standing. However, to illustrate the vast distinction between *fiqh al-aqalliyyāt* and classic religious law, I will present two religious decrees that are at the forefront of the doctrine. These two decrees have caused considerable tumult and dissention because they conflicted with the consensus held by the majority of religious scholars: a decree regarding enlistment in the army of the adoptive country at a time of war against Muslims, and a decree permitting an interest-incurring mortgage for the purpose of purchasing a house.[48]

Army Service for One's Naturalized Country against Fellow Muslims

Following 9/11, Captain Muhammad Abdul-Rasheed, a Muslim chaplain in the United States Army, broached an issue with al-ʿAlwani in his capacity as the chairman of the Fiqh Council of North America. Abdul-Rasheed wished to know if a Muslim could serve in a non-Muslim military that

[44] Ibid., 18.

[45] See the ECFR fatwa: http://e-cfr.org

[46] H. Dilwar, "Muslim Political Participation in Britain and the 'Europeanisation' of Fiqh," *Die Welt Des Islams*, 44/3 (2004): 385.

[47] Ibid., 386.

[48] Halawa, Hussein Mohammed. Interview by author. Dublin, February 12–13, 2012.

may fight against Muslims, and whether he should request to be reassigned to a non-combative role. Al-ʿAlwani referred the question to the religious scholars' forum administered by Dr. Mohamed Selim el-Awa. Upon deliberation and examination of the subject, the members of the forum, including Qaradawi, Tariq al-Bishri, Haytham al-Khayyat, and Fahmi Huwaydi, formulated a decree which el-Awa drafted and transmitted to al-ʿAlwani who signed and forwarded it the US Army.[49]

The fatwa opened with a declaration on the sanctity of life. It was based on Qurʾan verse 5:32 and referred to a terrorist act as a criminal act from both the moral and the shariʿa legal standpoints. The authors of the fatwa adopted the term *ḥirāba*, an armed attack on society, to describe an act of terrorism, albeit abstaining from a religious discussion on its meaning and implementation. In their view there is no distinction between Muslim and non-Muslim society, and the physical location in which the act was committed ought to be considered immaterial.[50]

The fatwa called on Muslim soldiers from the victimized society to bring the culprits to justice (not necessarily within the framework of shariʿa). As well as debating whether a Muslim soldier in the U.S. Army is permitted to fight an Afghan Muslim, the forum discussed a much more fundamental question: should the loyalty of a Muslim soldier lie in the great Muslim nation or in his country of residence? The fatwa acknowledged the legitimacy of the modern state and prioritized a Muslim's loyalty to his country during a time of war, when he is expected to actively demonstrate his allegiance. In this respect, deep and far-reaching significance may be attributed to the fatwa; however, one must bear in mind its timing as part of a response to the September 11 attacks. Religious scholars tend to minimize the significance to this fatwa, since after defining the World Trade Center attacks as criminal according to Islam, the fatwa effectively limited its scope to the issue of a Muslim soldier within a specific context.

The fatwa was based on two principles. The first, *aqalla al-ḍararayn*, or the lesser of two evils, indicates that Muslims should continue to fight for their country's army; the reasoning is that refusing service would result in a stain on the reputation of the country's entire Muslim community, causing Muslims soldiers to be considered unreliable. The second principle is intention (*niyya*) – if the intention behind the action is worthy, the deed itself is worthy regardless of consequences. Because the case

[49] El-Awa et al. Fatwa on Muslims partaking in a war against Muslims as part of the U.S. Army. http://www.aawsat.com

[50] Ibid.

had no precedent in traditional shariʿa literature, the authors of the fatwa accepted a certain degree of novelty and adopted a principle of intention, which relies on the intention of the actor rather than the nature of the act or its consequences.

The decree determined that Muslim soldiers are allowed to participate in premeditated campaigns against those their country has labeled as terrorists acting against it, or as harboring such terrorists. The soldiers should request to serve in supportive roles rather than on the front lines, yet if that request is denied, they should engage in direct fighting. They should uphold justice against abuse and protect innocents from harm. This permission serves as a declaration of loyalty by a Muslim to his country, thus averting certain damage to the Muslim community that would be incurred should Muslim soldiers refrain from fighting. Conversely, the resulting damage from fighting is not a certainty, and as decreed by the shariʿa, necessity revokes a prohibition and the minor damage should be accepted if it prevents a greater one.

Basheer Nafi inferred from the fatwa that it is permissible for Muslims to engage in war as part of the U.S. Army against terrorist organizations and countries. The argumentation behind it focused on the unique reality created by need (*ḍarūra*), and the circumstances that must be addressed. Basheer Nafi understood the fatwa as addressing the newfound situation in the international arena of Muslims who have naturalized in the West. The most significant facet of the fatwa was its homiletical and direct approach to the Qurʾan and the hadith. Disregarding the authority of the *madhāhib* or the accepted *fiqh* scholars, the authors of the fatwa felt bound only to unequivocal texts from the Qurʾan or the reliable sunna, and considered all other sources to be eligible for *ijtihād*. They utilized the aforementioned principles while ignoring their broader, more complex meaning in religious law tradition.[51]

The fatwa resonated strongly across the Islamic world. Salafis wholeheartedly objected to it, claiming it contradicts the religious scholars' clear prohibition against assisting non-Muslims in their fight against Muslims.[52] They deemed this prohibition to be absolute as it was unanimously accepted by religious scholars and based on unequivocal verses of

[51] B.M. Nafi, "Fatwa and War: On the Allegiance of the American Muslim Soldiers in the Aftermath of September 11th," *Islamic Law and Society* 11 (2004): 90–1.

[52] Shaykh Salman bin Fahd al-Odah, considered among the most prominent Saudi religious scholars, issued a religious decree that utterly prohibited all form of fighting against Muslims in the 2003 war against Iraq: http://www.onislam.net/arabic/newsanalysis/3008

the Qur'an. Hence, it was not open for interpretation, utilitarian considerations, or examination according to the interest (*maṣlaḥa*) of Muslims.[53] The fatwa was also harshly criticized by large swaths of the *wasaṭī* faction and proponents of the Muslim Brotherhood.[54] They conceded that shari'a does permit choosing the option of minimal harm, *akhaf al-ḍararayn*; however, they argued, American citizenship is not preferable to killing Muslims. Muslim religious law is clear in proclaiming that Muslim blood is sacred to God and is supreme to any citizenship or position held by a Muslim soldier in the American military. Moreover, they argued that this fatwa constituted a de-facto license to kill Muslims.[55]

Mortgages

The issue of purchasing a house in the West using a mortgage was first raised in 1986 following the hardships encountered by Muslims in Europe. Until that time, the majority of religious decrees prohibited the purchase of a house involving a mortgage with interest. The prohibition was met with unease due to the obvious difficulties of financing a home, which shifted the focus of the discussion from religious law to a question of identity. The issue had come up repeatedly, not by an individual, but by *'ulama'* council members encouraged by Qaradawi. The ECFR deliberated on the subject and examined studies submitted in favor of and against mortgages, including research from Shaykh Al-Arabi Al-Bichri. Al-Bichri claimed that Muslim minorities in the West were suffering from economic and social disadvantages and discrimination, particularly in terms of housing. In France, the percentage of Muslims residing in private houses was 12.82 percent compared to 55 percent of the general population; 10.68 percent of Muslims owned their own houses as opposed to 56 percent of the general population; and 55.7 percent of Muslims resided in small-scale homes as opposed to the average of 11.5 percent.[56] In

[53] Shaykh Hakim al-Mtiri, "al-ḥuriyya al-ṭuwfān," without a date. Al-Mtiri is a famous *salafi* preacher, www.dr-hakem.com/portals/Content/?info…jsp

[54] Al-Risuti, considered among the most prominent Muslim Brotherhood scholars, also believes that Muslims should not take up arms against Muslims as part of the army of their neutralization country, even though he did permit to pay taxes due to *ḍarūra* (necessity); see also, Muhammad bin al-Makhtar al-Shanqiti, "'An Fatwa al-Muslimin fi al-Jaysh al-Amriki," without a date, http://alarabnews.com/alshaab/GIF/19-10-2001/Mokhtar.htm

[55] Jamal al-Sharqawi, "'An al-Fatwa al-Amrikaniyya," *Majallat al-Sunna* 110, (November 2001).

[56] Shaykh Al-Arabi Al-Bichri, "Shira' al-Buyut 'an Tariq al-Qard al-Banki," *Al-Majallat al-'Ilmiyya li-l-Majlis al-Urubi li-l-Ifta'* 6 (January 2005): 159–78.

terms of religious law, Al-Bichri relied on Ibn Rushd (the grandson)[57] and Ibn al-Qayyim,[58] Ibn Taymiyya's[59] student, who argued that there are two types of interest (*ribā*): apparent, explicit interest and hidden interest. The apparent interest is forbidden in and of itself, while the hidden interest is forbidden because it causes the apparent interest. This distinction is important as it allows the religious scholar some malleability when ruling according to the well being of Muslims (*maṣlaḥa*) in a way that surpasses a lower level prohibition. Abd al-Rizaq al-Sanhuri[60] also references the two types of interests. Only that which exploits the needy is forbidden, while the rest are justified by either *sad al-dharā'i'* – avoiding the element that causes the sin (e.g. the lack of privately owned houses) – or the existence of a need or a necessity (*ḥajia* or *ḍarūra*). In light of this interpretation of religious law, al-Bichri believes that mortgages are not forbidden. Moreover, because safeguarding the Muslim's soul and his family is a necessity, the Muslim purchase of a house is considered to fortify Islam in Europe. By becoming homeowners, Muslims' influence over society grows. Thus, purchasing a house is vital to preservation of the religion outside the lands of Islam (*ba-l-ḥifāẓ 'alā al-dīn*). In addition, it increases the dignity, stability, and wellbeing of Muslim minorities. The purchased house should be adjacent to a mosque and a Muslim school, and should be big enough to accommodate the Muslim's needs.

Al-Bichri raises another argument in favor of mortgages: purchasing houses in the West is collectively necessarily in order that Muslims naturalize in the West and promote *da'wa*, the call to Islam. In his decree, he relies on essays by Al-Qarafi,[61] al-Imam al-Shatibi,[62] and Tahir bin 'Ashur,[63] particularly on the principles of the objective of the shari'a (*maqāṣid* al-shari'a), the prevalence of sins in society (*'umūm al-balā'*), and interest (*maṣlaḥa*). He believes the only avenue available to most Muslims who are otherwise unable to afford a house, is to borrow funds from a bank and pay back the amount in monthly installments, during which time the purchased house serves as collateral. Banks offer two forms of mortgages: those with fixed interest rates and those with variable interest rates.

57 Islamic thinker and philosopher (1126–1198).

58 A Syrian religious scholar (1292–1349).

59 A Syrian *Ḥanbalī* religious scholar (1263–1328), led innovative Islamic thinking that reconciles the text with common sense.

60 Egyptian jurist (1895–1971), a champion of civil legislation in Egypt.

61 Egyptian religious scholar (626–684 according to the *hijri* calendar) who specialized in *uṣūl al-fiqh*.

62 Andalusian religious scholar (died in 790 according to the *hijri* calender) who established the construction of religious law according to the objectives of shri'a (*maqāṣid al- shari'a*).

63 A Tunisian *Mālikī* religious scholar (1879–1972).

Only the former is permissible according to al-Bichri, as it is comparable to buying in installments. Following a thorough discussion on the subject, the ECFR adopted a fatwa that reiterated the prohibition on mortgages and encouraged Muslims to find religiously acceptable alternatives; these options range from loans without interest from Islamic financial institutions, to negotiating with Western banks for loans that abide by religious constraints, such as establishing an installment plan with a fee for a past-due payment. However, the fatwa continued, if a Muslim is still unable to obtain a religiously sanctioned mortgage, he is permitted to take an interest incurring mortgage in order purchase a house. For this final option, three conditions must be met: the buyer does not have sufficient funds to purchase the house by other means; he does not own another house; the house in question will serve as a residence only.[64]

The council based its decision on two guidelines: (1) necessity revokes a prohibition (*al-ḍarūrāt tubīḥ al-maḥẓūrāt*); (2) home ownership is, in the current climate of the West, a need that constitutes a necessity for Muslims, both on a personal level and in the broader sense. Although life is possible without the fulfillment of this need – differentiating it from a necessity or *ḍarūra* – its lack does indeed present a hardship (*ḥarj*), from which God has spared the Muslims. The personal need becomes a necessity when one considers that a rented house is a *ḥarj*; it does not fulfill the needs of a Muslim, as he may be evicted from it at any moment. Furthermore, residing in a rented house means paying rent throughout the years without receiving any form of ownership, while mortgage payments grant ownership. A house that is not considered a *ḥarj* is appropriate in terms of size and location – adjacent to a mosque, Islamic center, and a Muslim school. As previously mentioned, because necessity revokes prohibition, the permissibility of a mortgage is conditional on the suspension of a prohibition and does not constitute a sweeping endorsement of mortgages. Therefore, mortgages on commercial properties are prohibited.

The *Ḥanafī* School, preferred by Ibn Taymiyyah, is another source for the ECFR ruling on mortgages. The school asserts that a Muslim needn't adhere to shariʿa laws on civil, financial, and political matters that are beyond his control, i.e. determined by the regulations of the non-Muslim society. The prohibition on interest is dependent on the makeup of

[64] The ECFR, fatwa permitting interest incurring loans to purchase a house, 2009. http://e-cfr.org/new/fatwa/%D9%85%D8%A7-%D8%AD%D9%83%D9%85-%D8%B4%D8%B1%D8%A7%D8%A1-%D8%A7%D9%84%D9%85%D9%86%D8%A7%D8%B2%D9%84-%D8%A8%D9%82%D8%B1%D8%B6-%D8%A8%D9%86%D9%83%D9%8A-%D8%B1%D8%A8%D9%88%D9%8A-%D9%84%D9%84%D9%85-3/

country's society, its philosophy, and socio-economic trends. On other issues, Muslims must abide by religious law, or else immigrate to another country; these include ritual practices, food and beverages, clothing, and personal standing. Contrary to religious prohibitions, Muslims in non-Muslim countries are permitted to sign contracts in order to remain on par with the general population. Furthermore, adherence to shariʿa laws should minimize financial losses, as Islam seeks to benefit its believers rather than deprive them. Proper housing is a staple of modern Western society; therefore, because the prohibition on mortgages denies Muslims the ability to purchase a house, it is not applicable for Muslim minorities in the West.

Caeiro claims that financial transactions are among the most complex subjects tackled by Muslim religious law, especially because bank interest is considered *ribā* (forbidden interest). He outlines three approaches taken by religious scholars: (1) the idealistic approach; (2) the pragmatic approach; (3) the public interest leaning approach (*maṣlaḥa*). The idealistic approach limits the permission to transactions allowed by religious law. The pragmatic approach, which is the majority approach, copes with this issue in an unorthodox manner. According to the *maṣlaḥa*, modern day interest is not comparable to interest in the time of the Qurʾan and thus there is no obligation to oppose it. Caeiro believes that European interest laws stand in contrast to shariʿa interest laws. The solution lies in a voluntarily approach based on the will of the Muslim, as devout Muslims avoid loans with interest. In the absence of a shariʿa-based institution to allow for banking activity, the minority position serves as a catalyst for religious scholars (*al-fuqhāʾ*) to search for solutions.[65]

Muslims are divided over the validity of the fatwa allowing mortgages with interest. Some, like the "Islam online" website and Ebrahim Desai,[66] accepted it and even carried it a step further. Others opposed it, claiming it curtailed the development of religiously sanctioned Muslim financial institutions. They wondered what would become of Muslim butchers should Muslims be allowed to eat all local meats. Moreover, the detractors maintained that Islam is a universal religion applicable everywhere, and there is no imperative for Muslims to attain social and economic standing in Europe. In the December 1999 issue of "*al-Daʿwa*," the Muslim Brotherhood's journal, Mahmoud Rida Murad from Saudi Arabia wrote

[65] Caeiro, 2004, 351–75.

[66] South African Islamic thinker.

that this fatwa might result in the acceptance of prostitution and alcohol. The Standing Committee for Scholarly Research and Fatwa in Saudi Arabia ruled that loans with interest, including those for purchasing a house, are prohibited in every shape and form. This ruling was based on unequivocal verses from the Qur'an and the sunna of the Prophet, as the prohibition on loans with interest is critical, and its violation constitutes one of the major sins.[67] The *salafi* website "Islamweb," chiefly directed at Muslim minority communities, discussed this fatwa and determined that since interest is strictly forbidden, both in the lands of disbelief and the lands of Islam, many religious decrees have already forbade loans with interest, even for the purpose of purchasing houses in non-Muslim countries. These religious decrees were based on proof from the Qur'an and the sunna. Regarding the ECFR ruling, they claimed that a decree issued by anyone other than the Prophet could be discarded, regardless of the position and status of the presiding religious authority. Indeed, necessity can displace a prohibition, yet purchasing a house does not constitute a necessity, because if the Muslim is unable to finance it or go through a Muslim bank, he can always rent. Therefore, the ruling permitting interest is erroneous.[68]

Fiqh al-Aqalliyyāt and Personal Standing: Implementation of the Methodology

According its scholars, *fiqh al-aqalliyyāt* constitutes a method for constructing religious decrees and offers a comprehensive solution for all aspects of Muslim minority life: upholding religious rites and dictates, relationships with the non-Muslim other, involvement in the social and public spheres of their adoptive country, incurred obligations, naturalization, and the approach to the state's laws and to family law via the local judicial system. *Fiqh al-aqalliyyāt* thinkers, chiefly from the ECFR, have developed this methodology toward religious law in order to implement Islamic values and shariʿa laws; it is based on acknowledged, religious evidence that considers and balances religious objectives within the constraints of reality. In the eighteenth issue of "*al-Majallat al-ʿIlmiyya*" published in July 2011, the ECFR endeavored to apply the methodology to the

[67] The Permanent Committee for Islamic Research and Fatwa in Saudi Arabia, fatwa prohibiting loans with interest to purchase a house, without a date, http://islamqa.info/ar/ref/105331

[68] "Islamweb," fatwa prohibiting loans for purchasing a house, without a date, http://fatwa.islamweb.net/fatwa/index.php?page=showfatwa&Option=FatwaId&Id=49918

issue of waqf (an Islamic endowment of property). The research published in the journal was designed to adapt shariʿa law on the subject of waqf to the reality of life in the West, in order that Muslim minorities might manage their own endowment of property according to shariʿa laws, and adhere to the accepted legal practices in those countries.

In issues fourteen and fifteen of "*al-Majallat al-ʿIlmiyya*" (September 2009), the ECFR focused on applying the methodology to laws relating to money and credit. It emphasized that European financial laws contradict shariʿa laws, thus posing a challenge to Muslim minorities, who are left with two unfeasible options: either they must function within a financial system that negates their beliefs, or disengage from their surroundings and undergo substantial economic losses. In the research, the writers defined the goals of shariʿa within finances in such a way that the principles of the methodology were applicable beyond the field of economics.

As previously discussed, this book seeks to examine *fiqh al-aqalliyyāt* by using its approach to matters of personal status and family law as a case study. The personal sphere is considered the most vital and sensitive in Islamic religious law. With this in mind, the analysis of *fiqh al-aqalliyyāt* is conducted through the lens of contemporary dynamic transformations in familial arrangements, giving special attention to their inner relations. ECFR members and their work have thoroughly examined the field of personal status; these writings can be considered alongside the diverse array of challenges encountered by Muslim minorities. There is no consensus definition for this field and it varies according to the sovereign nation. Its earliest manifestations permeated legal systems in the Islamic world under article seven of the Ottoman shariʿa procedural law,[69] which declared that the sphere of personal status includes:[70] wills and inheritance (determining the identity of heirs, their stake in and division of the inheritance); guardianship and accountability for the soul; finances and education of minors and those incompetent to stand trial; legal competency (determining when a person is incompetent to stand trial and when one is legally competent and able); fatherhood; child custody, including visitation arrangements and accommodations; marital affairs, including marriage registration, proof of marriage, a wife's obedience to her husband,

[69] The Ottoman definition was introduced as an example, also because shariʿa courts in Israel are obligated by it.

[70] See Goiten, S. D., and A. Ben Shemesh, *Introduction to Muslim Law: Basic Principles and Laws* (Faculty of Law of the Hebrew University, Legal Studies, No. 3, Jerusalem: Mif'al Hashichpul and Gvilim Publishing Co. Ltd., 1957. The items are arranged according to the original article seven of the Ottoman shariʿa procedural law.

household and personal belongings, dowry and related affairs, and separation and divorce; alimony (for the wife, children, and other relatives) and the rights of the kin and spouse of an absent husband.

The current study examines the multiple facets of the family sphere as a test case for the comprehensiveness and applicability of *fiqh al-aqalliyyāt*. Moreover, the methodology is considered in light of its attempts to construct religious law solutions to newfound dilemmas, as well as the consistency of its adjudicators in implementation. An exhaustive discussion of all components of personal status relates broadly to other issues that affect Muslim minorities because it enables an analysis of the larger *fiqh al-aqalliyyāt* framework and its founding principles. Based on this framework, one can deduce and extrapolate the *fiqh al-aqalliyyāt* principles that are most relevant for Muslim minorities.

Among the issues raised in the case studies taken from the realm of family law, there are several areas of overlap: the validity of marriage and divorce, the affiliation of children, and child custody and alimony. Naturally, each ruling varies in accordance with the political-legal environment and the distinctive circumstances of each minority community. The examination of this field is highly important to *fiqh al-aqalliyyāt* because of instances when minorities endure state legislation that leads to civil arrangements contradictory to religious law.

Some of these circumstances include: whether men and women are granted equal rights in cases of arbitration according to shariʿa laws; the validity of civil marriage and divorce; determining the custodial parent by civil criteria different from religious laws; and a woman's accountability for her and her children's alimony, contrary to religious law in which this obligation is allotted to the husband or father. Another important issue is the paternal affiliation of a child according to Islam and according to civil law. Unlike the latter, the former states that a child born in matrimony is always affiliated with the husband of the biological mother. This might create a situation in which a child is affiliated with two different fathers: from a religious standpoint, the child would be affiliated with his mother's husband, but civilly, the child would be affiliated with his biological father.

As previously mentioned, issues pertaining to personal status are seminal to the shariʿa, as many such issues are categorized as *ḥuqūq Allah*, or the "rights of God;" these prohibitions are not to be ignored, breached, or even modified. They relate to public ordinances and interests, as well as the safeguarding of the shariʿa's five objectives: the preservation of religion, the preservation of the soul, the preservation of mental capacity, the preservation of affiliation of children to their fathers (*al-nasab*), and the preservation of property.[71] The application of shari'a to legal systems in the Muslim world was generally confined to matters of personal standing due to its prominence within Muslim religious law, despite being enacted by state legislation and not via classic religious law.[72] In the mid-nineteenth century, when the Ottoman legislator implemented comprehensive reforms (*tanẓīmāt*) within the empire's judicial and administration systems, even he deferred extension of the reform into family law. This last reform was completed only in 1917, half a century after the initiation of the civil law reform. The postponement derived from great trepidation in approaching shari'a laws in that manner. Therefore, the conclusions of discussions on personal status issues will serve as a significant measure for the comprehensiveness and integrity of the *fiqh al-aqalliyyāt* doctrine as it relates to Muslim minorities. These conclusions will enable this work to consider whether the doctrine is all-encompassing or if it supplies only limited solutions to specific questions raised by Muslims in the West, rather than proving comprehensive, consistent and systematic in its implementation.

Personal Standing and *Fiqh al-Aqalliyyāt:* Transformation in Shari'a Laws

The daily reality of Muslim minority families is fairly diverse in comparison to their counterparts in Muslim countries. Thus, they tend to possess distinctive characteristics that affect location- and circumstance-sensitive religious law. Ahmad Jaballah[73] believes the family framework is paramount to the preservation of Islamic religious identity in non-Muslim countries. Therefore, utmost efforts should be made to safeguarding the family and surmounting its unique obstacles, as the family is responsible for educating the next generation. Islamic education differs from education in the surrounding society, and the need to provide adequate Islamic education puts considerable pressure on the family, which must create an approach that instills a Muslim identity while enabling children to become properly immersed in society, with all the nuances and complexities that entails.[74] The tendencies of the general society permeate the minority

[71] Abd al-Karim Zidan, *Madkhal li-Dirasat al-Shari'a al-Islamiyya* (Beirut: 16th ed., 1999), 41.

[72] Ibid., 7.

[73] Tunisian religious scholar, president of the Union of Islamic Organizations in France (UOIF), and director of the European Institute of life sciences in Paris (IESH).

[74] Ahmad Jaballah, "Al-Usra al-Muslima fi Europe bayn Ta'thirat al-Bi'aa al-Ahtima'iyya wa-l-'Adat al-Murutha," *Al-Majallat al-'Ilmiyya li-l-Majlis Urubi li-l-Ifta' li-l-Buhuth* 7 (July 2005): 231.

group that lives among it. This influence can occur subconsciously and unintentionally, and can affect the personality, feelings, positions, and even the principles of members within the minority group. For example, surveys have shown that the longer Muslim women reside in the West, the more their birth rates decrease, becoming closer the standard rates in those countries.[75]

Western culture adheres to complete gender equality without considering the unique traits of each gender. Jaballah claims that while Islam does not oppose the notion of equality, it acknowledges the divergence in function between husband and wife: the wife is exempt from the burden of providing for her family and is designated for motherhood. This disparity between Islam and the West affects the Muslim family and requires an appropriate response from the adjudicators.[76] In terms of civil liberties that do not hinder freedom of choice, Western culture does not forbid extramarital sexual relations and those activities are not considered illegal or disruptive to public order. This Western sexual permissiveness affects family life to the degree of disintegration of the classic family structure in favor of alternative, non-marital-based family arrangements. Moreover, it contributes to mounting rates of divorces, single men and women, single parent families, and people favoring individuality over a committed relationship.[77] Whether consciously or subconsciously, these Western social norms influence Muslim youths and create behavioral patterns that shape the distinct characteristics and religious identity of the Muslim community. Therefore, an appropriate religious law approach is required such that young Muslims learn to recognize the environmental factors that may inform their behaviors and, in this way, eliminate unfavorable influences and preserve their distinct identity as Muslims.[78] Abdul-Majeed Al-Najjar compares the exceptional predicament of the Muslim minority family to its vis-à-vis in a Muslim country with five defining characteristics: test of temptations, family isolation, educational burden, serving as an emissary, and subordination to the laws and regulations of non-Muslim sovereigns.[79]

Test of temptations: everyday hard-to-resist temptations lie in wait for the Muslim minority family, particularly in the West. These include

[75] Ibid., 234–7.
[76] Ibid., 236–7.
[77] Ibid., 242–3.
[78] Ibid., 234–43.
[79] Abdul-Majeed al-Najjar, "Maqasid al-Shari'a fi Ahkam al-Usra Muwajahha li-Ahkam al-Usra al-Muslima fi al-Gharb," *Al-Majallat al-'Ilmiyya li-l-Majlis Urubi li-l-Ifta' li-l-Buhuth* 7 (July 2005): 70–75.

sexual permissiveness, economic consumerism, and food and beverage related cultural and social temptations. Other temptations, such as individual freedom, liberty, and individual responsibility are manifested in deviation from the traditional family framework. All of the above factors threaten the Muslim family, its cohesion, and the continued adherence by the young generation to the Islamic religion.

Family isolation: In contrast to families in Islamic countries, where each family unit may be considered a link in a chain with other families to form a cohesive whole, the Muslim family in the West stands alone. It is not a part of a larger familiar spectrum or continuum, and its borders are delineated by its children. This isolation affects the family's stability and sense of security; it may also limit the younger generation's commitment to Islamic social customs, due to the absence of a supportive communal system that socializes individuals and pressures them to act according to the prevailing norms.

The educational burden: the Muslim minority lacks educational and cultural institutions to instill Islamic values and customs in the younger generation. Instead, children absorb the general population's cultural and educational norms, which are so often foreign to Islam. This creates a heavy burden for the family, which must supplement what is missing and intensify efforts to ingrain Islamic values, traditions, and culture in the younger generation via education. This burden becomes even heavier when the family patriarch is uneducated and ignorant of Islamic customs and values.

Serving as an emissary: the family in Muslim minority communities is tasked with serving as a role model. This is especially important due to the disintegration of family values and lack of cohesion in non-Muslim societies, primarily in the West. The role of Muslim families is therefore to attract other families to Islamic family values, thus bringing them closer to adopting the Islamic religion.

Subordination to non-Muslim sovereign: Muslim families in minority communities are subjugated to a non-Muslim sovereign. As a result, they are also subject to a constitution, laws, and norms that reflect principles, values, and customs foreign to Islam. Such a situation necessarily generates substantial social and cultural strain upon the family. Unfamiliar to Muslim families in the lands of Islam, these influences are also manifested as a financial burden on the individual and the family due to the prominence of consumerism in the West. At times, civil laws can contradict shariʿa, further complicating matters for Muslim minorities. In this sense, a religious law approach is needed to reconcile the contradiction and assist the Muslim minority. For instance, German law, which differs from shariʿa law, affords special protection for marriage and the family. The German public has expressed concern that the contradictions between religious law and civil law will result in injury to a German citizen through the application of shariʿa law, especially in instances when one of the relevant parties is a German citizen or a naturalized citizen. German jurist Mathias Rohe has summarized the topics deliberated by German courts regarding issues of the personal standing, highlighting the contradiction between the two legal frameworks.[80]

Gender equality: German law does not accept religious norms that grant women a different, separate, or inferior role compared to men.

Marriage: the age of consent for marriage in Islam can be at times nine years old, while the minimum age of consent according to German law is eighteen. In special cases marriages are allowed at the age of sixteen. Another issue pertaining to marriage is the religious prohibition for Muslim women to marry non-Muslim men accepted by the courts in 1976. However, to Rohe, this acceptance contradicts the principles of equality and freedom of religion within German law.

Polygamy: monogamy is a staple of German law. Nonetheless, if polygamous marriages are recognized by the law in the state of origin, German courts acknowledge these marriages so as not to deny women the rights to which they are entitled. Civil rights, however, are given only to the first wife.

Dowry: the role of the dowry is unclear. According to Rohe, it should be considered part of the marriage contract, while the courts have yet to decide whether it belongs to contract law or is part of religious customs that are not legally binding. A 1980 verdict opposed the mandatory provision of dowry, despite Rohe's belief that a ruling against dowry constitutes a ruling against Muslim women.

Divorce: because the authority to issue a divorce lies exclusively with the German family court, unilateral divorces are rejected on principle and considered null and void. Concurrently, divorces that are recognized by foreign law may be accepted so long as they adhere to the stipulations of German law. For instance, if a couple has lived separately for at least a year and one party informed the other about the divorce in an appropriate manner, German courts will acknowledge this unilateral divorce, regardless of whether the divorcing party is the husband or the wife.

[80] M. Rohe, "Islamic Law in German Courts," *Hawwa* 1/1 (2003): 49–50.

Alimony: religious courts in Muslim countries tend to decide on lower alimony settlements in comparison to those passed by German courts, particularly for divorced women who reside in Germany with their young children and are without earning potential. Muslim men might resent this discrepancy, since they would pay less in their country of origin.

Child custody and guardianship: German law views the well being of the child as paramount in custody cases, as opposed to Muslim religious laws founded on legal principles which favor the father and determine custody arrangements contingent upon the status of the parents and the children's age.

Adoption of minors: Muslim religious law does not acknowledge adoption which it views solely as a legal institution with ensuing obligations and rights; in contrast, German law recognizes adoption and its consequences for the adopter and adoptee.[81]

Personal Standing: Development of Religious Law Methodology based on the Goals of Shariʿa

Abdul-Majeed Al-Najjar believes that classic Islamic religious law is uncharacteristically specific on issues of personal standing. In other areas, religious law tends to restrict itself to setting norms and general guidelines, rather than enumerating on minor contingencies and instances.[82] This is due to the uttermost significance attributed to personal standing, which dictates the structure of the family – the building block of the nation. The specificity of details in this field reflects the necessity of avoiding mistakes that might inflict great harm on society, and even on humanity at large.[83] To al-Najjar, personal standing-related shariʿa laws strive to fulfill their objectives,[84] which in turn should dictate the *ijtihād* in the personal standing field. The objectives of the shariʿa as they are portrayed in texts should be applied to cases that have no textual basis. Subsequently, religious laws that achieve these objectives should be constructed. If the adjudicator is

[81] Ibid., 51–5.

[82] Al-Najjar, "Maqasid al-Shariʿa fi Ahkam al-Usra Muwajahha li-Ahkam al-Usra al-Muslima fi al-Gharb," 67.

[83] Ibid., 68.

[84] Halawa explicates Al-Najjar's methodology by using the secondary objectives of the five objectives of shariʿa. To him, the secondary objectives can be used in all walks of life to generate religious rulings that fulfill the primary objectives. He exemplified with one of the five objectives– protecting the knowledge of the Child's affiliation– from which derives the religious permission to marry and the prohibition to commit adultery, as the latter leads to children with no affiliation.

not entirely familiar with the objectives, his decree might cause great damage to society as a whole and to the Muslim family in particular.[85] In the religious law tradition, essays dealing with the objectives of the shariʿa have not always appreciated the tremendous importance of their project. Such essays have dealt exhaustively with the general objectives of the shariʿa, but without delving into the specific details of the personal standing objectives or substantiating them in an independent manner.[86] This was due to the great specificity of shariʿa laws on matters of personal standing, and the narrow interpretation of *ijtihād* in this field. In his book, *Maqasid al-shariʿa al-Islamiyya* (Objectives of Islamic Shariʿa),[87] Tahir bin ʿAshur[88] dedicated for the first time an independent chapter to shariʿa objectives in terms of personal standing, albeit without giving them the proper scope.[89] Due to the shifting circumstances of Muslim minorities, an *ijtihād* is still required to attain the unique interests of the family as well as the objectives of the shariʿa in matters of personal standing. Al-Najjar specifies the objectives of family related shariʿa laws:[90]

1. Preservation of mankind: shariʿa laws must ensure the continuation of the human race through procreation between the two sexes. Every personal standing decree should be mindful of this imperative.
2. Closeness and devotion (*al-ifḍāʾ*): marriage generates extreme closeness that results in a spiritual merger between the couple. Every personal standing decree must aspire to invoke the utmost physical and spiritual closeness between the couple.
3. Sexual pleasure (*al-ifḍāʾ al-jinsī*): religious law encourages pleasure, as it is one of the aims of coupling. Lack of sexual relations in a couple's life might ruin a marriage and result in separation. Therefore, every decree on personal standing must encourage sexual relations between the couple, deriving the utmost permissible pleasure from it.
4. Social cohesion: because the family is the nucleus of society it must be cohesive. Family cohesion affects and strengthens the entire society,

[85] Al-Najjar, "Maqasid al- Shariʿa fi Ahkam al-Usra Muwajahha li-Ahkam al-Usra al-Muslima fi al-Gharb," 69.

[86] Ibid., 69.

[87] Tahir bin ʿAshur, *Maqasid al- Shariʿa al-Islamiyya* (Jordan: Dar al-Nafaʾis, 2nd ed., 2001), 345-end.

[88] Tunisian scholar (1879–1973), renowned for his religious law reforms, he served as president of the Al-Zaytuna institute. Called for *ijtihād*, mainly based on the objectives of shariʿa.

[89] Abdul-Majeed al-Najjar, "Malat al-Afʿal wa-Athruha fi Fiqh al-Aqalliyyat," *Al-Majallat al-ʿIlmiyya li-l-Majlis al-Urubi li-l-Iftaʾ* 4–5 (2003), 69,www.e-fcr.org

[90] Ibid., 75–87.

and a unified and robust society will strive to attain the good and the moral while rejecting the evil. Thus, every decree in the realm of personal standing must promote the cohesiveness of the family and prevent its disintegration.

5. A shining example: the family must serve as a beacon for other families so that in imitating its example, others can learn what is good and moral, and follow in that path. When a family ceases to function as dictated by religious law, it should be dismantled so as not to serve as a negative example to other families. Therefore, every decree in the realm of personal standing must guide the family unto the Islamic path and prevent them from deviating from it.

The weight and significance of each of the five objectives of the shariʿa alters according to the five distinct characterizations of Muslim families in non-Muslim countries. Whereas an objective might be of minor consequence to families in the Islamic world, its importance to Muslim families in non-Muslim countries can be immense. The reverse is also true. Therefore, shariʿa law must shift according to the unique challenges and tasks that each family faces. This shift will be manifested in favoring or rejecting a certain objective, in expanding or diminishing its meaning, as well as in its application.[91]

Personal Standing and Changing the Law According to the Objectives of the Shariʿa

Analyzing the objectives of shariʿa laws regarding personal standing through the lens of the distinctness of the Muslim family in non-Muslim countries demonstrates that the goal of preserving mankind within Muslim countries becomes even more important in the West. Western culture abounds with trends that are contradictory to Islam: bachelorhood, avoiding marriage and procreation, and the disintegration of families. These trends have brought about a decrease in the overall population, while the percentage of the aged has risen. Hence, the preservation of mankind is a real and pressing concern among Muslim minority communities. Unlike the lands of Islam, some of which must take measures to limit birthrates due to exponential population growth, Muslim minorities need to encourage family building and procreation in order to maintain a balance between the older and younger generations in society. Achieving this goal necessitates lenient religious ruling in terms of procreation and

[91] Ibid., 87.

population growth, while taking a stand against bachelorhood, childlessness, and extramarital sexual relations. Moreover, in order to preserve the integrity of the family and prevent its disintegration, it is vital to strengthen the bond between children and parents, and increase parental commitment to their children.[92]

Many temptations jeopardize the Muslim family in non-Muslim countries, chiefly sexual permissiveness and extramarital sexual relations. Simultaneously, the pressures of consumerism and financial burdens also plague the family. Thus, although it is less relevant within the conservative environment of Islamic countries, the objective of intimacy and devotion is of extreme significance in Muslim minority religious laws. The objective was intended to encourage the couple to derive the maximum sexual pleasure within the limitation of religion, thus inoculating them from surrounding temptations. Aside from prohibiting sodomy and sexual relations while the woman is on her menstrual cycle, religious decrees should be flexible and lenient on the matter of sexual pleasure. In addition, the decrees should encourage closeness and spiritual devotion between the couple in order to provide mutual support while simultaneously diminishing their desire to engage in an extramarital affair bred by emotional bankruptcy.[93]

The Muslim family suffers from isolation due to dissimilarities with its non-Muslim surroundings. This can cause seclusion, eroding the family's social standing. Therefore, the objective of social cohesion is an imperative, which compels adjudicators to allow the family to assimilate into society in two ways: (1) abolishing ethnic, religious, or nationalistic barriers so that a Muslim family can integrate into another Muslim country geographically adjacent to their own; (2) expressing openness toward non-Muslim society such that relations and integration become possible. Being receptive and building relationships with non-Muslims on the basis of mutual respect can assist in that goal, which is also served by partaking in their celebrations, mourning, and public life. This will bring stability and a sense that a Muslim family's residence in that country is not temporary but rather constant, thus transforming the family into a positive, productive element of society.[94]

Being an emissary to non-Muslim countries is also a valid consideration. Indeed, it is a heavy burden to serve as a role model for the non-Muslim

[92] Ibid., 88–9.
[93] Ibid., 89–93.
[94] Ibid., 93–7.

public – presenting the Islamic model and drawing society closer to it. This objective compels the adjudicator to rule beyond shariʿa rights and obligations, encouraging mutual dependency within the family and, in particular, good deeds wherein a person goes without to give to another. In this manner, the family becomes a warm nest, as opposed to Western families that entertain a weaker understanding of familial responsibility. In addition, since abiding by the law is seminal to Western society, the adjudicator must insist on the fulfillment of private, civil, and public obligations.[95]

Personal Standing: Dealing with Obligatory Civil Law

Following the framework developed by al-Najjar for Muslim minority religious law on matters of personal standing, as well as the supplements provided by Jaballah, Mohammed al-Amrani[96] endeavored to develop the religious law methodology of *fiqh al-aqalliyyāt* at its intersection with the laws and legal systems of non-Muslim countries.[97] To al-Amrani, legislation is designed to fulfill the public good, and dictate behavioral norms among the individual members of society, thus facilitating justice and equality. These goals are common both to manmade and divine legislation, yet the former relies on experience and knowledge that are confined by time and place, whereas God's legislation is absolute and transcendent. Striving to achieve the same objectives, manmade legislation can overlap with divine legislation, although they may differ and even contradict one another in their logic or leaning.[98]

Therefore, al-Amrani believes Muslim adjudicators are obliged to seek the points of interaction between religious and civil laws, thus avoiding the perplexing contradictions Muslim minorities face on a daily basis.[99] Although there is no complete congruence between them, the points of interaction create a common ground which the expert adjudicator can use to mediate the contradiction and stabilize the lives of Muslim minorities.[100] Al-Amrani illustrates this claim through the example of illicit marital

95 Ibid., 99–100.

96 Yemenite qadi and religious scholar, considered the most prominent Yemenite religious scholar in the modern age. Lectures at various universities in Yemen and at the High Judicial Institute; published dozens of books and researches on shariʿa related topics.

97 Mohammed al-Amrani, "Al-Usra al-Muslima fi al-Gharb bayn al-Tashriʿ al-Islami wa-l-Qawanin al-Wadʿiyya," *Al-Majallat al-ʿIlmiyya li-l-Majlis al-Urubi li-l-Iftaʾ li-l-Buhuth* 7 (July 2005): 175–227.

98 Ibid., 206.

99 Ibid., 207.

100 Ibid., 207–8.

relations: Muslim religious law prohibits one to marry a blood relative (e.g., mother, sister, aunt, or niece), a relation through breastfeeding (i.e., a wet nurse), and extends this prohibition to terminated unions (e.g., even after a couple is divorced or the wife passes away, it is prohibited to marry her mother). These prohibitions are absolute and not dependent on changing circumstances and time. Other prohibitions such as marrying the wife's sister are provisional and may be annulled in the case of a couple's divorce or the passing away of the wife. Legal systems in non-Muslim countries incorporate similar prohibitions adopted from Christian or Jewish traditions. French law, for instance, prohibits marrying mothers and daughters both biological and through adoption. In addition, the law forbids marrying uncles and nephews, or marrying the parents of the wife or husband. Another example for such intersection between Muslim law and civil law is guardianship. In France, both legal systems charge guardians to protect the interests of minors and those incompetent to stand trial, including in matters of marriage and divorce.[101]

Al-Amrani offers another method to reconcile Muslim minority tradition with the laws of the country: filtering out non-Islamic customs that have permeated the tradition. These sinful customs misrepresent Muslim tradition as negative and primitive, deserving to be replaced with the "enlightened" Western tradition, especially in the field of personal standing.[102] Viewing women as inherently inferior to men is an example of a custom that justifies unseemly conduct and even violence toward women, including limiting their freedoms. This misrepresentation can jeopardize the Muslim minority family and lead the next generation to reject Islamic tradition. Furthermore, it can bring the legal and social welfare authorities to intercede, and dismantle the Muslim family. If a man beats his wife under the guise of religious law, he breaks local laws which may result in criminal proceedings against him; his punishment may involve social welfare authorities intervening to dismantle the family.[103] Another custom mistakenly believed to be rooted in Islamic tradition is discrimination between boys and girls. Should girls feel discriminated against, and lacking in opportunities to progress, they might choose to abandon the unequal system in search of other, fairer systems. This can gravely harm the Muslim community, pushing away those who do not wish to play a part

101 Ibid., 207–18.
102 Jaballah, "Al-Usra al-Muslima fi Europe bayn Ta'thirat al-Bi'aa al-Ahtima'iyya wa-l-'Adat al-Murutha," 243–4.
103 Ibid.

in a religion or culture that discriminates against women.[104] Guardianship for women for the purpose of marriage is also misinterpreted, as Islam forbids forcing an adult woman into marriage against her will.[105] By contrast, it is customary according to common tradition for the father to choose his daughter's husband. This is no longer accepted by the younger generation, potentially causing them to feel alienated from the family and the community.[106]

When religious law negates or contradicts civil law, particularly in the field of personal standing, Muslims must tread cautiously and avoid civil legal proceedings.[107] Al-Amrani illustrates this through the subject of paternity: According to Muslim religious law, fatherhood outside of wedlock is not recognized and a child born from such a relationship is attributed to the husband of the biological mother, as paternity tests to determine the identity of the father are inadmissible. These religious laws contradict civil legislation that recognizes paternity tests to determine the father's identity, albeit the legislation differs from country to country. For instance, the majority of states in America have adopted inclusive laws that explicitly, or through legal interpretation, grant the recognized father the right to custody through clear and compelling evidence. By contrast, several states have adopted the counter-inclusive Uniform Parentage Act of 1973, which prohibits recognized fathers from claiming custody under any circumstances. Nevertheless, in the 2000 edition to the law it was stated that the alleged biological father of a child may take legal actions to affirm or disprove the existence of a parental relationship.[108] The disparity between shari'a and civil law also derives from the religious prohibition on committing adultery and engaging in extramarital sexual relations, as in non-Muslim civil societies there is no legal standing on sexual relations outside of marriage. Moreover, civil society has accepted alternative arrangements to marriage and the classic family structure. One can also

104 Ibid., 245.

105 Within the scope of *wilāyat al-ijbār* (the guardianship that grants the guardian absolute power to compel the protégé to do a certain thing), religious law permits to marry a woman who is a minor without her consent. Predominantly, this permission is not relevant to Muslim minorities in the West because most Western countries prohibit marriage under the age of consent.

106 Jaballah, "Al-Usra al-Muslima fi Europe bayn Ta'thirat al-Bi'aa al-Ahtima'iyya wa-l-'Adat al-Murutha," 245.

107 Al-Amrani, "Al-Usra al-Muslima fi al-Gharb bayn al-Tashri' al-Islami wa-l-Qawanin al-Wad'iyya," 218.

108 Ron Shaham, *The Expert Witness in Islamic Courts: Medicine and Crafts in the Service of Law* (Chicago: University of Chicago Press, 2010): 162–3.

add the Islamic rejection of adoption, which is a common and accepted practice in Western civil societies.[109]

Implementation of the *Fiqh al-Aqalliyyāt* Methodology in Matters of Personal Standing

In order to cope with the influences of the surrounding society, religious scholars believe that the adjudicator must study the lived realities of Muslim families in non-Muslim countries; he must consider how changes and developments affect the Muslim minority. Moreover, the adjudicator must possess a comprehensive outlook on Muslim minorities and a deep understanding of their sociolegal realities. His ruling must be given in such a way that the public identifies with and reacts to the elements at play, shying away from the negative elements and embracing the positive ones.[110] This will allow the adjudicator to protect Muslims from undesirable influences and fortify the family structure, enabling it to educate the next generation in light of Islamic values and the preservation of their religious identity.

The obligations of Muslim minority religious law should be modified according to the distinct characteristics of the Muslim family in non-Muslim countries, and the objectives of shariʿa. In the field of personal standing, a new type of religious law has emerged, one that differs both from classic religious law and laws customary to Muslim countries. This is the result of constructing religious laws that take into account the unique predicaments of Muslim minorities, while also adhering to the objectives of the shariʿa. This method – utilizing the objectives of shariʿa after the examination of the unique predicaments of the Muslim family in minority communities – is one of the pillars of *fiqh al-aqalliyyāt al-muslima* methodology in the field of personal standing.

In a dual legal system, civil laws are at times concurrent with and at times contradictory to shariʿa law. Thus, the adjudicator seeks the points of interaction and correspondence between the two systems.[111] In cases in which shariʿa laws contradict civil laws, the adjudicator should minimize the discrepancies so that Muslims do not break religious prohibitions, on the one hand, nor state laws, on the other.[112] Nonetheless, the position of

[109] Ibid., 218–225.

[110] Jaballah, "Al-Usra al-Muslima fi Europe bayn Ta'thirat al-Bi'aa al-Ahtimaʿiyya wa-l-ʿAdat al-Murutha," 248.

[111] Ibid., 207.

[112] Ibid., 175–6.

women in Islam is extremely sensitive. According to Caeiro,[113] the position of Muslim women in Europe is exceptionally problematic. The disparities between reality and the general *fiqh* on the topic of women are immense. Women are more concerned with their treatment within the religion and tend to ask more questions; newcomers to Islam as well ask many questions pertaining to women. Examples of questions raised by women are: can a woman get a haircut without her husband's permission? Can they participate in Islamic conferences? Can they marry without a *walī*, a guardian for marriage? The ECFR tends side with women on family matters, such as the right to meet their parents or take a maternity leave. Caeiro believes that this feministic approach by the ECFR extenuates high regard for women. In his opinion, the superiority of men over women, *quwāma*, also refers to the superiority of women over men. A woman serves her husband out of her own free will and not out of necessity. For instance, a husband does not have the right to the following: to force his wife to deposit her earnings into a joint bank account; to prohibit her from seeing her Christian parents; to prohibit her from speaking with male guests; to prohibit her from resting after childbirth or sickness; to prohibit her from participating in Muslim women conferences; to prohibit her from adhering to a different school of thought than his own (*madhab*). In addition, a woman is allowed to marry without a *walī* (a permission originating in the Ḥanafī School). Furthermore, the ECFR maintains that women should be encouraged to work and engage in the political arena. Caeiro believes that despite the ECFR's feministic leanings, it has also produced decrees that are detrimental to women, such as permitting polygamy and obliging women who divorce through *khulʿ* to pay compensations in exchange for a divorce. However, the ECFR does encourage conducting civil marriage ceremonies and divorces alongside the religious ones in order to ensure women's financial rights.

The adjudicators are asked to endow women with the esteem they deserve by filtering out the Muslim customs that infringe on their position and rights. In order to enable women to participate in Muslim minority public life, the adjudicators must strive to annul deeply rooted customs that negate the spirit of Islam. The adjudicators should seek to inculcate the importance and value of the family in the younger generation,

[113] Caeiro, "The European Council for Fatwa and Research" (paper presented at the Fourth Mediterranean Social and Political Research Meeting, European University Institute, Florence, Italy, March 19–23, 2003), 12.

attributing great significance to the institution of marriage and glorifying it in their eyes.[114]

The Methodical Implementation of *Fiqh al-Aqalliyyāt* in Ruling on Personal Standing

To explore the consistency and methodicalness of the implementation of the *fiqh al-aqalliyyāt* methodology, I will examine selected religious decrees that boast religious innovation in comparison with classic religious law.

The Sanction of Continuing the Marriage: A Female Islamic Convert and her Non-Muslim Husband

Religious scholars were in consensus (*ijmāʿ*) about the necessity to separate a woman who converted to Islam from her husband if the latter keeps his religion and does not convert. The separation should be instantaneous upon her conversion or at the end of *al-ʿidda* (a three month waiting period from the day of conversion) or until the end of the pregnancy were she pregnant at the time of the conversion.[115] Nevertheless, Qaradawi's ruling deviated from the aforementioned consensus. His point of departure was Ibn al-Qayyim, who quotes conflicting decrees by two authoritative religious scholars.[116] Some scholars decreed that a woman's marriage to a non-Muslim man became null and void the moment the woman converted. According to another decree, the marriage is null and void if the husband refuses the offer to convert, making the waiting period of the *ʿidda* superfluous. Some decrees annul the marriage of a woman who converted to Islam upon the termination of the *ʿidda* period counted from the day of her conversion. Some maintain that the marriage is valid as long as the woman remains in the land of her non-Muslim husband, and as long as the sovereign did not annul the marriage. In such a case, the woman remains with her husband but is not allowed to engage in a sexual relation with him. Thus, the marriage is valid in theory but not in practice, and the woman choosing to remain with her husband rather than separate must wait until he converts. If the husband does convert then she reverts to being his wife, both in theory and in practice. Qaradawi believes this

[114] Ibid., 246–8.
[115] Qaradawi, *Fi Fiqh al-Aqaliyyat al-Muslima*, 105.
[116] Ibid., 106–8.

position to be the most accurate – supported by the Prophet's sunna and adopted by Ibn Taymiyya.[117]

Qaradawi believes that there is no unequivocal text or *ijmāʿ* on this subject, and that the marriage predating the conversion is still in effect. Discrepancy in the couple's religious beliefs does not necessitate an automatic annulment, despite the fact that it may become a motivating factor to terminate a marriage.[118] He further maintains that even the Prophet did not separate a converted woman from her non-Muslim husband, basing his claim on the hadith of the Prophet's daughter Zainab, who asked her father if she could host her infidel husband who immigrated to the country. The Prophet replied that he was still her husband and she could host him, but not engage in intercourse. After six years, the husband converted to Islam and the Prophet allowed him and his daughter to reunite without constructing a new marriage agreement. Furthermore, Qaradawi claims that Caliph ʿUmr ibn al-Khattab was undecided on the subject, opting between separating a couple and allowing the wife a choice whether to remain with her husband or part with him.[119]

Qaradawi believes that in such a case the marriage is not annulled, even though it can be terminated, as the choice lies with the woman who converted; she can continue to live with her husband and wait for his conversion, or separate and marry another man after the waiting period (*al-ʿidda*) is over.[120] He rationalizes his decree by the need to safeguard newly converted women who remain with their husbands in a non-Muslim country, as well as concern for their children. In addition, such a situation preserves the hope that the husband will also convert to Islam. The ECFR decision number 8/3 has adopted Qaradawi's approach, decreeing that a woman who converts to Islam can remain with her non-Muslim husband if she so wishes, as long as the couple has already consummated the marriage. In a case in which the husband does not discriminate against her because of her religion, and she wishes for him to convert and is willing to wait until he does, the wife then must undertake all obligations and receive all rights pertaining to marriage.[121] This decree constitutes a considerable alleviation for newly converted Muslim women and is a direct derivative of the

117 Ibid., 105.
118 Ibid., 124–5.
119 Ibid., 110.
120 Ibid., 116.
121 Ruling 8/3 of the ECFR, which allows a woman who converted to Islam to remain with her non-Muslim husband: http://articles.islamweb.net/media/index.php?page=article&lang=A&id=4527

implementation of the formerly discussed *fiqh al-aqalliyyāt* methodology. In this instance, Qaradawi prioritized Muslim interests, specifically, those of women who convert, enabling them to remain with their non-Muslim husbands and thus preserve the integrity of their families. By assuaging a woman's fear that she might have to separate from her husband and leave her family were she to join Islam, this decree also acts to fulfill the objective of calling non-believers to Islam. Thus, the unique predicament of Muslim minorities has brought forth a most revolutionary shift in religious law.[122] The ECFR decree also inspired much dissention among religious scholars. It was harshly criticized by Al-Zuhayli who argued it contradicted the *ijmāʿ*, the consensus of the four schools that a woman who converted to Islam must separate from her non-Muslim husband, both in the lands of Islam and anywhere else.[123]

Marriages between Muslim Men and Women of the People of the Book (*Kitābiyāt*)

According to an *ijmāʿ* by religious scholars based on unequivocal verses from the Qur'an, it is permissible (*mubāḥ*) for a Muslim man to marry a Christian or a Jewish woman because both fall within the category of People of the Book. This was practiced by the *ṣaḥāba*, the companions of the Prophet; in modern times, Muslim minority website "Islamweb" decreed that a Muslim is allowed to marry a woman of the people of the book if she is pure and shies away from adultery.[124] Nevertheless, these marriages are considered obscene (*makrūh*) by the *Ḥanafī*, *Shāfiʿī* and segments of the *Mālikī* Schools, and are not deemed as preferable by the Ḥanbalī School.[125] Qaradawi concurs that religious law does allow for such a marriage, but there are five stipulations: (1) the woman was not merely born to observant parents, but she wholeheartedly believes in a monotheistic religion; (2) the woman is virtuous; (3) the woman keeps herself pure and abstains from extramarital sexual relations; (4) she does not belong to a nation hostile to Islam; (5) her marriage to a Muslim will not cause

[122] Ibid., 120–1.

[123] Islam Muhammad abu al-ʿAta, "Anqisamat Hawl Shariʿa Baqaʾ al-Zawja al-Kitabiyya al-lati Aslamt maʿ Zawjiha al-Ghayr Muslim fi al-Dul al-European," 2010.

[124] The fatwa allowing a Muslim man to marry a woman of the People of the Book, http://www.islamweb.net/mainpage/index.php

[125] Wahba al-Zuhayli, *Al-Fiqh al-Islami wa-Adillutih* (Damascus: Dar al-Fikr, 2007), ch. 9, 6653–5.

any harm to Muslims. The fifth stipulation derives, according to Qaradawi, from the inherent authority of the Muslim sovereign to veto the permission laws in cases where they may cause harm.[126]

Based on these stipulations, Qaradawi argues that the spirit and objectives of the shariʿa dictate that these marriages be rejected because of the damage they inflict on Muslims in non-Muslim countries. Because only Muslim men are allowed to marry non-Muslim women, this would lower the chances of Muslim women finding husbands outside the lands of Islam. Moreover, marrying a non-Muslim woman in a non-Muslim country may bring the children to forsake the Islamic religion, language, and tradition of their father due to their close relations with their mother. In addition, the influence of the non-Muslim environment can result in a loss of faith both by the father and his sons. These various threats are nonexistent when such marriages occur within the lands of Islam.[127] Qaradawi's decree is based on the rules that preventing harm is preferable to bringing benefit, and that minor damage is preferable to massive damage. Analysis of this demonstrates how the doctrine's methodology, as manifested in the framework of al-Najjar and Jaballah, was almost completely implemented. Furthermore, the decree echoes the shariʿa personal standing objective that every Muslim man and woman is entitled to have an intimate, devoted, and sexually pleasurable marriage. All of this drove Qaradawi to prohibit Muslim men from marrying non-Muslim women, so as not to decrease the chances of a Muslim woman getting married and thus fulfilling the objectives of the shariʿa with her husband.

To conclude, the isolation and dislodgment of the Muslim family from an Islamic environment in the West serves as a distinct characteristic that modifies Muslim religious law. The plethora of temptations in the West necessitates marriages to Muslim women so they are not forced to break shariʿa laws due to a shortage of eligible Muslim men. Education also necessitates marriage to a Muslim woman so the children are raised according to Islamic values, and do not utterly assume the culture and values of their non-Muslim surroundings. In summation, the detrimental influences of the environment have led religious scholars to prohibit marriage with non-Muslim women (i.e. Jews and Christians), despite it being allowed within the lands of Islam.

126 Caeiro, "The European Council for Fatwa and Research," 97–100.

127 Ibid., 100–4.

Marriage Guardian

All religious scholars, except for the *Ḥanafī* School determined that a guardian's consent is a prerequisite for marriage, and without his consent a marriage is null and void. This decree is grounded in the Prophet's hadith which states that "a woman marrying without the consent of the *walī* [guardian], her marriage is annulled, annulled, annulled, and in a case of a difference of opinion, the Sultan is the *walī* of those who do not have one."[128] If a woman does not have a relative who can serve as her guardian, shari'a law grants the Prophet the right to assume that role, after him comes the Sultan as the leader of the Muslim people, and after him his delegates in the different provinces, representatives, and appointed qadis.[129] By contrast, when Muslims do not have a sultan, as is the case for Muslim minority communities in the West, the authority to serve as a guardian is given to the certified leadership of the minority community. If there is an Islamic center, its Imam will serve as the guardian. In a case where the shari'a ordained guardian opposes the marriage with no reason substantiated by the shari'a, and there is no Muslim qadi, then the Imam is requested to approve the marriage.[130] In ruling number 4/3, the ECFR has adopted this decree and recommended that Imams of Islamic centers serve as guardians for women who do not have anyone to perform that duty. Nonetheless, it also ruled that the marriage of a woman of consensual age to a man whose virtue and religious devoutness are beyond reproach is valid.[131]

This religious decree coincides with the *fiqh al-aqalliyyāt* methodology since it takes into consideration the distinctiveness of the Muslim minority, the isolation of the family, and the various temptations it faces in a foreign country. Moreover, it takes into account civil law which allows a woman of consensual age to wed in civil marriage without the need for a guardian. Therefore, through the façade of granting a guardian's consent to marriage for women who either lack a guardian or whose guardian opposes their marriage, the decree has allowed women to marry whomever they wish. Thus, the decree promotes women's independence, freedom of choice, and women's rights in general.

[128] Al-Zuhayli, *Al-Fiqh al-Islami wa-Adillutih*, 6572–4.

[129] Umar Sulaiman al-Ashqar, *Ahkam al-Zawaj* (Jordan: Dar al-Nafa'is, 1997), 149.

[130] Mohammed al-Ghalayini, *Al-Marakiz al-Islamiyya fi North America* (Jordan: Dar Amar li-l-Nashr wa-l-Tawzi'a, 2009), 252–60; see also, al-Ashqar, *Ahkam al-Zawaj*, 149–50.

[131] *Decisions and Fatwas Issued by the European Council for Fatwa and Research*, 2002, 123–4.

Divorce and Marriage Annulment

Muslim religious law is divided over the annulment of marriage in the case of an absent husband. The *Ḥanafī* and *Shāfiʿī* Schools determined that in such a case, the woman had no right to request an annulment. On the other end of the spectrum, the *Mālikī* and the *Ḥanbalī* Schools permitted the annulment, albeit with a stipulation from the *Ḥanbalī* School that the husband's absence be unjustified and a minimum of six months. According to *Mālikī* School, the duration of the absence must be over a year, and in some cases over three years; however, if the husband is missing and his whereabouts are unknown, a qadi can annul the marriage immediately upon the request of the wife. If his whereabouts are known, he is then required to appear and present his testimony; failure to do so results in an immediate annulment.[132]

Religious scholars are faced with cases of Muslim men who came to the West seeking education or employment, took wives with them, and later returned to the lands of Islam leaving their Muslim wives behind. Al-Ghalayini[133] determines that Muslim minorities in the West, as well as their religious scholars, should adopt the *Mālikī* approach, enabling women to annul a marriage that de facto does not exist.[134] The school sequesters the husband's right for divorce and endows the arbitrators with the authority to exact it. Al-Ghalayini is a proponent of this more lenient approach also in cases of acute disagreement between the couple. Civil courts, he points out, grant separation in cases of conflict between the couple, especially in cases when the woman is harmed during the marriage; he implores arbitrators in Islamic centers to do the same.[135]

Al-Ghalayini tends to be more lenient in the separation procedures and annulment of marriage, especially when a woman appeals on account of harm incurred during the absence of her husband or a prolonged dispute. In shariʿa, the adoption of a more lenient and beneficial *Mālikī* approach is referred to as *takhayyur*. It coincides with *fiqh al-aqalliyyāt*, which favors religious laws that reduce the burden on the believer and are appropriate to his or her circumstances. This approach renders affiliation to a specific school inconsequential. In addition, this decree copes better with the

132 Al-Zuhayli, *Al-Fiqh al-Islami wa-Adillutih*, ch.9, 7066–7.

133 President of the North American Imam Federation, and member of the Assembly of Muslim Jurists of America.

134 Al-Ghalayini, *Al-Marakiz al-Islamiyya fi North America*, 256–64.

135 Ibid.

contradiction between religious and civil law, which annuls marriages even without the husband's consent.

The Validity of Divorce Issued by a Non-Muslim Judge

The validity of a Muslim couple's divorce when it is officiated by a non-Muslim judge alters according to the couple's circumstances. A couple that resides in a non-Muslim country, but who are citizens of and were wed in a Muslim country, must appeal their case to a shariʿa court in a Muslim country. Unless compelled by their circumstances, the couple is not allowed to voluntarily appeal to a non-Muslim civil court, as by doing so they commit an infringement of religious prohibitions. If the legal proceedings are taking place in a non-Muslim country, the couple must demand to be judged according to shariʿa law of the country in which they were married.[136]

Nevertheless, if shariʿa law is not recognized by the country of residence, or the marriage was conducted in a non-Muslim country, then civil law is paramount in cases of marriage and divorce. The question then arises: is this verdict religiously binding?[137] The annulment of a Muslim couple's marriage by a civil court in a non-Muslim country will be upheld by the enforcement agencies; a husband who fails to abide by the verdict will be breaking the law. Religious law encourages a person to become accustomed to the laws of his country of residence while still observing religious prohibitions. To spare the Muslim believer from hardships, Muslim minority religious adjudicators must try and bridge religious law and civil law.[138]

Through the story of a Muslim husband who got married in a non-Muslim country and left his wife and children for another woman, Mohammed Al Amrani demonstrates how under certain circumstances, divorce verdicts by a non-Muslim judge are granted a religious sanction. Following their strife, the husband had refused to divorce his wife or pay her and his children alimony. In order to guarantee quality of life for herself and her children, the woman had no other choice but to turn to a civil judge. In such instances, the need to protect the disenfranchised outweighs the prohibition of an appeal to a non-Muslim judge.[139]

[136] For a broader discussion on the subject see al-Amrani, "Al-Usra al-Muslima fi al-Gharb bayn al-Tashriʿ al-Islami wa-l-Qawanin al-Wadʿiyya."
[137] Ibid., 188–90.
[138] Ibid., 199–202.
[139] Ibid., 198–9.

The ECFR decreed in resolution 5/3 that a Muslim who got married according to the laws of a Western country must abide by the divorce verdict issued by that same legal system. This is because getting married according to non-Muslim law implies the Muslim's acceptance of the possible consequences of this act, including the annulment of the marriage by a non-Muslim judge. According to the ECFR, the husband delegated the right to divorce his wife to the prevailing legal system in that country. Although the husband may not have openly declared his relinquishing of this right, the guiding principle is that common practice is valid as a prerequisite condition. Upholding the decree of a non-Muslim judge is allowed in order to prevent injustice and chaos.[140]

The shari'a appeals court in Amman, Jordan has deliberated on this issue on several occasions, its ruling changing from case to case. In a precedential ruling, the court rejected the divorce verdict supplied by a civil court in Sweden for a Muslim couple that got married in Damascus. Despite being decreed by a Swedish court and endorsed by the Islamic center in Stockholm, Sweden, the divorce was invalidated by the Jordanian court. The reason given was that the divorce had been decreed by a non-Muslim judge; the court explicated the decision by the position of the Ḥanafi School, which is prevalent in Jordan, that the presiding judge in legal proceedings between Muslims must be Muslim as well. In a dissenting opinion, Qadi Al-Rawajba argued that an *ijtihād* was necessary because the previous religious scholars were unfamiliar with the circumstances of Muslim minorities living under non-Muslim sovereigns, and could not have anticipated the lack of a Muslim qadi to rule on their affairs. Qadi Rawajba added that by settling in those countries, Muslim couples had in fact granted the civil courts the power to annul their marriages. Since these countries do not recognize shari'a law, the divorce of a Muslim couple by a non-Muslim judge must be upheld.[141] In a later appeal, the shair'a court in Jordan overturned its previous decision, and the minority voice was unanimously accepted, as was the validity of the divorce.[142]

140 Hussein Mohammed Halawa, "Al-Talaq wa-Ahkamuh," *Al-Majallat al-'Ilmiyya li-l-Majlis al-Urubi li-l-Ifta' li-l-Buhuth* 8–9 (June 2006): 165.

141 Appeal no. 409/2004–59704, Na'im al-Sahli v. 'Abir al-Tahir wa-'Iysa Abu Murad. Personal communication with al-Rawajba, a qadi at the Jordanian Court of Appeals.

142 Appeal no. 336/2007–66725, Musa Khabbas Wafa' al-Khatib versus Ahmad Qasim. Personal communication with al-Rawajba, a qadi at the Jordanian Court of Appeals.

Muslim Inheriting from a Non-Muslim

Religious scholars from all four schools have unanimously decreed that due to a contrast of religions, a Muslim may not inherent anything of wealth from a non-Muslim and vice versa. This ruling is founded on the hadith that a "Muslim shall not inherit from an infidel, nor an infidel from a Muslim."[143] Nevertheless, in a decree upheld only by a handful of previous religious scholars, Qaradawi permitted a Muslim to inherit from a non-Muslim, but not the other way around.[144] His justification was based on the hadith that Islam seeks to heap benefits on its believers rather than deny them. Therefore, much in the way that the Islamic permission for a Muslim man to marry a woman of the people of the book does not apply to a Muslim woman, so too should a Muslim be allowed to inherit from a non-Muslim without the reverse being permissible. In his decree, Qaradawi aspires to draw the people of the book closer to Islam, as some wish to convert to Islam but are wary of losing their inheritance; he has heard this fear echoed by many in non-Muslim countries. The decree might assuage the fear of relinquishing an inheritance, and thus encourage potential converts. In terms of shariʿa there is a clear-cut interest to allow Muslims to inherit from non-Muslims,[145] particularly when civil law entitles it.[146]

The ECFR adopted this decree in resolution 5/1, ruling that the aforementioned hadith meant that the prohibition on inheritance between a Muslim and an infidel is only in effect if the infidel is in a state of war with Islam. Hence, the decree that allows a Muslim to inherit from an infidel is in line with the Prophet's hadith.[147] This decree is another manifestation of the implementation of *fiqh al-aqalliyyāt*. The new religious law, which differs from the accepted, classic religious law tradition, accomplishes the objectives of shariʿa in matters of personal standing as manifested by the doctrine's thinkers – taking into consideration the unique circumstances of the Muslim family in the West. The methodology also fulfills the principle of Muslim interests, the role of Muslim minorities as emissaries of Islam, and the calling upon non-Muslim to join the religion.

143 Al-Zuhayli, *Al-Fiqh al-Islami wa-Adillutih*, 7718–9.
144 Al-Ghalayini, *Al-Marakiz al-Islamiyya fi North America*, 126.
145 Ibid., 129–30.
146 Ibid., 131.
147 *Decisions and Fatwas issued by the European Council for Fatwa and Research*, 2002, 137–8.

Adopting Abandoned Children

Muslim religious law prohibits the adoption of children based on an explicit verse in the Qur'an (33:4–5). Nonetheless, for the sake of the children, it is permissible to raise children that are not one's own until they become adults. In such cases, the children will remain estranged to the people who raised them, as they are not entitled to any right enjoyed by the biological children, and are under the prohibitions that befall foreign children in terms of marriage.[148] Contrary to this specific religious law, in a decree issued on October 7, 2003, al-ʿAlwani determined that if there was no other way to preserve the Muslim identity of children who immigrated to non-Muslim countries, Muslims were allowed to adopt them. Al-ʿAlwani believes that there is no objection to a couple adopting and civilly registering children, as long as private documentation is drafted such that it articulates the entire array of rights according to religion, and makes clear that the adopted child is not their own. In his decree, al-ʿAlwani draws on shariʿa law that the lesser damage should be preferred to the greater one.[149]

According to al-Ghalayini, because non-Muslim countries such as the United States do not permit one to raise orphaned children (*kafālat yatīm*) without adopting them, al-ʿAlwani's revolutionary ruling was obtained despite the strict prohibition in the Qur'an. In this sense, the decree is designed to prevent a situation wherein a Muslim orphan, raised by Christians or Jews, might replace his religious identity with another. Al-Ghalayini further suggests that adoptive mothers should breastfeed their adopted children so that they become breastfed children.[150] Breastfeeding ameliorates the position of the child within the family in terms of rights, permissions, and prohibitions. The adoptive parents may specify in their will if the adopted child is to be excluded from any inheritance, or if he will be counted among the inheritors, along with the biological children, regardless Islamic inheritance laws.[151] This decree implements the framework of the *fiqh al-aqalliyyāt* doctrine in the issue of orphaned and abandoned Muslim children in non-Muslim countries. It determines that for Muslim minorities in non-Muslim countries, fulfilling the general shariʿa objective of preserving the religion outweighs the prohibition against adopting.

[148] Al-Zuhayli *Al-Fiqh al-Islami wa-Adillutih*, 7247–50.

[149] Al-Ghalayini, *Al-Marakiz al-Islamiyya fi North America*, 269–70.

[150] According to Muslim religious law, a woman who breastfeeds a child is granted a mother's status, as the child receives her DNA. Thus, her biological children are considered the brothers or sisters of the breastfed child, and are prohibited from marrying.

[151] Al-Ghalayini, *Al-Marakiz al-Islamiyya fi North America*, 269–70.

3

Muslim Minorities: Implementation of Shariʿa in General and *Fiqh al-Aqalliyyāt* in Particular

In this chapter I will examine the applicability of shariʿa as a legal framework of rules and norms in general, and of *fiqh al-aqalliyyāt* in particular, vis-à-vis Muslim minorities in the West. I will furthermore examine their effectiveness and pervasiveness in the lives of Muslim minorities. In addition, the chapter will focus on Western public and administrative attitudes toward the application of shariʿa in the West – special attention will be given to the influence of a pluralism that accepts the application of more than one legal system for a specific case. Thus, this chapter explores the practices adopted by Muslim minorities in order to implement shariʿa and develop pluralistic civil law. Pluralism is achieved through arbitrators, mediators, and religious conciliators who are appointed by civil courts, or advise civil judges over cases involving Muslim couples. Through the establishment of independent Islamic institutions for ruling and arbitration according to shariʿa law, Muslim minorities have achieved pluralism external to the existing legal frameworks. The question this chapter wishes to resolve is whether religious pluralism is a reality for Muslim minorities in the West.

In keeping with these goals, the current chapter will focus on the work of Islamic centers and shariʿa councils in the field of personal standing, particularly on marriages, divorces, and arbitration between Muslims; the analysis will also consider the approach that civil law takes toward Muslim minorities, and the latter's relation with the general legal system. These lines of inquiry consider the extent of the congruity between *fiqh al-aqalliyyāt* and the pluralistic legal model. As a legal model, pluralism rejects the centralist understanding of a legal system as hierarchical, monolithic, and uniform, and the law of the land as the only normative arrangement by which society operates. According to legal pluralism, there are additional normative arrangements that may dictate conduct, such as tribal laws or the legislation of private corporations and institutions. This approach views the legal system as polycentric, internally contradictory, and not necessarily logical or unified in its rationale.[1]

The Muslim minority in Britain will serve as a test case for the applicability of shariʿa; the population will then be compared with the Muslim minority in the United States. The British Muslim minority is well documented, although religious affiliation is not always included in the personal information collected about each of its some 80 million citizens. Britain has a well-established Muslim minority, and in 2001 the Office for National Statistics added to its ten-year census a question regarding religious affiliation. In 2001, 1.6 million citizens declared themselves Muslim; a newspaper poll conducted in 2009 determined that Britain had 2.4 million Muslim citizens; and according to current estimates, Britain today has about 3 million Muslim citizens.[2]

The Muslim minority in Britain is also noteworthy due to its religious cohesion and endeavors to implement shariʿa through shariʿa councils: voluntary institutions for ruling on intra-Muslim disputes according to shariʿa law. A comparison will be drawn to the Muslim minority in the United States, which contrary to Europe, is a liberal country with absolute separation of church and state. Muslim thinkers, chiefly those residing within the United States, have established the Fiqh Council of North America with the exclusive goal of exploring religious law that pertains to the distinct circumstances of Muslims in North America.

Muslim Minority Position on Shariʿa in the West

There is no conformity among Muslims in Europe in terms of their religion, identity, and resolving their affairs according to shariʿa. Muslims subjected to the legal frameworks of the secular, democratic European state vary in their approach, and five viewpoints are discernible.[3]

The erstwhile Muslim approach: critical of Islam to the point of individual resentment toward traditional religion. This approach is characterized

[1] For more on legal pluralism, see J. Griffiths, "What Is Legal Pluralism?" *Journal of Legal Pluralism and Unofficial Law* 24 (1986): 1–55; B.Z. Tamanaha, "The Folly of the 'Social Scientific' Concept of Legal Pluralism," *Journal of Law and Society* 20 (1993): 192–217; and G. R. Woodman, "Ideological Combat and Social Observation: Recent Debates about Legal Pluralism," *Journal of Legal Pluralism* 42 (1998): 21–59.

[2] Amin, Mohammed. Interview by author. London, October 16, 2011.

[3] M. Rohe, "Islam and the Law in Europe," *Orient* 2 (2010): 31–6.

by extreme anti-religious sentiments, demands for extensive reforms, and the total assimilation of Muslims in their adoptive countries, forsaking religion in the process.[4]

The pragmatic approach: according to Rohe, employment and cultural hardships notwithstanding, many Muslims in Europe accept the status quo and view the democratic state as the best form of governance. Because the rules of democracy do not clash with their traditional religious lifestyle, many adopt a casual approach toward religion.[5]

Religious approaches for civil integration: advocating for Muslim integration in Europe and acceptance of prevailing norms, while still preserving the unique Muslim identity. Because the European state is considered enlightened and just, and because the status of Muslim minorities in it is extant and irreversible, there is no need for a dramatic revision or creation of a parallel social system. Freedom of religion enables active religious life both personally and publicly. Modern scholars reject the Middle Ages' distinction between *dār al-Islām*, *dār al-ḥarb*, and *dār al-ʿahd*. Extensive cooperation and adoption of joint legal norms have eliminated past antagonism. The scholars behind this approach support the abolishment of inappropriate social norms found to be more influential than religious decrees. Furthermore, they call for a revised legal reading of the Qurʾan and shariʿa.[6] This is manifested in the ruling by Faisal Kutty[7] that Islam is a gender-equal religion. The assertion would appear to contradict Qurʾan inheritance laws that allocate to a male heir double the portion of a female heir, yet Kutty claims that because in the past the man was the sole breadwinner, he was granted a larger portion of the inheritance; conversely, contemporary men and women carry a similar financial burden, thus they are entitled to similar inheritance privileges.

The traditional approach: typically rejects violent and extreme ideology, on the one hand, while concurring with an Islamist view on gender standing according to shariʿa, on the other. Although they do not represent the majority, these thinkers belong to highly organized groups that cooperate with non-Muslims on public and social issues, yet maintain very strict and traditional outlooks on gender relations and religious practices. While regarding their countries as *dār al-ʿahd*, namely, a foreign regime that

[4] Ibid., 32.
[5] Ibid., 31–2.
[6] Ibid., 34–6.
[7] A Muslim thinker and adjudicator residing in Canada.

should be cooperated with, they are proponents of social isolation and adherence to clear-cut social and religious Islamic characteristics.[8]

Islamist approaches: to Rohe, a fringe faction of Muslims in Europe adhering to a total rejection of European legal and social frameworks, seeking to impose Muslim norms in the belief that divine law should be favored over immoral norms. Although the use of violence is a minority position, the lion's share of Islamist approaches, represented by the *salafi* faction, utilize radical rhetoric calling for the extermination of the prevailing order. Muslim religious law distinguishes between three groups of Muslims: (1) Muslims who refuse to litigate according to shariʿa law and opt for civil proceedings that do not follow the shariʿa; (2) Muslims who do not discern between religious law and civil law; (3) Muslims who wish shariʿa to govern all their dealings and proceedings.[9]

A Muslim in the first of the aforementioned groups, who uncoerced and of his own free will refuses to uphold shariʿa law, rejecting it for other legal systems, is considered a heretic or an apostate. This position is held exclusively by thinkers who adhere to *al-takfīr wa-l-hijra*.[10] However, al-Amrani maintains that the majority of Sunni religious scholars mitigate judgment by viewing these actions as violations of a prohibition rather than as heresy. Members of the second group should be more aware of the religious obligation to litigate according to shariʿa laws. Opting for the civil law framework due to their leanings or a desire to defend private interests is comparable to a refusal to accept shariʿa laws. Religious scholars determine that Muslims belonging to the third group have not broken the divine decree because they seek and request to litigate according to shariʿa laws, and refrain from appealing to nonreligious proceedings unless forced upon them by an adversarial party. They are also innocent because they are unable to deviate from the general rules of society that compel them to litigate under civil law and cope with the norms to which they are subjugated. They appeal to civil court not out of choice or sympathy, but as a result of compulsion and coercion. *Fiqh al-aqalliyyāt* scholars believe that most Muslim minorities are coerced and subjugated to civil laws, and therefore belong to the third group. Being a minority in a society whose

8 Rohe, "Islam and the Law in Europe," 33–4.

9 Ibid.

10 A Muslim religious group formed in Egypt in 1971. The group holds the belief that a Muslim is a heretic and no longer considered a Muslim if he does not uphold all religious decrees or merely performs them partially. The groups' followers should segregate themselves from the heretic society.

beliefs and perceptions are foreign – at times even hostile – to Islam, they are unable to litigate according to the dictates of their religion.[11]

A prevalent approach in legal anthropology is that litigation is an interactive framework within the boundaries of which people maneuver in order to achieve optimal results, particularly when faced with a variety of legal systems at their disposal. They must account for diverse and often competing interests, such as relationships, access to resources, psychological factors, and financial ramifications. Their primary objective is to resolve the dispute locally, as proceeding to state litigation provides the prosecuting party with leverage to achieve the best deal possible. Similarly, Muslims make strategic decisions when deciding between the available legal institutions in Muslim societies, adapting the coexisting and reciprocal legal systems to their social and political goals.[12]

Implementation of Shariʿa in Britain

British legal history suggests that Britain employs a unified legal system overseeing all of its territories – a trend that is unlikely to change. The claim that freedom of religion according to the European Convention on Human Rights (ECHR) connotes the right for a distinct legal system of shariʿa courts has been rebuffed, and government policy does not sanction it. Moreover, British jurists claim that Islamic law is not a monolith framework of rules, and thus there is no single shariʿa court that would be accepted by all Muslims.[13] Nevertheless, some Muslim leaders believe that according to the Human Rights Act of 1998, Muslims in Britain are entitled to live according to shariʿa; this includes recognition of Muslim marriages and divorces. Some go so far as to claim that shariʿa councils can be transformed into shariʿa courts, drawing their authority from the mutual consent of the litigating parties. They further maintain that the position of Shaykh al-Islam of the British Isles, conceived by Queen Victoria in the nineteenth century, should be staffed. Were this the case, the exact commencement of the month of Ramadan and the collection of zakat could be determined by Shaykh al-Islam. Furthermore, this would enable the

11 Mohammed, al-Amrani, "Al-Usra al-Muslima fi al-Gharb bayn al-Tashriʿ al-Islami wa-l-Qawanin al-Wadʿiyya," *Al-Majallat al-ʿIlmiyya li-l-Majlis al-Urubi li-l-Iftaʾ li-l-Buhuth* 7 (July 2005): 177–87.

12 Ron Shaham, "Enjoying from all the Worlds: Legal Forum Shopping in Islamic Societies," *The New East* 46 (2006): 76–7.

13 Hajj A. Thomson, "How Some Elements of Shariah Can Be Accommodated in British Legal System," Seminar on Sharia: A Way of Life (London: The Islamic Culture Centre, 2008), 4–6.

institution of shariʿa courts and the appointment of qadis authorized to rule on all matters pertaining to family and inheritance laws, in addition to marriage and divorce, albeit not on criminal law.[14]

The Archbishop of Canterbury, Dr. Rowan Williams, believes that a partial concurrence should exist between the religious and legal duties of the state; thus, religious duties should be recognized by British law. Rowan bases his position on the commitment to universal human rights that allows for permissive regulation. The concept of citizenship in a multi-cultural society varies, and religious freedom also necessitates the accommodation of the individual's religious sensitivities. People entertain several concurring social identities, and often their religious identity is paramount. Archbishop Rowan wonders whether a certain form of "complementary law" is required. Although he rejects the establishment of a separate legal system for religious rulings, such as Muslim religious law, he suggests that Muslim law should in some manner be practiced in Britain.[15]

Former President of the Supreme Court of England and Wales, Lord Phillips, examined the initiative of the Archbishop of Canterbury to discuss the British legal system's recognition of Muslim law. He determined that British law was founded on the principle of liberty: any citizen holds the right to pursue fulfillment, provided that his actions do not contradict public policy or the law. People are allowed to practice their religion freely; therefore, contingent on mutual accord of the involved parties, partial modifications could be made to state laws in mediating conflicts according to Muslim religious law. Nonetheless, Much like Rowan, Lord Phillips proclaims that this must be performed within the confines of British law, and those residing in Britain must follow its laws to the letter. In this way, the freedom and flexibility afforded by British law enable the implementation of Muslim law in several fields, with no need for a comprehensive external shariʿa framework.[16]

Arbitration cases provide an example of instances in which British courts may acknowledge proceedings conducted according to shariʿa. The British Arbitration Act of 1996 allows both sides to appoint the arbitrator of their choice, and abide by any mutually agreed upon law or legal system. Civil courts are compelled to accept, ratify, and enforce these verdicts;[17]

[14] Hajj A Thomson, "Applying Islamic Fiqh in UK Arbitration Law," Seminar on Arbitration First (London: The Islamic Culture Centre, 2005), 17.

[15] I. D. Edge, "Family Law, Minorities and Legal Pluralism: Should English Law Give More Recognition to Islamic Law?" *Temple Church, DRAFT* (November 12, 2008): 2.

[16] Ibid.

[17] Thomson, "Applying Islamic Fiqh in UK Arbitration Law," 17–23.

matters pertaining to personal standing are the exception, as they are outside the scope of arbitration as they affect the position of the individual vis-à-vis the state.[18] Many Muslims utilize the arbitration process for inheritance and financial matters, as long as all parties agree to conform to shariʿa laws. Despite not being recognized by the court, arbitration by shariʿa councils is in fact civilly valid (contingent on the consent of all parties involved). This is true even if a male heir stands to receive double the portion of a female heir with equal rights to the inheritance, which would seem to contradict civil law on gender discrimination.[19]

Arbitration proceedings that conform to the principles of Islamic religious law are permitted as part of civil and commercial laws only if conducted in accordance with British law and particularly with the Arbitration Act of 1996. In a precedential verdict in 2004, the United Kingdom's Supreme Court decreed that according to the Contracts Act of 1990, a contract is subject only to state laws and not to general legal frameworks such as shariʿa, because unlike the legal system, it is not possible to contractually activate shariʿa in cases of dissension. Nevertheless, section 46 (1)(B) of the Arbitration Act allows the arbitrating body to employ legal tools separate from the laws of the land, thus enabling the utilization of Muslim law. The resolutions of such arbitration proceedings are recognized and enforced by the courts as long as they adhere to the stipulations set forth in the Arbitration Act.[20]

Inheritance is another legal field in which shariʿa laws can be implemented. British law is on the liberal end of the spectrum in regards to inheritance – allowing the individual almost complete freedom to arrange for inheritance as he sees fit. This freedom has recently been somewhat curtailed by the rights of those financially dependent on the deceased, such as minors, to seek continued support regardless of what is specified in the will. The practical manifestation of this liberal approach is that Muslims can divide their property according to shariʿa inheritance laws. In this sense, a Muslim can discriminate against women in his will, whereas according to British inheritance laws, unless otherwise specified, all successors are entitled to an equal share. All legal arrangements pertaining to personal standing are part of public policy; as such, they are subject to the exclusive legal jurisdiction of British civil courts, which impose on all

[18] I. D. Edge, "Family Law, Minorities and Legal Pluralism," 3.

[19] A. M. Hutchinson, "Arbitration/Mediation in Family Law and Children's Cases in the UK," *Seminar on Arbitration First* (London: The Islamic Culture Centre 2005), 35–9.

[20] Edge, "Family Law, Minorities and Legal Pluralism," 7–8.

citizens a uniform set of legal principles, regardless of race and religion. It is worth noting that although Muslim law and British civil law share some similar features on the issue of marital relations, there are also several points of contention between them.

In practice, the law acknowledges extralegal arrangements, chiefly in the field of marriage. For instance, the law recognizes, with some qualifications, the validity of various marriage ceremonies. In conjunction with the official record of marriage in the registry office which disallows any religious symbolism, there may be religious ceremonies: in the Anglican Church the minister serves as the marriage cleric; a marriage ceremony conducted by the Society of Friends (also known as Quakers) is considered valid; a Jewish marriage ceremony is valid if both partners are Jewish. The Marriage Act of 1949 determined that Quakers and Jews are not required to undertake a separate civil registration of marriage, but it did not make specific reference to other religions. Therefore, Islamic marriages are not recognized by law and require a separate civil registration. Although several mosques followed the Marriage Act, which enabled religious communities to register a building for the purpose of marriage, a ceremony conducted in such a building must meet several criteria in order to be considered valid.

Shariʿa marriage ceremonies held outside Britain are accepted providing they are recognized by the origin country. Even if the woman was not yet the age of consent according to British law, the marriage is accepted if the age of consent is different in the country of origin. These marriages can be substantiated with various evidence, such as witnesses or documentation, even in the absence of a marriage certificate. Nevertheless, if the marriage was conducted without the consent of one of the parties, or if one of the parties did not possess the ability to adhere to the marriage, it can be annulled. Muslim marriages are not valid without civil registration, leaving significant portions of the Muslim population out of the realm of British family law. This is detrimental to Muslim women who operated under the assumption that Muslim marriages were sanctioned by law, yet upon divorcing realized that British law did not acknowledge their marriages, rendering them effectively single and without the full protection allotted to spouses and their children. However, it must be acknowledged that the protection afforded to common law marriages by British law is more robust than in the past. In effect, Muslim marriages conducted in Britain are devoid of legal standing without civil registration; in instances where the couple is not recognized as married, they are unable to claim reciprocal rights toward one other, nor are they covered by state sanctioned rights or eligible for child support. Therefore, many Muslims opt to construct a shari'a marriage agreement alongside a civil one in order to gain recognition. As mentioned, a civil marriage can be conducted in a mosque if the registrar is authorized to perform a civil ceremony, and the place is certified for that purpose by British law.[21]

Civilly registering the marriage grants statutory recognition to the legal outcomes of marriage, to the couple's children, and to any associated civil rights: the annulment of marriage in court, the right to sue for property and finances, access to the deceased spouse's pension, and the right of inheritance in the absence of a will. In polygamous marriages, only the official wife receives the rights that derive from marriage. In deliberating on children custody, British law judges according to the well-being of the child: the child's preferences, physical and emotional needs, background, gender, potential exposure to damage or danger, effects of the shifting circumstances, and the parental capabilities of each parent. Additional considerations for Muslims are the provision of halal food and a religious upbringing. British courts tend to grant custody to the mother, believing it to be in the best interest of the child; however, Muslim religious law also takes into consideration the age of the children.[22]

If a disagreement persists between the couple regarding joint property, the court divides it equally. Because the dowry is considered a prenuptial agreement based on the Contracts Act, the law may compel the husband to pay the deferred dowry. In cases where a couple has been married for many years and possesses considerable joint property, the court assigns lesser significance to the prenuptial agreement and greater significance to the egalitarian division of property. The court can order one side to return property, sell joint assets, or pay reparations for damages incurred by the other side, such as a confiscated passport or personal belongings. Were the marriage conducted outside Britain, the woman is entitled to the deferred dowry; however, should she be the party initiating the divorce, she must demonstrate damage (*ḍarar*) or faultiness of the marriage agreement (*fasād*) in order to receive the deferred dowry.[23]

British law considers the dowry a prenuptial agreement, hence the husband's obligation to pay his wife the dowry upon divorce. In addition, the courts tend to compound the dowry with auxiliary fees and

[21] Hajj A Thomson, "Accommodating the Islamic Dissolution Law of Marriage within English Law," *Seminar on Dissolution of Marriage* (London: The Islamic Culture Centre, 2006), 24–5.

[22] Ibid., 29.

[23] Ibid., 30–2.

compensations, and a judge may rule that half the property belongs to the wife, and compel the husband to pay her alimony if he can afford to do so. In contrast, Muslim law obliges the husband to pay alimony alone upon the termination of *al-ʿidda* period.[24]

British law permits the annulment of a marriage under the following circumstances: if the couple's marriage is illegal (e.g., immediate blood relations), if one of the partners is not yet sixteen years of age, if the couple does not consist of a male and a female, if one of the partners is already married, if the marriage has not been physically consummated, if the marriage was not consummated out of free will, if the marriage was not consented to, if one of the couple suffers from a debilitating mental or sexual disease, if the woman is pregnant by another man without the knowledge of her husband.[25] Marriages recognized by British law can be annulled based on British law; this does not include marriages that were held outside of Britain. shariʿa divorces in which the husband divorces the wife are not compatible with British divorce laws and are therefore not recognized by the courts. Acceptable causes for divorce according to British law are: infidelity, abandonment for a period of at least two years, a two-year period of separation and consent for divorce, a five-year period of separation (in which case consent for divorce is not required), unreasonable conduct.[26] Divorces conducted outside the British territories, including shariʿa divorces, are accepted and upheld in Britain providing they are valid according to the law of the place in which they were given as specified in the 1986 Domicile and Recognition of Foreign Divorces Act.[27] *Talāq* divorce by a Muslim husband might also be recognized; however, this is contingent on specific conditions being met: the husband can show substantial ties to the land in which the divorce was given, the judge has exercised his discretion, and the wife was sufficiently notified.[28] From all of this, it is apparent that British law subjugates all citizens – regardless of religion, race, or gender – to uniform legal territorial norms; as well, this evidences that British courts are punctilious is exacting civil laws. The relationship between the courts and Muslim individual laws is a dynamic

24 Shaykh Abu Sayeed, "Polygamy and Islam," *Seminar on Shariʿa as Way of Life*, (London: Islamic Culture Center, 2008), 1–3.

25 Thomson, "Accommodating the Islamic Dissolution Law of Marriage within English Law," 27–8.

26 Suhaib Hasan, "Al-Tafriq al-Qadaʾi min Khilal Qanwat al-Shariʿa al-Islamiyya," *Al-Majallat al-ʿIlmiyya li-l-Majlis al-Urubi li-l-Iftaʾ li-l-Buhuth* 8–9 (June 2006): 250–3.

27 Thomson, "Accommodating the Islamic Dissolution Law of Marriage within English Law," 27–8.

28 Edge, "Family Law, Minorities and Legal Pluralism," 9.

one, and the former are inclined to accept shariʿa laws providing they do not directly oppose existing laws. This allows for the flourishing of a more pluralistic legal system in Britain.

Shariʿa Councils in Britain

Islamic centers in non-Muslim countries began to appear in the latter decades of the twentieth century; they are designed to serve as focal points for the surrounding Muslim communities. In Britain, voluntary shariʿa councils were established by the boards of Islamic centers and mosques for the purpose of shariʿa guided arbitration in intra-Muslim disputes, mainly in the field of personal standing. Each council is independent and adopts its own legal procedures and religious methodology. In some councils there is a triumvirate of adjudicators, while in others there is only one. Their rulings are neither legally binding nor enforceable, but rather serve as a recommendation whose acceptance is contingent on the religious fidelity and devoutness of the interested parties. Thus, the councils' rulings constitute a fatwa rather than a verdict.[29] Shariʿa councils do not take legal precedence into account; thus, the ruling in one case does not infer on other cases. Because they harbor the belief that the unique and transformed circumstances of Muslims in the West must be taken into account, shariʿa adjudicators are neither reliant on nor compelled by the religious law tradition. For instance, a woman may not be forced to preserve her marriage, and if she so wishes, should be granted a divorce in exchange for relinquishing her shariʿa rights (*khulʿ* divorce).[30] Shariʿa councils' rulings are not published due to the confidentiality of the proceedings. Among the fatwas published on their websites, some reflect rulings, while others reflect responses to queries brought to the council; because confidentiality is maintained, it is impossible to discern which is which. Thus far, about twenty shariʿa councils have been established in different cities around Britain, particularly where Muslim communities flourish. Following the initiative of the chairman of the Islamic council in London, British shariʿa councils decided to unite under one umbrella organization to align their activities and unify their rulings.[31] According to anti-Islamic British sources, there are eighty such councils in Britain. These numbers seem to

[29] Suhaib, Hasan. Interview by author. Leyton Shariʿa Council, London, October 15, 2012.

[30] Ibid.

[31] Alongside the councils, the imams in mosques and Islamic centers assist the Muslim public in solving its problems, albeit not considered religiously ordained judges.

be exaggerated and designed to incite panic among the non-Muslim public, stoking fears about the expansion of Islam in Britain.[32]

Shariʿa councils receive grievances not only from Muslims within Britain but also outside of Britain, provided that at least one party is a European resident or citizen, as not all European countries have or approve of shariʿa councils. In cases received outside its territorial jurisdiction, the council is assisted by imams from other cities and countries, in some cases requesting the local imam to attempt and reconcile the couple's dispute. If a resolution is not attained, the council asks for the imam's evaluation of the case and a recommendation on whether the couple can be reconciled, or if they are best suited for divorce; if necessary, this method may be used to determine the dowry. Based on the imam's position, the council rules on the dispute in question.[33] Since its inception in 1982, the shariʿa council in Leyton, London has processed 7,835 cases. The council in Birmingham, established in 1988, receives around fourteen cases a month. The panel of adjudicators in those councils meets monthly to rule on all plaints previously deliberated upon.[34] Around 90 percent of these plaints come from women, and the vast majority (about 95 percent) are for the termination of marriage agreements that were not registered in the state, or religious approval for divorces obtained from a civil court. The rest of the plaints are for marriage permissions and arbitration due to a conflict between the couple. In general, arbitration cases are scarce because the council lacks the authority to compel the sides to uphold its ruling and enforce its implementation; as previously mentioned, the council's rulings serve as mere recommendations.

Upon visiting Leyton, I was invited by Shaykh Suhaib Hasan to observe deliberation on two cases. The council's chambers resemble a regular courtroom – the judge's pulpit is elevated from the crowd, which is seated to either side. Each case consists of a claim form filed by the plaintive, various corroborating documentation, and the position papers submitted by imams at the request of the council. One case was a divorce proceeding initiated by a Muslim Norwegian woman of Somali descent, who wished to divorce her husband with whom she had been living for over eight years. Despite promising to grant her a divorce if a medical examination proved he could not procreate, the husband recanted upon receiving several professional opinions from doctors that he was sterile. Because she wished to

32 Amin, Mohammed. Interview by author. London, October 16, 2011.
33 Shah-Kazemi, 2001, 80.
34 Suhaib, Hasan and Amra Bone. Interview by author. London, October 14–15, 2012.

have children, the woman could not continue to live her husband knowing that procreation was not possible. At the end of the discussion, Shaykh Hasan decided to direct the plaintive to an imam at the Oslo mosque; he would consult with both sides in hopes of attaining an understanding, and afterward provide his ruling. Notwithstanding, the council decided to contact the husband via telephone in order to convince him to reach a compromise with his wife. Shaykh Hasan also instructed the woman to commence divorce proceedings in a Norwegian court. Further deliberations in the case were halted.

The second case also involved a Muslim couple. The woman was of Somali descent and held British citizenship; the man, also Somali, was considered an illegal immigrant from Germany, and was about to face deportation hearings. The couple requested a permit from the council confirming their shariʿa marriage, as they were married in front of an imam in Athens, Greece. They presented Shaykh Hasan with a document from said imam confirming they were married. Upon both husband and wife signing an oath testifying that they indeed entered into shariʿa wedlock in Athens, the Sheik approved their signatures and drafted a letter to the husband's attorney, stating the couple was married according to the shariʿa. The letter sought to prove that the man was in fact married to a British citizen, and thus able to obtain citizenship status rather than be deported.

The majority of Muslims in the West resolve their conflicts in civil courts, since such courts possess legal authority and their rulings can be enforced by the state. Moreover, Muslims regard the civil system as accessible and just, and they operate under the assumption that it will grant women a greater range of rights than available through Muslim religious law. In fact, only a handful seek the councils' rulings as those are not binding. In addition, there are several factors that lead many among the Muslim population to regard the shariʿa system as feeble: a woefully inadequate knowledge of the shariʿa laws governing relations within and beyond the family; weak religious commitments; and a shortage of eligible candidates to serve as shariʿa adjudicators.[35]

Nonetheless, Muslims in the West still seek religious guidance and approach the councils on a myriad of issues. Muslim couples may request a shariʿa wedding contract (*nikāḥ*) to obtain a religious authorization for civil marriages.[36] In such cases, the council confirms the couple is married

[35] Hasan, "Al-Tafriq al-Qadaʾi min Khilal Qanwat al-Shariʿa al-Islamiyya," 242–4.

[36] Thomson, "Accommodating the Islamic Dissolution Law of Marriage within English Law," 25.

according to the shariʿa; this can serve them in the Islamic origin country, if relevant, as well as for intracommunity purposes.[37] Another cause for approaching a council is obtaining a religious permit for civil divorce. Women, fearing that a civil divorce is not sufficient in the eyes of the religion, tend to approach shariʿa councils to ascertain that they are indeed divorced according to religious law, and thus there is no hindrance to their marrying another man.[38] In addition, the councils are approached by couples who were married in religious weddings but were not civilly registered, and now wish to separate. In cases of the latter, the marriage agreement was drafted exclusively according to the shariʿa, and is therefore not recognized by state institutions that require renewed registration in accordance with civil law; according to the state, the couple is not married. In such instances, it is impossible to file a plaint to annul the marriage in civil courts,[39] and the parties' sole option is a religious proceeding, which includes the shariʿa councils.[40]

As previously stated, according to the state, a couple is not considered married if their marriage was not registered by the appropriate civil registry. In such cases, a religious annulment is sufficient, and the council can rule in favor of a divorce based on the husband's absence or harm inflicted upon the woman over the course of the marriage. The council can issue a divorce if the husband consented to appear before the council and grant his wife a divorce, or if he empowered the council to do so. If the husband has received three written notices, yet still failed to appear before the council to present his position on divorce or compensation, the council may commence a *khulʿ* procedure – divorce in exchange for the wife relinquishing the benefits to which she is entitled from her husband. At the end of the procedure, the council members can annul the marriage; the divorce will appear only in the council's records, not in the civil registry; the woman will receive a permit stating she is divorced and eligible to marry another man upon the termination of *al-ʿidda* period. In these instances, the council attempts to resolve cases that civil courts do not.[41]

[37] S. N. Shah-Kazemi, *Untying the Knot: Muslim Women, Divorce and the Shariah* (London: University of Westminster, 2001), 5–11.

[38] Suhaib, Hasan. Interview by author. London, October 15, 2012.

[39] In terms of religion, the husband is allowed to divorce his wife unilaterally, without her consent or knowledge. Contrarily, a woman requires a shariʿa qadi or an authorized religious court to divorce her husband.

[40] Shah-Kazemi, *Untying the Knot: Muslim Women, Divorce and the Shariah*, 34–8.

[41] Hasan, "Al-Tafriq al-Qadaʾi min Khilal Qanwat al- Shariʿa al-Islamiyya," 244.

Muslims who were married according to a shariʿa contract, yet did not register in the state registry office, often erroneously believe that their marriage is valid and recognized by the state. Therefore, Islamic centers strive to encourage couples to officially register in order to comply by the law and preserve their rights.[42] Another reason to approach shariʿa councils is the couple's wish to resolve matters of personal standing solely according to the Muslim shariʿa and in front of a Muslim adjudicator, rather than in a civil court that upholds foreign rules. Upon receiving the council's ruling, the couple can civilly validate the ruling in a civil court and uphold it through the state's authorities. Civil courts do not acknowledge the legitimacy of shariʿa councils and their rulings; however, with the consent of the parties involved, the courts can uphold these rulings. Hence, albeit not having authority de jure, shariʿa councils are endowed with it de facto.

On occasion, there are instances of couples who were married according to shariʿa outside of Britain, but who have a dire need to undergo arbitration in marriage and divorce by British shariʿa councils, despite the fact that their unions are technically subject to the shariʿa laws of the country in which they were married. British law acknowledges these marriages,[43] and when there is strife and the couple must produce a valid marriage contract, the court entertains evidence supported by the shariʿa and hears expert opinions from the shariʿa council. If proven that the constraints of shariʿa have been upheld, the court approves the marriage, and its binding verdict will be registered at the General Register Office, which holds such records in Britain.[44]

At times, the appeal to the council is concurrent with divorce proceedings in a civil court, or even prior to them. In cases where the marriage was civilly registered, the council instructs the wife to file for divorce in a civil court – the lawful authority on such matters. Since annulling a marriage without the consent of the court might be construed as breaking the law, Islamic centers wait for a complaint to be filed before attempting to guide

[42] Ibid., 254–5.

[43] Thomson, "Accommodating the Islamic Dissolution Law of Marriage within English Law," 31–42.

[44] Ian Edge presented a case of a British woman of Egyptian descent who requested that her marriage to a Muslim man from Dubai, officiated by an imam and two witnesses in Dubai, be validated by a British court. Seemingly, all of the shariʿa stipulations were met for the marriage to be recognized as valid. However, the husband failed to appear in front of the court, and the burden of proof fell to the woman who was unable to prove that they were married according to the shariʿa. In the absence of the husband, the court decreed that they were married, but did not recognize that specific marriage agreement and in the eye of the court the woman was not entitled to any rights.

the couple through their shariʿa obligations toward an agreement. Only once a civil complaint is filed will the council issue a ruling that annuls the marriage contract or issues a divorce. Annulments reached by the couple by their own accord are then transmitted for the approval of the court.[45] Only on rare occasions, such as a husband physically threatening his wife, does a shariʿa council issue a divorce in advance of the civil court. In such a case, the council seeks to prevent abuse or harm to the woman, even though the divorce is not yet recognized by a civil court.[46]

When the wife requests that the council sanction a divorce already issued by a civil court, the council considers whether the husband filed for divorce, and whether the court issued a final verdict in favor of divorce. If both these criteria are met, the council sanctions the divorce. In addition, before issuing an Islamic divorce certificate, the council ascertains that the wife was granted her full rights according to the shariʿa. If the wife did not receive her rights or the deferred dowry in its entirety, the council will not issue the husband a divorce, despite the civil court's verdict. Even though the divorce is both civilly and religiously valid, the council pressures the husband to grant the wife her full rights.[47]

In cases where the husband did not defend himself in court against a divorce filed by his wife, the council probes the reasons behind his absence via court documents and subpoena. If indeed he signed the subpoena and refrained from making his case, the council regards it as a *khulʿ* divorce, granting the wife the Islamic divorce certificate; in exchange, she must return the dowry and jewelry she received for the marriage. However, in cases where the wife filed for divorce and the husband was not informed of the hearing, nor was he present to defend himself, the council will not sanction the divorce but will attempt to reconcile the couple. If the reconciliation fails, or if one of the parties fails to meet the council's terms, the council will approve the divorce. If the wife insists on a divorce, the council deliberates and approves the request should they find sufficient shariʿa grounds.

In a persisting conflict between a couple (*nizāʿ wa-shiqāq*), the adjudicators confer with each party alone in an attempt to mediate, granting the couple an extension to try and reach reconciliation (*ṣulḥ*); however, if this is not achieved, the council issues a divorce. If the husband is adamant to

45 Hasan, "Al-Tafriq al-Qadaʾi min Khilal Qanwat al- Shariʿa al-Islamiyya," 256–8.

46 Suhaib, Hasan. Interview by author. London, October 15, 2012.

47 S. Hasan, "Shariʿa: A Way of Life," *Seminar on Shariʿa as Way of Life*, (London: The Islamic Culture Centre (2008): 14–7.

neither reconcile nor grant his wife a divorce, one of two things may happen: either the council will separate them, or the wife will opt for a *khulʿ* divorce, relinquishing her shariʿa rights in exchange for a divorce. The council is authorized to conduct the proceedings without the presence of the couple, via correspondence or their local imams. In such instances, the council ascertains the reasons for divorce, and whether the woman is willing to return the dowry and jewelry to the husband. When the husband is the one seeking the divorce, the council confirms that he is willing to pay the dowry, and that the wife will allow the husband regular child visitation rights. Only then will the council issue a ruling in the divorce case.[48]

The Religious Qualification of Shariʿa Councils According to Muslim Religious Law

It is essential to establish whether shariʿa councils possess the religious authority to rule on intra-Muslim disputes and annul Muslim marriages, since classic religious scholars believed that a qadi must be appointed to resolve such matters – his ruling being binding, at least in the religious sense. By contrast, in the absence of a Muslim sovereign, modern religious scholars believe that the authority figures among the Muslim community (*ahl al-ḥal wa-ʿaqd*) can appoint talented, capable men to judiciary positions. These judges can rule on all matters pertaining to Muslims, including intricate issues such as marrying a woman who does not have a marriage guardian (*walī li-l-zawāj*), providing a divorce for a woman whose husband is missing, as well as separating a couple due to a conflict (*nizāʿ wa-shiqāq*) or harm that has befallen the wife.[49] This position coincides with Ibn Nujaym, the *Ḥanafī* jurist who maintained that Muslims must petition the infidel sovereign to appoint a Muslim adjudicator and respect his jurisdiction. *Ḥanafī* jurist Ibn al Hammam also argued that in lieu of a sultan or a representative appointed by him, as was the case in fifteenth-century Spain, Muslims must appoint one of their own as a guardian to serve as qadi resolving their disputes.[50]

48 Ibid.

49 Mohammed al-Ghalayini, *Al-Marakiz al-Islamiyya fi North America* (Jordan: Dar Amar li-l-Nashr wa-l-Tawziʿa, 2009), 245–52.

50 Mohammed al-Amrani, "Al-Usra al-Muslima fi al-Gharb bayn al-Tashriʿ al-Islami wa-l-Qawanin al-Wadʿiyya," *Al-Majallat al-ʿIlmiyya li-l-Majlis al-Urubi li-l-Iftaʾ li-l-Buhuth* 7 (July 2005): 195–7.

Even in the anthology of religious decrees compiled by fifteenth-century Maghrebian mufti al-Wansharisi, it was reinforced that in the absence of a qadi the town's elders would officiate marriages. Abu Jaʿfar Ahmad bin Nasar al-Dawudi[51] determined that a woman who wishes to be married, but who has no access to a qadi or a guardian, could do so after the worthiest and most distinguished men in the land gather and proclaim her marriage. In the absence of a sultan, the most trustworthy and knowledgeable men in the land fulfill his role.[52] Al-Qabisi[53] believed that Muslims forced to immigrate and settle in a non-Muslim country must appoint a figure that holds the authority to rule on their affairs. They are allowed to wait for a mandate from the sovereign, particularly if he is not a Muslim. When there is an appointed authority who rules in accordance to Islam, his rulings are binding to those who accepted his authority and are settled within his dominion.

Shaykh Ashraf ʿAli Thanwi (1863–1943), the famous Indian religious scholar who lived under British rule, believed that the ruling of a Muslim qadi appointed by a non-Muslim government is as valid and binding as the ruling of a Muslim qadi in the lands of Islam. Nevertheless, when a Muslim qadi is not present or the state legal system does not uphold shariʿa law, one should act solely according to the shariʿa. For instance, according to the *Ḥanafī* School that is prevalent in India, a wife cannot divorce her husband without his consent. In cases where the husband refuses to consent to divorce, or is absent, missing, or mentally disabled, the wife is allowed to undergo Muslim arbitration and demand a divorce according to the *Mālikī* School, which under such circumstances and in the absence of a qadi in that land, grants a divorce.[54] Religious scholar Al-Salih al-Tunisi[55] also believed that in the absence of a sovereign, separation of a couple should be performed by a group of at least three Muslims. Established by Muslims during British colonialism, the shariʿa emirate in the region of Bihar is an example of a shariʿa legal system coexisting alongside India's legal system. To this day it arbitrates on intra-Muslim disputes and proceedings.[56]

[51] Eleventh-century *Mālikī* religious scholar of Libyan descent.

[52] Hasan, "Al-Tafriq al-Qadaʾi min Khilal Qanwat al- Shariʿa al-Islamiyya," 246–8.

[53] Tunisian *Mālikī* religious scholar (936–1012 A.D.).

[54] Hasan, "Al-Tafriq al-Qadaʾi min Khilal Qanwat al- Shariʿa al-Islamiyya," 249–50.

[55] Tunisian religious scholar (1877–1957), was head of the Jamiʿ al-Zaytuna mosque in Tunisia.

[56] Hasan, "Al-Tafriq al-Qadaʾi min Khilal Qanwat al- Shariʿa al-Islamiyya," 248.

British Law's Approach to Shariʿa Councils

British law does not acknowledge shariʿa councils; however, they are registered at the Charity Commission for England and Wales as public organizations specializing in Islamic marriages and divorces. Previously, the British government offered shariʿa councils a status identical to that of Jewish religious courts. According to the 2002 Divorce Act, Jewish couples seeking divorce must first be referred to a Jewish religious court, and only afterwards can a civil court rule on the case. This is due to the Jewish obligation according to which the woman must receive a divorce from her husband. Not wishing to relinquish their ability to annul a marriage without the consent of the husband, shariʿa councils rejected the offer, seeking different recognition than was awarded to Jewish religious courts. They harbor the belief that the jurisdiction of shariʿa councils is broader than that of Jewish religious courts, also owing to the latter's dependence on the husband's consent to the divorce. Hence, Shaykh Hasan also believes it is not fitting to receive a status identical to that of Jewish religious courts.[57] Nonetheless, since British law aspires to be equal toward all religions, it did not approve the Muslim request.

It is fair to assume that if British law were to recognize Muslim marriages, it would result in a positive shift in which Muslims, sensing the state's willingness to incorporate them into general British law, would appeal to the state's courts. As mentioned, Islamic divorces issued by shariʿa councils are not recognized by law, yet they do affect the ability of both partners to remarry in a religious ceremony. In this sense, shariʿa councils and Islamic religious courts will continue to enjoy legal jurisdiction over religious divorces, much like Jewish courts do. The Divorce (Religious Marriages) Act can be extended to Muslims, wherein a complete and total divorce for a woman would be attained only if conducted according to shariʿa. Indeed, in presiding over a case, civil court judges must abide exclusively by state laws. However, they do acknowledge the need to be acquainted with shariʿa law; for this reason, they consult shariʿa council members in a non-official capacity over matters of religious law, at times inviting religious authorities as witnesses or expert witnesses. Although civil court judges do not acknowledge shariʿa councils' rulings, a few do take them into account, at times even discussing and referring to

[57] Suhaib, Hasan, Mohammed Amin, and Amra Bone. Interviews by author. London, October 15, 2012. On this matter, their position differs from that of Yilmaz.

them directly. However, only in a handful of cases have judges referred the divorcing couple to a shariʿa council.[58]

On occasion, the councils are approached by lawyers who seek the expert opinion of its members and their position on issues of personal standing. In addition, the councils strive to translate the laws of Islam on matters of personal standing to the native language of the respective country, taking into account the circumstances of Muslim communities in the West.[59] Shariʿa councils can assist in marriage annulment proceedings. Section 1 of the 1996 Family Law Act stipulates the principles that orchestrate the annulment of marriage, which include arbitration within the family. However, despite the courts' attempts to encourage voluntary arbitration, this practice has not become widespread. Based on the provision that mediators can help formulate a divorce agreement to be adopted by the court, community arbitrators have the ability to assist in a Muslim couple's separation process and divorce. Arbitration can be performed by individual Muslim arbitrators or by a set of procedures set forth by an Islamic institute; in the case of the latter, the institute encourages consultation with the community-initiated shariʿa council. Each council employs numerous volunteers, both men and women, trained in arbitration techniques and educated in the basics of family law vis-à-vis the shariʿa and state law. The agreement achieved through arbitration should be submitted and approved by the court, which ascertains that it was indeed signed by both parties out of free will.[60]

It is worthwhile to note that a bill for a law prohibiting gender discrimination (alongside other forms of discrimination) in arbitration procedures was submitted to the House of Lords. The proposal stated that any such discrimination constitutes a criminal offense punishable by a prison sentence. The law was designed to prevent shariʿa hearings that are considered discriminatory toward women; examples of this include inheritance proceedings and the lesser significance ascribed to a woman's testimony as opposed to a man's. Despite the miniscule chances of this bill passing, it still poses a threat to shariʿa councils in upholding shariʿa law.[61]

[58] Thomson, "How Some Elements of Shariah Can be accommodated in British Legal System," 1–7.

[59] Hasan, "Al-Tafriq al-Qada'i min Khilal Qanwat al-Shariʿa al-Islamiyya," 29.

[60] Shah-Kazemi, *Untying the Knot: Muslim Women, Divorce and the Shariah*, 9–13.

[61] Amin, Mohammed. Interview by author. London, October 15, 2012.

Implementation of Shari'a in the United States

In the United States there are no authorized Islamic religious institutions accepted by the Muslim public that determine the obligatory shari'a laws for the local population. If such institutions do indeed exist, they are in the early stages of formulation and development. The active center for the advancement of religious rulings for Muslims in the United States is the Fiqh Council of North America, a source of spiritual and moral authority for Muslims, albeit devoid of any legal standing. The council's scope consists of clarifying what is religiously permitted and prohibited to the Muslim community. The council does not publish its religious rulings consistently; some are published in its website, some in the newspapers, and others are transmitted directly to the public.[62]

The variety and heterogeneity of Muslims in the United States hinders the acceptance of one religious authority. Some Muslims are African Americans; others are new and long-settled immigrants of varying descent, from a variety of countries in the Arab world. Some are Sunni, following its various schools, while others are Shi'ites. There are also affiliates of various religious factions: Sufi, *salafi*, Muslim Brotherhood, and al-Jama'a al-Islamiyya. Nonetheless, Muslim activists in America believe that the affinity among Muslims is discernable. The first wave of immigrants, divided by origin or by affiliation to a religious faction, is waning; in their stead emerges a new generation of Muslims that were born in America. This generation considers itself and identifies as American, having integrated in public life and into American organizations, including political parties. The importance allocated to ethnic origin is fading, in part due to mixed marriages of Muslims from different backgrounds, and of various religions, as well as an overall increase of assimilation in American society.[63]

Following the precedent of the establishment of religious courts by the Jewish community to perform arbitration between Jews within the community, several Muslim activists aspire to establish Muslim American tribunals. Among Muslims, there is a vibrant and active sense of personal obligation stemming from the public movement advocating civil and religious responsibilities for one's life. Such attitudes have brought about

[62] Hendi, Yahya. Interview by author. Washington, DC, November 1, 2012. Member of the "Fiqh Council of North America," a religious counselor and lecturer at Georgetown University on comparison between religions.

[63] Khalil, Asim. Interview by author. New York City, October 23, 2012. Head of the Muslim Bar Association of New York.

the establishment of Islamic organizations set to promote the various concerns of Muslims in America, such as the National Association of Muslim Lawyers, which has become the formal organization in charge of affairs pertaining to Islam and civil life in America.[64]

The most religiously influential element in the lives of Muslims is the imams in the mosques established in various cities by Islamic organizations. The United States lacks a governing body that oversees the imams, and any Muslim can try and perform the duties of imam, become a leader of the community, and implement the religious laws as he sees fit. This is manifested in the highly diverse implementation of Islamic law.[65] In fact, there is a vast spectrum of imams – some are trained in Muslim religious law, civil law, and possess consultation and mediation skills, whereas others do not. A talented and capable imam, particularly in the large urban centers, fulfills a significant role for the community, including reconciling couples and educating and guiding the community. He also serves as a preacher, and at times even as a qadi in disputes, although his rulings are not legally binding and compel the parties only a voluntary basis.[66]

Efforts by Muslim thinkers and in academia to create a new religious methodology for Muslims in America notwithstanding, the absence of an acknowledged and influential religious authority, compounded by the extreme diversity among Muslims in America, has resulted in discord over a unified religious law. In contrast to Muslims in Great Britain, Muslims in the United States are, in general, interested in a more egalitarian model of religious law that would assuage disputes within the family. Islamists have been unable to restrict interpretations to those of scholars that exclusively represent the school of their own country of origin. Through the experience of integrating into modern society, second generation immigrant communities challenge perceptions about the preservation of customs and religious attitudes of their countries of origin. For the purpose of this discussion, one must acknowledge certain features of the Muslim American experience within the context of a secular and democratic society. For instance, in America, women are an integral part of the activist and intellectual movements, mainly on issues pertaining to abuse within the family and women's standing in general.[67]

64 A. Quraishi A. and N. Syeed-Miller, "No Stars: A Survey of Islamic Family Law in the United States," in *Women's Rights & Islamic Family Law: Perspectives on Reform*. Lynn Welchman ed. (London: Zed Books Ltd, 2004), 213–17.

65 Ibid., 181–2.

66 Hendi, Yahya. Interview by author. Washington, DC, November 1, 2012.

67 Quraishi and Syeed-Miller, "No Stars: a Survey of Islamic Family Law in the United States," 213–17.

Nevertheless, Islamist thinkers and activists are still hesitant about promoting an open and liberal religious law approach. Any deviation from classic religious law might result in Muslim scholars losing the recognition of the main religious faction. The need to differentiate between culture and religion is another problem. The Muslim community still does not distinguish between customs and religious traditions; in the interest of more progressive and flexible religious laws, a decision must be reached regarding which customs should be preserved and which should be discarded contingent on their compatibility with lived realities and circumstances. The goal is to create a unified approach and agenda in order to promote a consensus in the field of religious law. This poses the ultimate challenge for minority religions: strict preservation of their values and traditions, while adjusting to the cultural, legal, and social contexts of the place in which they aspire to put down roots and flourish.[68]

Concurrently, as stated in the Constitution, the United States practices complete separation of church and state, particularly in its legal system. Thus, courts in the various states subject all citizens exclusively to civil law, without a trace of formal religious influence. Perhaps because of this, the perception of shariʿa in America is for the most part unfavorable – Americans have no real sense of shariʿa, and harbor negative prejudices against it, claiming it discriminates against women and non-Muslims. These attitudes are evidenced in the founding of a public movement against the implementation of shariʿa in America. Factors such as these have limited the propagation of shariʿa in America, both in civil court procedures and in the establishment of shariʿa institutions, for fear their establishment might rouse the general American population against Muslims, hindering their acceptance.[69]

American law enables mutually consensual arbitration procedures. An imam or a Muslim religious figure can act as the arbitrator in a conflict if both parties consent to his role in front of a civil judge. His ruling will be binding and enforceable by civil courts. Because it does not constitute a framework with clear rules that are generally knowable beforehand, arbitration performed according to shariʿa is not recognized by American law. However, the law does recognize arbitration performed according to the shariʿa-based laws of foreign countries, because in these cases, shariʿa is transformed into a clear framework of laws that are knowable in advance.

[68] Quraishi and Syeed-Miller, "No Stars: A Survey of Islamic Family Law in the United States," 218–19.

[69] Khalil, Asim. Interview by author. New York City, October 23, 2012.

In order to curtail shariʿa-driven arbitration, some states have legally banned arbitration based on religious laws. However, following petitions to constitutional courts, these bans did not come into effect.[70]

In the field of personal standing, the laws in the United States vary from state to state. However, the majority of states limit the officiating and registering of marriages to state authorized individuals. In this sense, only a Muslim imam who is licensed by the state can officiate a marriage ceremony and register the couple. In the United States, marriages must first be registered at the state registry office, only then can a licensed imam officiate a shariʿa marriage and supply the couple with a shariʿa marriage certificate. Marriages that are ineligible for registration in the state due to issues of age of consent or bigamy are unable to be registered as shariʿa marriages.[71]

While numerous Muslim religious figures are authorized by the state to register a marriage, some are not, and registering a marriage without authorization constitutes a felony and results in the annulment of the marriage by the law.[72] The approach for these unofficial marriages also varies from state to state. The state of Virginia acknowledges private marriages that were not registered in the state registry office; therefore, a divorce claim can be filed even in instances when the marriage was a privately arranged shariʿa marriage. Nevertheless, the majority of states do not acknowledge shariʿa marriages that were not legally registered, regarding them as null and void. Because in such cases filing for divorce is impossible, women must turn to their local imam. As well, Muslims must consult an imam to obtain an authorization that a divorce issued by a civil judge is viable in terms of the shariʿa.

American family courts do not exhibit any consistent legal approach in regards to the legal standing of a dowry. Whereas some states regard a dowry as a pre-nuptial agreement and enforce it, others do not recognize its legal standing. In this sense, approaches vary: a dowry may be considered a prenuptial agreement, a valid contract, or a contract containing ambiguous religious stipulations and clauses.[73] Most Muslim couples that divorce, do so in adherence to the civil statute in order to obtain legal validity. They ascertain their rights both by shariʿa law and civil law. A small minority

70 Ibid.

71 Abdul Rauf, Feisal. Interview by author. New York City, October 18, 2012. Head of the Cordoba Initiative.

72 Quraishi and Syeed-Miller, "No Stars: A Survey of Islamic Family Law in the United States," 192–4.

73 Ibid., 207.

opts for Islamic, non-civil divorces; however, shariʿa *ṭalāq* divorces, in which the husband divorces his wife in front of an imam, are not recognized legally, and should be carried out by state laws alone. Regardless, the American legal system applies the divorce laws of the couple's place of residence. Thus, if a divorce is requested outside the territorial borders of the Unites States, an American court will uphold the foreign laws of the country in which it was issued.[74]

In custody cases, American law rules only according to the well-being of the child, taking no heed of shariʿa considerations such as age and gender. The courts are inconsistent in pursuing the dictates of foreign ruling in cases of child custody, yet they always rule according to what they perceive to be the best interest of the child. In some states, the courts take into consideration the children's religion in determining their best interest, and thus the religious component plays a part in the verdict. Courts also tend to consider that Muslims are not bound to a single place of residence for long, due to their high mobility between the Islamic state of origin and their place of residence in the United States. In this sense, courts regard marriages and divorces conducted outside the United States as complicating the legal standpoint of Muslims.[75] In terms of inheritance, the law compels the author of the will to detail the exact distribution of his estate; in this sense, a division of the inheritance according to shariʿa is possible. However, stating in the will that the division of property will be conducted according to the rules of shariʿa is problematic, both because it is not recognized by American law, and because it implies guiding principles contradictory to the American Constitution, such as the dissimilarity between the portion of the inheritance given to a male, as opposed to that of a female heir.[76]

Imams can serve as expert witnesses in civil procedures and testify to shariʿa laws in cases of disputes between couples where the judge requires elucidation of the shariʿa to reach a verdict. Imams can also assist the defense in criminal cases, testifying whether the line of defense, for instance a husband striking his wife claiming he has the religious authority to do so, is acknowledged religiously or not. This testimony is paramount because the state respects the religious beliefs of its citizens and through the separation of state and church is forbidden to intervene in them. In addition, imams can serve as regular witnesses for cases in which they are

[74] Ibid., 197–8.

[75] Ibid., 210–11.

[76] Khalil, Asim. Interview by author. New York City, October 23, 2012.

involved, for instance, upon performing arbitration between two parties, particularly a couple, in an attempt to reconcile them.[77]

A recent study examined verdicts by appeals courts in several states. The conclusion was that shariʿa laws have permeated legal decisions and were in fact implemented within those verdicts. Nevertheless, the implementation of shariʿa in America still faces at least one substantial hurdle: its clash with the Constitution. An example of this conflict can be found in the prohibition to discriminate between men and women, which exists in conflict with shariʿa inheritance laws. Thus, issues resolved via mutual consent of the parties require examination and legal scrutiny of their congruence with public policy.[78] An examination of the study reveals that courts in various states do not employ a unified approach to shariʿa law. The courts tend to acknowledge shariʿa when the actions of one party are rooted in his expression of freedom of religion, or in accepting verdicts passed by foreign legal systems that are shariʿa-based. The common thread for such cases is the desire to safeguard freedom of religion on the one hand, while on the other, ascertaining that shariʿa-based verdicts do not deprive women and children or their rights, nor contradict public policy.

This approach is manifested in the State of Arkansas Court of Appeals that upheld a verdict by a lower court decreeing that, based on the First Amendment to the Constitution which protects the freedom of religion, a Muslim community cannot be compelled to keep an imam in his post. In another verdict, a New Jersey appeals court refused to issue a restraining order against a Muslim husband who mistreated his wife and verbally divorced her in front of an imam, because the court believed the husband's actions originated from his religious obligations had no criminal intent. In another example, the New Jersey Court of Appeals overturned an initial verdict that had not recognized a couple's divorce according to Pakistani law. In a custody case, the Maryland Court of Appeals upheld a Pakistani court ruling in favor of the father in an ex parte hearing because the mother could not return to Pakistan, where she would be arrested for adultery. The Maryland court argued that the Pakistani court ruled in line with the benefit of the child. The Minnesota Court of Appeals upheld a court ruling that acknowledged arbitration by a committee that reached a decision based on a mutual agreement to resolve a conflict according to the shariʿa. The Florida Court of Appeals ruled that a husband should compensate his wife based on a marriage agreement that contained a dowry

[77] Hendi, Yahya. Interview by author. Washington, DC, November 1, 2012.
[78] The Center for Security Policy, *Shariʿa Law and American State Courts*, 2011.

clause, even though the wife initiated the divorce. The California Court of Appeals overturned a ruling by a lower appellate court, decreeing that the verdict in a custody case by a Lebanese shariʿa court should be upheld since it ruled according to the children's best interests, even if the children were living in a Western society rather than a Muslim one.

On other occasions, American courts refused to accept the implementation of shariʿa law when it jeopardized the fair-mindedness of legal proceedings, and impinged upon the rights of women and children. This approach is manifested in a verdict by the Maryland Court of Appeals. The court refused to accept a divorce between an American woman and a Pakistani husband issued by a Pakistani court according to the rules of shariʿa, claiming that a Muslim *ṭalāq* divorce is detrimental to women's rights. The Washington Court of Appeals overturned a custody verdict in favor of the husband substantiated by a shariʿa ruling from a court in the Philippines. The Washington Court of Appeals decreed that in this case, shariʿa law contradicts public policy and the initial ruling did not demonstrate consideration for the child's best interest. In another case, the Washington Court of Appeals refused to enforce an Iranian court's verdict regarding a divorce that gave custody to the Iranian father. Once more, the American court's argument was that the foreign court did not take into consideration the interests of the child. In Michigan, the court of appeals overturned a court ruling acknowledging a divorce verdict by a court in India, arguing that the wife was unaware of the *ṭalāq* and the infringement on her rights.

A ruling by a lower Arizona court in a joint property dispute applied Muslim-Moroccan laws to reach a verdict. The Arizona Court of Appeals reversed the verdict based on Christian-Syrian laws, claiming that implementing Muslim-Moroccan laws is a contradiction of Arizona law, which states that property purchased by either spouse constitutes joint property. In a lawsuit by an American woman who sustained injuries in a hotel in Saudi Arabia, a court in Massachusetts refused to implement the shariʿa-based law of Saudi Arabia on the grounds that it does not adequately represent the rights of women and non-Muslims.

The California Court of Appeals overturned a previous ruling which gave an Iranian court jurisdiction over the inheritance of an Iranian man, arguing that in Iran the rights of the plaintiff would not have been preserved because she is a woman and because she belongs to the Baha'i faith. The same court determined that a Shi'ite couple married in California in a temporary marriage (*mutʿaa*) that was not legally registered is not considered married by California state law. The Virginia Court of Appeals also refused to acknowledge the shariʿa marriage of a British couple that did not legally register their marriage; the status of the marriage as null and void was determined by its standing in the place the ceremony was conducted, not the laws of Islam.

The Religious Validity of a Verdict by a Non-Muslim Judge According to *Fiqh al-Aqalliyyāt*

The Western public adheres to a separation of religion and government, and regards religion as a private element that does not belong in the legal public sphere. Thus, establishing Muslim religious courts in non-Muslim countries is impractical. The general public tends to oppose the establishment of shariʿa courts, usually on the grounds that such courts would undermine the pillars of government and public order.[79] Moreover, Muslim religious law regards the establishment of shariʿa courts as illegitimate, since without the consent of the sovereign charged with the execution of the law, Muslims are not authorized to form a court and oblige the public to litigate in it.[80] Even when a member of a Muslim minority appeals to a shariʿa court in his country of origin, he is not exempt from turning to the civil court in his country of residence to ratify the ruling and imbue it with binding legal validity according to the laws of that land. In such instances, Muslims are required to appeal to two forms of litigation: a religious one in their country of origin and a civil one is their country of residence. This arrangement is therefore impractical, particularly when civil courts are more accessible and efficient than the remote religious option;[81] thus, Muslims must often resort to state courts that abide by civil laws. As previously mentioned, civil courts are accessible and committed to upholding justice without bias or delay; they operate with a predetermined set of comprehensive laws, free from bureaucratic and administrative impediments. Furthermore, Muslims do not feel estranged in these

[79] Buhuth wa-Darasat, "Kuwibik Tarfud Iqamat Mahakim Shariʿa li-Muslimi Canada." The sole attempt to establish shariʿa courts in Canada was recorded in 2004 in Ontario. Capitalizing on the Ontario 1991 Arbitration Act, the Islamic Institute of Civil Justice announced its intention to form a shariʿa based arbitration court. This announcement was publicly criticized, mainly by Muslim organizations and the Muslim Canadian Congress who warned that strict observance of shariʿa laws contradicts Canadian Bill of Rights. Upon much deliberation, the National Assembly of Quebec decided to desist religious-based arbitration in family affairs.

[80] Al-Amrani, "Al-Usra al-Muslima fi al-Gharb bayn al-Tashriʿ al-Islami wa-l-Qawanin al-Wadʿiyya," 190.

[81] Ibid., 188–9.

courts because the younger generation – second- or even third generation immigrants – was raised according to the values of their adoptive countries, removed from the world of Islam.[82]

Therefore, the question arises: given the dearth of Muslim religious courts in the West, can the verdict of a non-Muslim judge be considered religiously valid in an intra-Muslim legal dispute? This question becomes even more crucial in cases that determine the personal standing of an individual in both the civil and religious spheres. The religious validity of a verdict by a non-Muslim judge is relevant to three groups: (1) Muslims who do not litigate by the shariʿa as they are unfamiliar with it; (2) Muslims who believe shariʿa laws are ill-suited for their surroundings and circumstances; (3) Muslims who wish to litigate according to shariʿa law, but are prevented from doing so, perhaps because state laws force them to appeal to a non-Muslim judge. Cases in which Muslims purposefully refuse to litigate by the shariʿa are irrelevant because by doing so, they have sinned and transgressed against religious prohibitions.[83] According to Muslim religious law, a Muslim is forbidden from willfully appealing to a non-Muslim judge or to non-shariʿa laws; thus, in principle, a verdict by a non-Muslim judge has no religious validity or applicability. This position has brought previous religious scholars to prohibit Muslims from settling disputes in non-Muslim countries for fear that they will commit a transgression by being bound to appear in front of judges who do not follow shariʿa law.

However, in current times, numerous Muslims have settled in non-Muslim countries and, for a variety of reasons, have no plans to return to the lands of Islam. Solutions must then be offered to treat the accompanying problems that come with living under a non-Muslim regime and being subject to litigation in front of non-Muslim judges and in accordance with non-shariʿa laws.[84] In this respect, Doctor Mohammed al-Amrani, member of the International Union of Muslim Scholars, makes the distinction between Muslims who live as a minority in the non-Muslim land of their birth, and immigrant Muslim minorities. Al-Amrani believes that the indigenous Muslim minority must establish a shariʿa legal system; either the minority leader or the Muslim public must appoint those who are authorized to be Muslim judges. He further maintains that, so long as Muslims can sustain legal religious systems, they should not submit to non-Muslim laws. He bases his opinion on previous religious scholars – Ibn ʿAbdin, Ibn

[82] Ibid., 189.
[83] Ibid., 177–8.
[84] Ibid., 179–91.

Nujaym, and Ibn al Hammam – who determined that in a land ruled by non-Muslims, the qadi is awarded authority because of his appointment by the Muslim population. Even when nominated by a non-Muslim ruler, his tenure is still legitimate and his verdicts binding due to the need to conduct trials and prevent wrongdoings. This is accepted by the religious scholars of various schools,[85] yet, when the sovereign elects a non-Muslim to officiate in Muslim affairs, his ruling is illegitimate, except for in cases of necessity (*ḍarūra*), when it is not possible to appoint a Muslim qadi.[86]

Due to their inability to appoint a qadi, immigrant Muslim minorities are permitted to litigate in front of a non-Muslim judge whose ruling is religiously valid and civilly binding.[87] Nevertheless, Muslim minorities are requested to strive and establish Islamic institutions of shariʿa arbitration, particularly in the personal standing field. These institutions will employ Muslims who are well versed in religious law and can arbitrate in conflicts without threatening society's foundations and civil order. This arrangement is accepted by most countries' legal systems, subject to the rules and stipulation of the respective systems.[88] For that reason, *fiqh al-aqalliyyāt* operates under the working assumption that Muslim minorities in the West cannot have a shariʿa legal system, even on the most private, internal issues in their lives, that is, personal standing matters. Rather, they should strive for legal pluralism through the construction of institutions for arbitration within the Islamic centers; in this way, Muslim religious law will be introduced to the civil legal system through consultation and counsel provided by the institutions in Islam-related cases. This legally pluralistic framework is manifested in ECFR decrees that encourage minority communities in Europe to bring their respective countries of residence to recognize shariʿa-based arbitration between Muslims, and to involve the Islamic centers in the legal proceedings of Muslim couples, particularly in matters of personal standing.[89] As will be discussed hereinafter, Islamic centers strive to expand their scope of arbitration, primarily within the family and on matters of personal standing. Nevertheless, *fiqh al-aqalliyyāt* scholars still regard civil court rulings as binding, including divorce verdicts by non-Muslim judges.

85 Al-Amrani, "Al-Usra al-Muslima fi al-Gharb bayn al-Tashriʿ al-Islami wa-l-Qawanin al-Wadʿiyya," 196–7.
86 Ibid., 196.
87 Ibid., 198–9.
88 Ibid., 203–6.
89 For instance, al-Amrani, "Al-Usra al-Muslima fi al-Gharb bayn al-Tashriʿ al-Islami wa-l-Qawanin al-Wadʿiyya."

Implementation of Shariʿa and *Fiqh al-Aqalliyyāt* in the Muslim Population in the West

From the aforementioned discussion we can infer that the West employs a system of legal pluralism through which, depending on the country, shariʿa is partially implemented for Muslims. This applies both to the state legal apparatuses as well as independent organizations that work within the Muslim community. The degree and depth of the plurality vary from country to country, contingent on the conditions of diverse legal systems. Therefore, we may be compelled to ask: What is the role of *fiqh al-aqalliyyāt* doctrine in those fields where shariʿa is implemented? As well, does such a doctrine strengthen plurality by calling upon Muslims to assimilate in the public sphere? Furthermore, we must consider the scope of its acceptance by Muslim minorities, and determine to what extent the doctrine influences Muslims' lives and the realization of their religious identity in the West.

As previously mentioned, Muslim populations in the West are comprised of diverse religious factions, including the Muslim Brotherhood founded in Egypt by Hassan al-Banna in the 1920s, and al-Jamaʿa al-Islamiyya, founded in Pakistan by Abul A'la Maududi in the 1940s. The movements' respective religious perceptions are akin to the *wasaṭī* faction and the proponents of *fiqh al-aqalliyyāt*. There are also *salafi* Islamist groups that oppose *fiqh al-aqalliyyāt*. These groups are close to the Wahhabi faction and Jamaʿat al-Daʿua wa-l-Tabligh; founded in India by Muhammad al-Kandhlawi in the nineteenth century, this faction calls for the upholding of religion as it is represented in the Qurʾan and the sunna, rejecting any form of renewal. Other Islamic factions, such as the Sufi faction, are ambivalent toward *fiqh al-aqalliyyāt*. In addition, there are devout Muslims who do not identify with a specific religious faction, and secular Muslims who view religion through a cultural lens.[90]

In my European and American fieldwork, I have determined that it is a common practice for Muslims to resist adherence to a specific faction, and instead amalgamate the religious practices and conventions of several factions. They might pray at a mosque with a *salafi* imam, seek the answers to their questions from *wasaṭī* leaning religious adjudicators, and read *salafi* literature, all while imitating the general, non-Muslim population in their everyday lives. For instance, the board of the mosque in Edinburgh, Scotland is not affiliated with any faction, albeit the imam is of

[90] Al-Ghalayini, *Al-Marakiz al-Islamiyya fi North America*, 32–43.

Egyptian descent and a *salafi* faction proponent. When Muslims contact the mosque to obtain a religious decision they are referred to the available adjudicator regardless of the faction to which they themselves are affiliated. Those seeking guidance may be referred to, among others, Shaykh Abdullah Al-Judai, the vice chairman of the ECFR and an affiliate of the *wasaṭī* faction.[91] What's more, a visit to the mosque's library reveals that the lion's share of books has a *salafi* leaning, some of which, whether directly or indirectly, criticize the *wasaṭī* and *fiqh al-aqalliyyāt* doctrines, claiming they deviate from Muslim religious law.[92]

The positions of the Muslim activists I have encountered in the United States and Europe vacillated between supporting and rejecting the doctrine, its leading scholars, and their rulings. Some were simply not familiar with the doctrine. Attitudes toward the doctrine can be categorized into four groups. One group is comprised of Muslim activists and public figures who know and accept the doctrine, identify with its scholars, and abide by their rulings. I have, for example, encountered such a position in Islamic centers in Los Angeles and Maryland in the United States,[93] as well as in Dublin.[94] These public figures and imams declared that they identify with the *wasaṭī* faction, adhere to *fiqh al-aqalliyyāt*, and abide by its scholars' rulings.

Among the intellectuals supporting the doctrine of *fiqh al-aqalliyyāt* is Doctor Abu Bakir al-Shanqiti, the head of the International Institute of Islamic Thought in Virginia.[95] According to Shanqiti, the institute provides a nurturing environment for a Muslim intellectual movement that – in light of the challenges brought forth by modernity, shifting realities, and local circumstances – would promote the process of mending society (*iṣlāḥ*) and the renewal of Islamic thought (*tajdīd al-fikr al-Islāmī*). The center supports any activity that strengthens organizations dedicated to Islamic thought and the rejuvenation of religious law, including the Fiqh Council of North America. Al-Shanqiti clarifies that the center has adopted the *wasaṭī* faction through the Islamization of science, which seeks to interpret the Qur'an and the sunna vis-à-vis science and

91 Secretary of the mosque in Edinbrugh. Interview by author. Scotland, February 16, 2012.

92 See Ahmad Mursi, "Al-Muwasasat al-Islamiyya fi Mujtamaʿ al-Jaliyat wa-l-Aqalliyyat Nazra Mustaqbaliyya," *Multaqa Khadim al-Haramayn al-Sharifayn al-Malik Fahd bin ʿAbd al-ʿAziz Al Suʿud al-Islami al-Thaqafi* (Copenhagen, 2001).

93 Meetings with Muslim activists and community leaders in mosques and Islamic centers in Maryland and California, between March 15 and April 9, 2011.

94 Meetings with Muslim activists and community leaders in mosques and Islamic centers in Dublin, and Scotland between February 10 and February 15, 2012.

95 Al-Shanqiti, abu Bakir. Interview by author. Virginia, November 2, 2012.

modern life, amalgamating religion and reality. Thus, one of the objectives of the center is to formulize this perception into an action plan capable of directing the center's researches and publications. To al-Shanqiti, the methodology of *fiqh al-aqalliyyāt* is more aligned with public needs than text-based Wahhabi and *salafi* religious law. Religious law according to the *salafi* faction is based on segments (*juz'iyyāt*) rather than the whole (*kulliyyāt*); thus, their interpretations are necessarily partial, unable to integrate the various texts. To al-Shanqiti, those opposing *fiqh al-aqalliyyāt* are mostly of the *salafi* leaning. They refer to the proponents of the doctrine who favor common sense over primary sources as "new *Mu'tazila*," and to the doctrine as "*fiqh mu'tazila*."

The second group consists mainly of *salafis* who oppose any form of rejuvenation in shari'a law. Such Muslim activists and imams reject *fiqh al-aqalliyyāt*, claiming it deviates in its ruling and negates the principles of the religion. The young *salafi* representatives I met with at the al-Sunna Mosque in Bradford, Britain, claimed that Muslim religious law is absolute and valid regardless of time or place; thus, there can be no specialized religious law for Muslim minorities in the West. There is no need for a specialized minority *fiqh* because the laws of Islam, as reflected in the practice of al-Salaf, should be upheld in the West as in the lands of Islam. The young activists demonstrated a dismissive attitude toward *fiqh al-aqalliyyāt* and its scholars, claiming they deviated from Muslim religious law and the practice of al-Salaf. They unequivocally reject the rulings both of the ECFR and Yusuf al-Qaradawi on the grounds that they contradict shari'a law from the Qur'an and the sunna, which should be followed to the letter, even at the price of discouraging others to turn to Islam. For instance, they discard Qaradawi's reasoning in one of his religious decrees that by allowing Muslims to send Christmas cards, they bring Christians closer to Islam. In addition, they reject the ECFR ruling that permits Muslims in Europe to take mortgages in order to buy a house and improve their quality of life, since this contradicts an explicit verse in the Qur'an prohibiting mortgages or interest-incurring loans.[96]

The young activists preach obedience to the Qur'an and the sunna as interpreted by the first generation of Muslims and the founders of the various schools.[97] Although they claimed not to discern between the four

[96] See also, Shavit, "The Wasati and Salafi Approaches to the Religious Law of Muslim Minorities," *Islamic Law and Society* 19/4 (2012): 32.

[97] Young *salafi* representatives. Interview by author. Bradford, al-Sunna Mosque, February 17, 2012.

schools, they demonstrated affinity and identification with the *Ḥanbalī* School. One explained that in Pakistan he was a follower of the *Ḥanafī* School; however, after time spent in Saudi Arabia studying the religion of Islam, he abandoned it for the practice of al-Salaf. For them, every religious decree must be scrutinized for the sources upon which it has drawn. A religious decree that is based on the Qurʾan and the sunna of the Prophet, as well as the *ijmāʿ* of the *ṣaḥāba* and *al-tābʿūn* (the generations succeeding the death of the Prophet up to the tenth century), is accepted and followed regardless of its school of origin. In contradistinction, they reject decrees that do not rely or draw upon the primary sources or on *qiyās* and secondary sources, namely *maṣlaḥa* and *istiḥsān*. For matters that require a fatwa, they turn to religious scholars in Saudi Arabia, who for them represent the true Islam. When confronted with the issue of how familiar Saudi Arabian scholars would be with the specific circumstances of Muslim minorities, particularly in the West, they replied that the scholars comprehend reality anywhere, and added that any query would include a description by the applicant of the issue and his circumstances.

Another group of activists, mainly Muslims from the Indian Peninsula, reject *fiqh al-aqalliyyāt*, and embody a traditional religious approach with a distinct religious doctrine that is based on the *Ḥanafī* School. The representative of this group is Shaykh Shams ad-Duha Muhammad, founding director and principal of the Ebrahim College in London,[98] who argues that the original national identity of the minority outweighs its religious identity, influencing their behavior and lack of cohesion. Muslims in the West have yet to come together over a unified religious law because not enough energy has been committed to Muslim cohesion and unification. He claims that the majority of students in the college do not accept *fiqh al-aqalliyyāt*, though they do learn from it.

According to members of this group, Muslims in Britain do not display a uniform religious methodology because of their heterogeneity in terms of country of origin and affiliation to a school of thought. The majority of the group hails from the Indian Subcontinent and is influenced by the Deoband tradition, a religious movement originating in an Islamic college

[98] Muhammad, Shams ad-Duha. Interview by author. London, October 13, 2012. Member of Jamaʿat al-Tabligh, and founding director and principal of the Ebrahim College in London. The college was established in 2003 for the purpose of teaching the religion of Islam and currently has one hundred full-time students and about one thousand part-time students. One of the objectives of the college is to enable students to learn about the challenges facing Muslims in Britain due to their life circumstances and to initiate long-term enlightened thinking.

in the city of Deoband, India. Markedly based on the *Ḥanafī* School, it distilled religious law from the influences of the modern age, generating the religious scholar (*ʿulama'*) and movements such as Jamaʿat al-Tabligh.

According to this group, India previously developed Muslim minority religious law, although it is not referred to as such. Unlike European *fiqh al-aqalliyyāt*, religious law in India strictly adheres by the *Ḥanafī* School, avoiding infringement on religious decrees by erring on the side of caution (*al-iḥtiyāṭ*). This form of religious law, observed by Muslims in the West who originate from the Indian Peninsula, shies away from the methodology of alleviation (*taysīr*) found in European *fiqh al-aqalliyyāt*, which accepts decrees by all religious schools rather than committing to a specific one.

This Indian Islamic faction differs from the *salafi* faction, which is extensively influenced by the Wahhabi movement in Saudi Arabia. They believe that followers of the *salafi* faction adopt the *Ḥanbalī* School and its rules, and regard Saudi scholars as the religious authority, approaching them for all matters and for any fatwa. In contradistinction, the Deoband movement believes authority to lie with *Ḥanafī* religious scholars from the Indian Subcontinent, and approach them consistently and follow their rulings. This traditional faction is susceptible to change and alternative Islamic approaches, more so than the *salafi* faction, which is characterized by seclusion and aversion to religious dialogues and disputes with other factions.

Another representative of the group rejecting *fiqh al-aqalliyyāt* is Dr. Muzammil Siddiqi, Chairman of the Fiqh Council of North America, who endeavors to mediate the supporters and opposition of *fiqh al-aqalliyyāt*. Siddiqi is more akin to the Wahhabi faction in that it opposes religious law according to the objectives of the shariʿa, which is seminal to the *fiqh al-aqalliyyāt* methodology.[99]

A third group to consider is the Muslim activists who are unaware of *fiqh al-aqalliyyāt*. According to Doctor Amra Bone, a female adjudicator in the shariʿa council in Birmingham,[100] the doctrine is unfamiliar to the majority of Muslims in Britain. shariʿa councils are not affiliated with the ECFR and have not adopted a religious law doctrine comparable to other

[99] Al-Shanqiti, abu Bakir. Interview by author. Virginia, November 2, 2012.

[100] Bone, Amra. Interview by author. London, October 13, 2012. Bone is an Islamist female activist of Pakistani descent who holds a PhD in Islamic Studies. The only female shariʿa judge in Britain, she maintains that women who approach the council are benefitted by that fact, as she understands their hardships better than a male judge.

Islamic organizations. To Doctor Bone, the plurality of Muslims in Britain has resulted in a tendency to adhere to the prevailing school in one's countries of origin, primarily the *Ḥanafī* School, often demonstrating an even stricter approach for fear of forsaking the faith. To Bone, due to shifting circumstances in the various European countries, it is impossible to accept the *fiqh al-aqalliyyāt* methodology and rule in a manner applicable to each specific country. She maintains that Islam is a religion of realism, not idealism, and thus it cannot be confined to a uniform framework of religious law.

Bone herself is not affiliated with a specific school, believing that the reality in Britain compels Muslim community leaders to conduct a specific *ijtihād* to construct shair'a laws befitting their needs. In the shariʿa council of which she is a member, there is an observance of equality between men and women. In general, the council does not adhere to the *Ḥanafī* School or any other school, but rather implements religious laws suitable to modern life. She illustrates this through the example of Muslim women marrying non-Muslim men, which according to religious law is strictly forbidden. Contemporary circumstances require us to rethink this prohibition, particularly because in our times, women are highly influential in their children's lives. Women are relatively present in the house, provide for their children, teach them, and enhance their faith. In cases of separation from the spouse, the wife has the power to expel her ex-husband from the home, and tends to receive custody over the children. To Bone, the reality necessitates a rescinding of the prohibition on this form of marriage. Even the secretary at the Edinburgh Islamic center was relatively uninformed regarding the ECFR and Qaradawi, only remotely familiar with their rulings. According to her, the *fiqh al-aqalliyyāt* doctrine is not prevalent in her community, many being unaware of it.[101]

The fourth group is those that claim *fiqh al-aqalliyyāt* is too conservative, advocating for a more liberal religious law. Among the representatives of this group is Mohammed Amin[102] who believes the ECFR is not a religious authority and has no clout over Muslims in Britain. He does not approve of the council, which he finds to be overly traditional.

101 Secretery of the mosque in Edinbrugh. Interview by author. Scotland, February 16, 2012.

102 Muhammad Amin, born in 1950, is a British Muslim of Pakistani descent, graduate of the Faculty of Mathematics at Cambridge University. Amin is a member of the board of the Muslim Council of Britain founded in 1997. It confederates about five hundred national, regional, and local Islamic organizations, such as mosques, shariʿa councils, and Islamic centers, but not individuals. Although it is a public organization, it is not recognized by the British government as the official Muslim representative body.

Proclaiming himself a Muslim liberal, Amin is an active member of the British Conservative Party. Shaykh Doctor Yahya Hendi maintains that members of Fiqh Council of North America hail from all Islamic schools and factions, including Shi'ite and Sunni; he asserts that the members are not in consensus over a single religious law methodology, including *fiqh al-aqalliyyāt*. Although it is mentioned in their discussions, council members have not adopted the doctrine. Hendi himself takes issue with the terminology; he claims minority religious law as it exists all over the world is in fact identical to Islamic majority law in that it is based on the objectives of the sharīʿa (*maqāṣid al-sharīʿa*). Thus, it should be considered flexible and pragmatic – applicable in every place and in any context. Owing to the lack of any viable alternatives to purchasing a house in the United States or obtaining a loan from Islamic finance institutions, the council's fatwa permits Muslims to take a mortgage with interest. Nevertheless, he does not regard this as minority religious law; rather, because the specific interest prohibited by the Qur'an is not bank interest, this decree is permissible. Thus, deciding whether to allow a mortgage is dependent on the lived reality of each Muslim.[103]

[103] Hendi, Yahya. Interview by author. Washington, DC, November 1, 2012.

4

The Evolution of Muslim Religious Law among the Muslim Minority in Israel and Its Linkage to *Fiqh al-Aqalliyyāt al-Muslima* Doctrine

In this chapter, I will discuss the development of religious law among the Muslim minority in Israel in order to elaborate the formulation of its identity, religious awareness, and law. The chapter will examine the actions, rulings, religious law methodology, and contribution of each of the active Islamic components to the formulation of Muslim religious law in Israel: the shair'a courts, the Southern and Northern branches of the Islamic Movement, and the Sufi order of al-Tariqa al-Khalwatiyya al-Qasimiyya al-Jamiʿa. Moreover, the chapter will discuss the linkage between *fiqh al-aqalliyyāt* vis-à-vis Muslims in the West and the development of religious law among the Muslim minority in Israel from the 1990s onward. It will demonstrate the existence of tendencies in Israel supporting the emergence of local Muslim religious law based on, and deriving from, classic religious law which takes into consideration the unique circumstances of Muslims in Israel.

Background on Islam in Israel

Islam propagated into the Southern Levant between 634 and 638 CE, following the defeat of the Byzantine army at the hands of the Muslim army. Henceforth – notwithstanding limited periods of Crusader or Mongol rule – Muslims constituted the majority and thus ruled the area. The defeat of the Ottoman Empire in World War I signaled the termination of the Muslim rule. Yet, despite the British mandate in Palestine, Muslims remained the hegemonic majority until the inception of the State of Israel in 1948.[1]

According to the Pew Research Center, in the last two decades the Muslim population in Israel has more than doubled. It grew from

[1] Ori Stendel, *Arabs of Israel: Between the Rock and the Hard Place* (Jerusalem: Academon, 1993), 38–44.

0.6 million people in 1990 to 1.3 million in 2010, an increase of 103 percent. By the year 2030, the Muslim population is projected to increase another 66 percent, from 1.3 million to 2.1 million. In 2010, Muslims comprised 17.7 percent of the Israeli population. According Pew Research Center estimates, by the year 2030 this percentage might rise to 23.2 percent.[2] From these demographic trends, it is possible to predict that Muslims will soon constitute over 90 percent of Israel's minority population – its ratio among the non-Jewish inhabitants prior to the establishment of the State of Israel. In this context, Muslims – the focal minority group of this book – in fact constitute the vast majority within the Arab population in Israel.[3]

The majority of Muslims in Israel are Sunnis with a leaning toward the *Shāfiʿī* School. However, the *Ḥanafī* School is prevalent in the cities, and as well in shariʿa courts tracing back to the provisions of the Ottoman Sultan, on which obligatory Ottoman legislation in shariʿa courts is based. The Ottoman legislation was absorbed into British Mandate law in Palestine, then subsequently into Israeli law.[4]

Despite ostensibly belonging to the *Shāfiʿī* or the *Ḥanafī* Schools, Muslims in Israel did not develop uniform religious awareness and practices that consciously and consistently followed one religious school. The majority of Muslims obtained limited knowledge in an unsystematic way: aggregating information from day school, religious radio and television programs, and local imams whose own knowledge might also be partial. Only a handful possessed comprehensive religious knowledge in its various avenues. There are a variety of reasons behind this deficiency:

1. The exodus of educated religious leadership from the territories that would become the State of Israel following the events of 1948. For instance, all qadis who served in shariʿa courts during the British Mandate left the country save for one.
2. The prevalent state of war between the Jewish state and the adjacent Arab countries, along with the majority of the Muslim world. The resulting disconnect between Muslims in Israel and the surrounding Muslim world has inhibited the development of cultural relations or an exchange of knowledge between the Muslim public in Israel and Muslims in the lands of Islam.

[2] This estimate includes the Muslim citizens of East Jerusalem.

[3] Pew Research Center, "The Future of the Global Muslim Population: Projections for 2010–2030." *The Pew Forum on Religion & Public Life* (January 2011): 92–93.

[4] Iyad Zahalka, *Shariʿa Courts: Between Identity and Adjudication* (Tel Aviv: Israel Bar Association Press, 2009).

3. The lack of higher education facilities for religious studies that could educate Muslim students on all facets of the Islamic religion, as well as qualify them to serve in a variety of religious capacities. This has led to a deficiency in an educated religious leadership that would teach and disseminate religious values that originate from the sources.
4. The awakening of the Muslim minority in Israel commencing relatively late in relation to the establishment of the State of Israel. The Muslim minority became noteworthy only by the late 1980s with the success of the Islamic Movement in the municipal elections. Furthermore, in the decades since its inception, the Islamic Movement has not focused on formulating an awareness of Muslim religious law, rather its efforts are focused on promoting a return to religious and political activity.

Thus, religion developed into a tradition passed down through generations based on the available religious education and independent of a preferred school's shariʿa laws. Commitment to a specific school became a purely symbolic gesture, uncorroborated by actual religious knowledge from the previous generation.[5]

In the early 1990s, there was a significant shift in religious law, as well as the activities and awareness related to religious law, among Muslims in Israel. Responsible for this shift are the active religious elements within the public: the shariʿa courts following reforms and innovations in the practice of shariʿa laws; the two branches of the Islamic Movement that established institutions and centers for religious studies and ruling; and the Sufi order al-Tariqa al-Khalwatiyya al-Qasimiyya al-Jamiʿa that established the shariʿa college in Baqa al-Gharbiyye which later became the al-Qasemi College, in addition to a center for religious ruling. These factors initiated the development of Muslim religious law for Muslims in Israel.

In actuality, the lack of a uniform and consolidated religious perception allowed the public flexibility in terms of religion and religious law, and in accepting, despite their diversity, the perceptions of various Islamic entities. For example, albeit belonging to the *Shāfiʿī* School, the Muslim public accepted shariʿa courts' commitment to decrees based on the *Ḥanafī* School. For that reason, the Muslim public in Israel was accepting of new interpretations of religious and shariʿa laws that deviated from a specific school without outright renouncing it, particularly in the rulings of shariʿa courts.

[5] In the early 1980s, representatives of the Islamic Movement educated by its leaders in the proper manner of prayer to appear in mosques. Incensed by it, the elders, considered it a deviation from the accustomed and time-honored tradition of prayer.

Shari'a Courts

The Ottoman Empire regulated litigation among its subjects in a structured, institutionalized system of shariʿa courts. The courts operated alongside the civil Ottoman *al-niẓāmiyya* courts, and ruled in accordance with shariʿa laws and the *Ḥanafī* School adopted by the Ottoman sultan and consequently by his subjects.[6] The courts had the authority to rule on personal standing affairs and other matters brought to them with the consent of all parties involved. The British Mandate opted to maintain the judicial autonomy of the religious factions on matters of personal standing. According to the King's decree in his council over the land of Palestine, 1922–1947,[7] the separation of religious and civil courts in the Ottoman legal system was adopted. Furthermore, the British assumed the Ottoman shariʿa courts' legislation and legal procedures on matters of personal standing. No significant changes were made to the nature and jurisdiction of these courts, notwithstanding the annulment of their jurisdiction regarding non-Muslims, and the establishment of a shariʿa court of appeals.[8]

After the establishment of the State of Israel, the Provisional Government, through article 11 of the 1948 Government and Law Order, assumed the British Mandate's legal system. This applied particularly to the prevailing law and jurisdiction of shariʿa courts, contingent on later amendments. In this sense, shariʿa courts in Israel today are a continuation of the shariʿa courts established by the Muslim Ottoman sultan.

In the last two decades, we have witnessed a renewal of shariʿa laws in the field of personal standing of Muslims in Israel. Following the initiative of qadi Ahmad Natur, the president of the shariʿa court of appeals at the time, Muslim religious law was innovated through consistent and intensive legal work. The renewal and rejuvenation were attained through adoption of laws from various schools and scholars external to the obligatory *Ḥanafī* School, in what is referred to as a selective *ijtihād* (*intiqāʾī*), designed to handle the needs and challenges faced by the Muslim society in Israel.[9] The innovations and alterations were made in accordance with

[6] See article 1801 of *Shirh al-Majla* in Salim Rustam Baz al-Lubnani (*Shirh al-Majla, Dar Ahya' al-Turath al-ʿArabi*, 3rd edition, Beirut, 1986).

[7] See State of Israel Laws, 3rd volume.

[8] Goiten and Ben Shemesh, Introduction to Muslim law: Basic principles and laws, (Faculty of Law of the Hebrew University. Legal Studies, No. 3) Jerusalem: Mif'al Hashichpul and Gvilim Publishing Co. Ltd., 1957.

[9] This is analogous to *takhayyur al-aḥkām*, choosing religious laws from the various schools. The term *takhayyur* is associated with the layman who chooses the most convenient laws and not with the religious scholars who perform *ijtihād*.

the principles and rules of religious law, and without deviating from the foundations of religious law (*uṣūl al-fiqh*).[10]

This reform utilized two major apparatuses: (1) Legal manifestos issued by a consensus of the league of qadis designed to directly alter the law on a specific matter by presenting their religious law positions on public affairs; (2) decrees by the shariʿa court of appeals that served as binding precedents over the regional courts. In addition, Qadi Natur issued his own decrees in response to public appeals on various matters, including appeals via *Kul al-ʿArab* newspaper. Qadi Natur's seminal religious decrees discussed, among other issues, the eternal sanctity of Muslim cemeteries and the holiness of mosques that no longer hold Muslims' prayers.[11]

Unlike religious decrees whose validity is voluntary, the legal manifestos were granted a binding validity of new shariʿa courts laws. Every manifesto contained a new law deviating from the prevailing law, which henceforth was to be implemented by shariʿa courts. The *ijtihād* performed through these manifestos generated change in two fields: (1) The first and fourth legal manifestos emphasized the collective rights of Muslims over their sacred properties (waqf) and their distinctiveness as a consolidated minority that aspires to preserve the uniqueness of its culture and laws, uncommon to its political and judicial surroundings. This applied to the first manifesto that focused on the Islamic waqf and the need to preserve it and preempt any threat to its existence or legal and religious standing. The fourth manifesto called for arbitration within the confines of the courts on conflicts that are not under the jurisdiction of shariʿa courts. (2) The second field in which the manifestos effected change was the liberalization of the approach toward women and children's rights via liberal interpretation of relevant shariʿa laws. The second manifesto abolished the institutionalized method of alimony informants; instead, the decision over the amount was entrusted to the qadi, based on the renewed conditions and needs. The third manifesto acknowledged the right of a child whose father passed away to his father's share in his grandfather's inheritance.

Nevertheless, the principle of binding precedents, which appeared in many of the shariʿa court of appeals' rulings, was essential to the reform in shariʿa law. According to the principle, the supremacy of the court of appeals as the legal policymaker for the regional courts was established by granting its rulings the status of binding precedent. In order to achieve justice and clarify for the public the official position on a subject, in cases

[10] Zahalka, *Shariʿa Courts*, 113–17.
[11] Ibid., 45–51.

of similar causes and circumstances, the regional courts must implement the shariʿa law principles outlined by the court of appeals. Nonetheless, the principle of binding precedents only compels the regional courts and not the court of appeals itself. In this manner, the rulings by the court of appeals had a direct and certain influence on the lower courts and the shariʿa legal system as a whole. The reasoning behind it was the need for a judicial policy, *siyāsa qaḍāʾiyya*, that in contrast to religious decrees which are open to *ijtihād*, would stabilize the judicial system. The innovation in the ruling of the court of appeals encompassed the entirety of subjects under the jurisdiction of the courts pertaining to personal standing and waqf.[12]

Concurrently, the shariʿa court of appeals maintained a defensive judicial approach in order to thwart any intervention in seminal shariʿa laws by the Israeli legal system. This policy disregards any judicial norm that negates the religion of Islam, while striving to embrace any binding civil norm under two conditions: first, if disregarding or ruling against legislation that directly engages with religious and shariʿa courts might result in Supreme Court intervention and annulment of the ruling;[13] and second, if the same principle enforced by the state legislator is already present within shariʿa law and can be mitigated with religious law.

In cases where the two aforementioned conditions are fulfilled, the court of appeals reinforces the civil concept which the shariʿa court deliberated on, instilling in it Islamic religious content. Thus, the ruling which stems from, and coincides with, Muslim religious law is concordant with the binding civil norm. In this way, the shariʿa court of appeals is able to safeguard shariʿa law and religious law from state intervention without breaching binding civil laws.[14]

The most prominent issue in this defensive judicial policy[15] was found in matters pertaining to the benefit of the minor.[16] In custody cases, religious courts are bound by article 25 of the 1962 Israeli Legal Capacity and Guardianship Law to rule solely according to the benefit of the child and not by religious laws.[17] Therefore, shariʿa courts were compelled to rule

[12] Ibid., 61–75.

[13] The Supreme Court of Israel 95/3269, Katz v. The Rabbinical Court of Jerusalem (1996) P.D. 50 (4), 590; Israel Supreme Court 92/3914, Lev v. Tel-Aviv Regional Rabbinical Court, (1994) P.D. 48 (2), 491.

[14] Zahalka, *Shariʿa Courts*, 117–24.

[15] For a detailed discussion see Zahalka, *Shariʿa Courts*, 83–103.

[16] The Supreme Court of Israel 04/8906, Jane Doe v. John Doe (2005) P.D. (3), 767.

[17] The Supreme Court of Israel 06/1129, John Doe v. Shariʿa Court of Appeals (2006) P.D. 06 (11), 729.

according to the interest of the minor and not by shariʿa laws. In order to counter this negation, the shariʿa court of appeals argued that the minor's interest is a legal principle that exists in Muslim law and is one of the objectives of shariʿa laws in cases of child custody. Judging by its Islamic interpretation, it reinforced this principle, giving it supremacy and instilling in it Islamic content.[18] Thus, the shariʿa court of appeals was able to uphold the Israeli Legal Capacity and Guardianship Law without deviating from Muslim religious law and its guiding principles.

Nevertheless, when an Israeli law imposed on shariʿa courts contradicted Muslim religious law, such as gender equality as manifested in the Women's Equal Rights Law of 1951, the shariʿa court of appeals refrained from challenging this principle, choosing to ignore it instead. This is evidenced in the continued practices of equating the testimony of one man with that of two women, and of ruling by shariʿa laws, even if from a non-Muslim standpoint, they do not offer equal rights to women.

In these instances, where there is an intersection with Israeli law, shariʿa courts do not adapt shariʿa law to Israeli judicial principles. Rather, they uphold Muslim religious law directly, rejuvenating it by creating localized practices that draw on interpretation of various doctrines within Muslim law contingent on the spirit of the place and the time. The innovations were based on *ijtihād intiqāʾī* – constructing new religious laws by choosing the most appropriate law from the variety of schools and religious scholars, disparate from the obligatory *Ḥanafī* school. This has enabled shariʿa courts to alleviate the lives of the Muslim public in Israel by adopting religious laws that relate to its unique reality and conditions. Moreover, it has enabled shariʿa courts to creatively cope with binding civil law.[19]

Analyzing Qadi Natur's verdicts, the legal manifestos, and the innovation achieved through rulings of the shariʿa court of appeals reveals that – as opposed to other religious law doctrines and previous decrees by qadis – a more conservative approach was employed in the case of waqf. In this manner, Muslim cemeteries are deemed eternally sacred; their sanctity is not contingent on whether they are ancient or active, or whether the tombstones are disintegrating or not. Contrary to previous rulings, this decree takes into account life circumstances in Israel. At the same time, it is based on the same religious law principles and interest of the Muslim public that governed the decisions of classic religious scholars. On the

[18] Fakhr al-Din al-Zaylaʿi, *Al-Hidaya Sharh Bidayat al-Mubtadaʾ*, 939 (Dar al-maʿarfa, vo.3, 46 in "Al-Hadana fi al-Sharʿ"), 939. Muhammad Zayd al-Abyani, *Sharh al-Ahwal al-Shakhsiyya* (Beirut, 9th edition, 2002), 269–70.

[19] Zahalka, Shariʿa Courts, 113–6.

issue of abandoned mosques in Israel, the religious scholars' position was reiterated; accordingly, a place remains sacred even if the mosque has collapsed or Muslims have abandoned it.

Furthermore, religious law flexibility was also manifested in fields in which it was not possible to utilize selective *ijtihād* when implementing the religious tradition of previous religious scholars in a way that benefitted and befitted the unique circumstances of Muslims in Israel.[20] The novelty of this decree pertains to prevailing religious laws in shariʿa courts in Israel that tended to adhere to, and not deviate from, the *Ḥanafī* School. Consequently, this tendency diminished the standing of the *Ḥanafī* School.[21]

An examination of religious law innovation in the last two decades by the shariʿa court of appeals demonstrates how shariʿa courts established a religious law methodology designed to renew shariʿa laws,[22] based on religious law tradition and the utilization of the following shariʿa mechanisms:

1. **Freedom from obligation to a school** – the commitment to rule according to the *Ḥanafī* School, as ordered by the Ottoman sultan, has become more lenient, inducing shariʿa courts to digress from it in order to attain a ruling that acknowledges the public's newfound conditions and challenges. The most striking example is the adoption of Ibn Taymiyya's religious decree according to which, divorcing three times at a single session constitutes small Sufi divorce that enables the husband to remarry the wife, whereas the *Ḥanafī* School regards this form of divorce as a large Sufi divorce which are final and requires a *muḥalil* prior to the couple being allowed to re-marrying.
2. **Selective ijtihād (*intiqāʾī*)**[23] – Shariʿa courts regard all facets of Muslim religious law as highly relevant in terms of religion. They adopt religious laws from all four schools or from classic law literature aligning with the circumstances of the specific case and the renewed needs and conditions. For instance, obligatory inheritance (*al-waṣiyya al-wājiba*) in articles 76–78 of Egypt's obligatory Law of Inheritance performed through the Egyptian legislator's *ijtihād*, is partly based on Ibn Hazm al-Zahiri religious law depicted in his book *al-Muhala*.

[20] Ibid., 47–8.
[21] Ibid., 48–59.
[22] The response of Qadi Natur to a direct question I asked him on November 8, 2012.
[23] A term coined by Qaradawi, *Al-Ijtihad al-Muʿasir bayn al-Andibat wa-l-Anfirat*, (Cairo, 2nd edition, 1998), 20.

3. **Public interest (*maṣlaḥa*)** – The courts have accepted that the public interest is embodied in shariʿa laws regarding debt, permissions, and prohibitions. Thus, where shariʿa thrives so does the public interest. In this vein, in order to prevent damage to Muslim headstones and construction on Muslim cemeteries, the court deemed them eternally sacred.
4. **Purposeful interpretation to extract the goals of the texts in primary sources** – According to *fiqh al-maqāṣid*, shariʿa is designed to achieve five objectives: preservation of religion, health, mental capacity, lineage, and property. These objectives must be represented in the ruling of adjudicators who interpret primary source texts in light of these objectives. Thus, interpretation of the Prophet's hadith that granted a mother custody over her son ushered in the notion of supremacy of the minor's best interest in future verdicts.
5. **Altering religious law according to shifting circumstances** – Shariʿa courts adopted the religious law principle that religious law changes with the circumstances, whether in the accepted custom (*ʿurf*), or in conditions that require a change of the law. This is manifested in linking the deferred dowry to the cost of living index due to frequent fluctuations in currency strength as a result of the Western economy that is practiced in Israel.
6. **Acknowledging Muslims in Israel as a distinctive minority** – The characteristics of Muslims in Israel are distinct in comparison to Muslims in the lands of Islam and Muslim minorities. This is due to being simultaneously a religious minority and a national minority, vying for their collective rights. This realization led to an adjustment of religious law for Muslims in Israel. For instance, in Israel, Muslims reside in a pluralistic and liberal society which promotes gender equality. Thus, to prevent women from turning away from religion and refraining from appealing to shariʿa courts, religious courts have endorsed liberalization of women's rights, such as facilitating the burden of appointing arbitrators for marital disputes.
7. **Respecting basic human rights and dignity** – Muslim religious law acknowledges the human being as inherently entitled to basic rights; thus, his dignity should be upheld, and no harm should befall him. For instance, a woman should not be admonished nor lose her right to alimony for refusing to have intercourse with her husband. Alimony is not awarded in return for martial relations, but rather for the woman residing in her matrimonial house (*iḥtibās*).

Under these circumstances, shariʿa courts developed localized judicial practices that derive directly from general Muslim religious law, yet differ from prereform religious law and religious law customary to Muslim states, including neighboring ones. The Muslim public did not oppose the development of religious law, accepting and even supporting the changes and innovations.[24]

The Muslim public in Israel is divided over the standing of shariʿa courts, the acknowledgment of their legal authority in matters of personal standing, and their role in shaping the public's life experience and future. This division manifested itself in the 1990s, when segments of the public initiated a bill revoking shariʿa courts' unique jurisdiction over personal standing affairs of the Muslims in Israel.

There are three main discernable groups in the Arab public in Israel that vie over the character of society, the influence of religion, and the future and position of shariʿa courts: (1) The Muslim religious group headed by the two branches of the Islamic Movement; (2) The nonreligious group led by the Arab national organizations and movements; (3) The secular group, at its core the Communist Party of Israel and feminist organizations.

An analysis of processes within Arab society, as well as the public's perception of shariʿa courts and its willingness to appeal to them, reveals the standing of the courts is influenced by three major factors that affect their credibility in the public eye: (1) Their religious legitimacy as determined by their history, roots, reputation, and presiding qadis; (2) The scope of their independence vis-à-vis the state, meaning the capacity to rule according to shariʿa, prove loyal to Muslim society, and serve as a nursing bed for religious and national activities that advocate for Muslim society with an understanding of the leeway and autonomy provided by Israeli law; (3) Their legislative record, integrity of legal proceedings and upholding of justice, efficiency, treatment of women and children, and devotion to the more vulnerable members of society.

The two branches of the Islamic Movement regard shariʿa courts as Islamic religious institutions that uphold Muslim religion and its principles, and utterly conform with them. On February 20, 2004, in an extremely rare decision, both branches issued an op-ed in the local press[25] titled "An Important Announcement Regarding the Position of the Two Branches of the Islamic Movement in Israel on shariʿa Courts in Israel." It was signed

[24] Zahalka, *Shariʿa Courts*, 120–1.

[25] For example, see the journal of the Southern Branch of the Islamic Movement, "*Al-Mithaq*," February 20, 2004.

by Shaykh Ibrahim Abdullah Sarsur, head of the Southern Branch at the time, and Shaykh Hashem Abdul Rahman, mayor of Umm al-Fahm and spokesperson of the Northern Branch at the time.

In contradistinction to the Islamic Movement, the nonreligious elements (mostly associated with the educated sectors and Arab nationalism) are neutral toward religion. Nevertheless, these elements are sympathetic toward, and supportive of, shariʿa courts due to the latter's perception and religious-national stance that on matters of women and children's rights becomes liberal. shariʿa litigators and lawyers chose to continue to appeal to shariʿa courts despite the 2001 Fifth Amendment to the Israeli Family Court Law, which enabled them to appeal to civil courts. Even though historically these groups did not identify with shariʿa courts, in the last decade their approach became more sympathetic and favorable, regarding them as a symbol of autonomy for the Arab minority, and as an additional pillar in the fortification of the distinct identity of the Muslim minority in Israel.[26]

On the other hand, the Communist Party, which promotes an agenda of curtailing religion's influence, as well as women's organizations, both endeavored to restrict shariʿa courts' authority.[27] This is manifested in initiatives to offset the courts' unique jurisdiction over Muslims personal standing affairs in Israel and opening civil family courts to the Arab public. This endeavor was successful, paving the way for the 2001 amendment to the Family Court Law.

However, in the current climate, opposition to shariʿa courts by women's organizations and Arab seculars has subsided. Therefore, the aforementioned amendment that granted civil family courts equal authority over personal standing affairs was a de facto failure. The majority of Muslims, including women organizations, favor shariʿa courts over civil ones.[28] This is unmistakably evidenced in a speech given at a Hebrew University conference by Taghrid Jahshan, a lawyer and prominent activist in women's

[26] Taken from a speech by Laila Abed Rabbo, "Transformations in Muslim Family Laws in Israel – Historical, Comparative and Contemporary Outlook" (presented the conclusions of her doctoral diss. in a symposium by the Hebrew University's Nehemia Levtzion Center for Islamic Studies, May 7, 2009).

[27] Such as Aida Tuma, a prominent operative in MAKI and the Democratic Front for Peace and Equality, who heads a women's organization against violence, and Khulud Badawi, who headed the Action Committee for Equality in the field of Personal Standing, and others.

[28] See statistics from the management of the shariʿa courts indicating a consistent increase from 2003 in the number of cases, despite a one-time decline due to the fifth amendment to the Israeli Family Court Law: http://index.justice.gov.il/Ar/Units/TheShariaCourts/Pages/Reports.aspx

organization. She conceded the amendment's failure, stating that shari'a courts have maintained their hegemony as the principle judicial system for Muslims in Israel in the field of personal standing.[29]

Women's organizations also exhibit a hesitant attitude toward religious law and shari'a courts. In an article published at *al-Siwar*[30] journal, Shirin Bitshun – a lawyer and organizer of the feminist organization Kiyan's legal project – writes that according to shari'a courts, a woman, even a wealthy one, is entitled to alimony provided that all the requirements are met. However, she writes, if the same affluent woman appealed to a civil family court, her case would be dismissed should the court apply civil law and the principle of income equality. Her conclusion is that implementation of civil principles such as equality, instead of the patriarchal methodology employed by religious laws, constitutes a difficulty that must be thoroughly examined. Furthermore, the Fifth Amendment to Family Court Law has been unbeneficial for women.

It would seem that whether due to its religious imperative, its role in formulating and strengthening the collective identity of the Arab minority, or championing the rights of women and children, all of the various Muslim factions accept and trust the shari'a court. This tendency is supported by the gradual increase in the number of cases opened annually by shari'a courts, despite the fact that the public now has the option to appeal to civil family courts.

Shari'a courts' religious outputs are even more essential because the personal standing issues on which they rule are seminal to shari'a. A significant portion of personal standing affairs, including marriage and divorce, children's affiliation, and safeguarding the next generation, fall under the category of divine rights (*ḥuqūq Allah*). These rights, in the form of public norms that constitute a taboo which cannot be broken, overlooked, or even alleviated, are also revered by secular Muslims.[31] Due to the utter importance of personal standing in Muslim religious law, the application of shari'a by most legal systems in modern times has been reduced to this field, even if by state legislation and not through classic religious law.[32] In this sense, the conclusions drawn from the discussion on personal

[29] Abed Rabbo, "Transformations in Muslim family Laws in Israel."

[30] Shirin Bitshun, "Nafaqat al-Zawja wa-Mabada' al-Musawaa bina al-Mara'a wa-l-Rajul," *Al-Siwar al-Haraka al-Nasawiyya al-'Arabiyya li-Da'm Dahaya al-I'tida'at al-Jinsiyya*. 37 (2010): 6.

[31] Abd al-Karim Zidan, *Madkhal li-Dirasat al-Shari'a al-Islamiyya* (Beirut: 16th edition, 1999), 41.

[32] Ibid., 7.

standing can serve as an important indicator in examining the evolution of religious law for Muslims in Israel, especially since shariʿa courts' rulings are acknowledged by all active Islamic factions in Israel, who also refrain from overruling shariʿa courts' decrees.

Religious Decrees by the Southern Branch of the Islamic Movement

The Islamic Movement was split over participation in the elections for Israeli Parliament. The Southern Branch, located in Kafr Qasim and led by Abdallah Nimer Darwish, supported participation in the elections, whereas the Northern Branch, with headquarters in Umm al-Fahm and headed by Shaykh Raed Salah, demanded a boycott of the elections.[33]

In the wake of the rift, the majority of founders continued to spearhead the Southern Branch, which focused on promoting the call to Islam (*al-daʿwa*) in conjunction with political efforts and social work. It founded the al-Hiwar College for Islamic Studies in Tira in 2001 (granted, its activities are still somewhat marginal), as well as an ad-hoc religious ruling committee that converges upon request and does not have active or permanent members.[34]

The Southern Branch did not endeavor to develop religious law nor document the decrees issued by the movement and its leaders, although said decrees were sporadically published internally. Regarding the Jerusalem mufti as the highest religious authority, the movement believed that Muslims in Israel have no need for a special body for religious ruling, save for distinct concerns such as participation in the election. However, this position was reversed in the movement's sixteenth convention held on December 28, 2013 in Tira, and the decision was made to form a department for *fiqh*, religious ruling, and documentation, the mandate for which is the promotion of religious law for Muslims in Israel and the passing of religious rulings that take into account their unique circumstances. The movement is set to elect members to serve in this department.[35]

In the ideological sphere, the movement is not committed to a single school, but rather accepts the religious tradition of all four schools, favoring one over the other based on its relevance to the conditions of Muslims in Israel, while emphasizing the principle of alleviation originating from

[33] The religious ruling regarding participation in election was published by Haya't al-Fatawa wa-l-Buhuth al-Islamiyya- al-Haraka al-Islamiyya, an organization established specifically for that purpose and did not operate as a permanent council for religious ruling.

[34] Sarsur responds to questions asked by the author, July 29, 2012.

[35] Sarsur, Ibrahim. Interview by author. January 17, 2014.

these circumstances. Officially, the movement adopts the *wasaṭī* doctrine and rules according to its methodology. It regards Muslims in Israel as an indigenous minority – one which experienced hardships and suffering, and was in fact transformed from a majority in its homeland into a minority. This situation necessitates a specialized religious law that balances all aspects of life.[36]

The most intriguing ruling by the movement was a decree permitting the movement's participation in the parliamentary elections. The decree discussed in this chapter is a revised version of the original decree issued by the movement's leaders in preparation for the 1996 general elections. Both versions were signed by Haya't al-Fatawa wa-l-Buhuth al-Islamiyya-al-Haraka al-Islamiyya, the Religious Law and Research division of the Islamic Movement.[37] Ibrahim Abdullah Sarsur clarified that the movement periodically updates its religious decrees to account for developments in the country and the region, as well as in the treatment of the Muslim minority in Israel.

The Southern Branch refers to Muslims in Israel as an indigenous minority which secured its existence in its homeland, yet failed to secure its legitimacy in the eyes of the Israeli establishment; this stems from the inherent contradiction manifested in the country's insignia and self-definition as a Jewish and democratic state. The population further failed to impose the legitimacy of its existence on the official regional agenda, particularly on the Arab, Islamic, and even Palestinian agenda. The decree claims that Israel has become a democratic country for its Jewish citizens, and a Jewish and Zionistic country for its Arab and Muslim citizens. According to the decree, all diplomatic endeavors to resolve the Arab-Israeli conflict are based on UN Resolutions 242, 338, and their equivalents; agreements that recognize the State of Israel within the borders of the Green Line do not discuss the future of Muslim Arabs in Israel. This disregard compels the Muslim citizens of Israel to adopt objectives that correspond to their multifaceted reality.

The decree warns that the well-being of the Muslim and Arab minorities in their homeland is at risk, particularly at a time of worrisome increases in extremism by Jewish individuals, Jewish political parties, and government policies which have crossed many red lines in their treatment of this minority. This trend is manifested in a string of laws designed to oust

[36] Sarsur responds to questions asked by the author, July 29, 2012.

[37] In an interview on September 26, 2012, Shaykh Nimer Darwish explicated that in fact he drafted the fatwa and the shura council of the Islamic Movement signed it.

the Muslim minority from positions of power. It follows that the Muslim minority does not wish to lead a refugee life, and will not stand for discrimination or exploitation.

According to the decree, the reasoning behind the movement's political aspirations is twofold: first, political activity is part of a wide array of activities with the mutual goal of preaching Islam in order to fortify the individual and society, as well as safeguard the land and a sense of identity. In this way, judging by the movement's proclaimed policy, there is no contradiction between participation in the political arena and its other various activities. The movement's nonprofit organizations, institutions, and foundations continue their activities with gusto, as if the movement were not a player in the political arena. Moreover, its political participation has also produced positive results in the academic, cultural, social, and economic spheres, as well as accomplished long-term goals in social welfare, promoting religion and contributing to the protection of the mosque of the Temple Mount and the waqf.

The second motivation behind the decision is in the movement's credo: work in this world is the path to achieving heaven in the next, and political success promotes religious objectives. Hence, political activity represents one element within a larger shariʿa approach: in any place where Muslim interests exist, so does God's shariʿa. In other words, the movement based its decision on the interests of the Muslim public in Israel. Participation in the political arena is a means and a tool by which to offset racism and the exploitive policies of the Israeli government – both in the Palestinian arena and in the inner-Israeli one. Gaining representation in areas of power and public service will pave the way toward a resolution of the hardships faced by the Muslim public in Israel; in contrast, abandoning parliamentary ambitions will produce a void that would eventually be filled by non-Islamic elements.

The Islamic Movement is part of a triumphant global rejuvenation movement that thrives through adaptation of Islam to newfound realities. However, this is not sufficient, as some believe that the state of Islam in Arab and Muslim countries is even direr than that experienced by Muslims in Israel. Therefore, there is no reason why the Islamic movement is those countries continues to strive, while the Islamic movement in Israel regresses. In addition, political nonparticipation might be misconstrued by the Muslim public as indicating that Muslims are incapable of taking responsibility for their own lives, instead, busying themselves completely with religion; alternately, it might suggest that the purity of Islamic work is contingent on avoiding politics, which is grossly erroneous.

Upon surveying the positions of religious scholars for and against participation, the decree reaches the conclusion that in terms of religion, there is no contradiction between politics and the call to Islam. The possible damage incurred from participation is marginal, and does not impair the pillars of religion; furthermore, any damage is outweighed by the benefits garnered from participation. This is another case of opting for the lesser harm: to participate in elections is to make concessions necessitated by the exploitive reality, whereas ignoring the elections would constitute acquiescence to exploitation. Indeed, recognizing that participation is required and attainable due to Islam's flexibility, the Southern Branch chose to participate in the political arena.

Religious Decrees by the Northern Branch of the Islamic Movement

As oppose to the Southern Branch, the Northern Branch focused on internal Muslim affairs such as waqf, assisting prisoners, helping those in need, founding medical institutions, and promoting the individual and collective rights of the Arab public. In terms of religious education, in 1989 the Northern Branch established the al-Daʿawa al-ʿUlum al-Islamiyya college in Umm al-Fahm, which was academically recognized by academic institutions in the Muslim world, but not by the Israeli Council for Higher Education. Since its inception, the college has educated numerous youth, some of its graduates becoming teachers, imams, and preachers in mosques. Through the public impact generated by these graduates, who demonstrate knowledge and proficiency in the religion of Islam, the Northern Branch became a leader in the field and a destination for public appeals.

In 1996, the Northern Branch founded a religious ruling committee. The committee responded to appeals by the Muslim public directly or via the movements' journal, *Sawt al-Haqq wa-l-Huriyya*. In 2002, the movement institutionalized religious ruling by establishing the Islamic Council for Religious Decrees (al-Majlis al-Islami al-Ifta').[38] The reasoning behind the establishment was the religious demand that every Muslim community should have religious scholars who can adjudicate for their community, restrict those elements within society that lead the people astray, and provide answers in cases of emergency (e.g., an immediate, time-sensitive decision on whether or not to perform an abortion).

[38] http://www.fatawah.com

The Movement believes there is distrust and detachment between Muslims in Israel and religious scholars in the Muslim world. Religious decrees from abroad do not suffice, since religious scholars in the Muslim world are unfamiliar with the distinct features of life in Israel; such an understanding is imperative to comprehending a society's reality, its essential needs, and in order to examine issues that constitute a necessity (*ḍarūra*) or a hardship (*ḥarj*). The movement further maintains that harmony should prevail among Muslims in Israel over religious law, particularly due to the complex and newfound challenges faced by Muslims in Israel. Moreover, there is a need to decide the dates of Islamic religious holidays and the commencement of the month of Ramadan, as well as the sum of penance for committing a sin such as perjury or breaking the fast of Ramadan, and the ransom for killing a man (*diyya*). The movement explicates that the council's establishment was designed to create a ruling body for religious law that would answer questions originating from local committees and institutions, including those affiliated with the Islamic Movement itself, in order to align their work with the laws of shariʿa.[39]

The head of the council and its members are nominated by the national leadership of the Islamic Movement with the aid of an advisory committee consisting of prominent figures in the field of religious law, mostly from the occupied territories. The council has introduced compelling methodology for its members, based solely on religious law decrees by the four Sunni Schools. Thus, it is compulsory to examine the certified religious texts of each school on the topic in question, and indicate the authorized and preferable religious decrees in each.[40] Rulings on both clear-cut and complex cases that do not originate from the four schools must be brought to the general assembly of the council, and receive the backing of a majority of all the council members, as opposed to a simple majority of those present in the discussion.[41]

39 *Fatwa al-Majlis al-Islami al-Ifta'* (2005, vol. 1), introduction.

40 The council's decision from February 20, 2012, determined a detailed list of authorized books for each of the schools. The books on the list should be consulted in every decree.

41 The methodology of the movement's council was obtained from the two volumes of religious decrees, pamphlets, website and other publications by the Islamic Council for Fatwa, including an internal document titled: "Decisions of the Council Regarding Methodology for Religious Ruling," which includes decisions by the council on February 13, 20, 27, and March 3, 2012. The author obtained this document from Dr. Waleed Husayn, a member of the council during a discussion with him on July 22, 2012 at the al-Daʿawa college in Umm al-Fahm.

When the topic in question is new and no reference to it can be found in the religious law tradition of the four schools, it is mandatory to turn to the decrees of the Islamic Fiqh Academy (Majmaʿ al-Fiqh al-Islami) and the Muslim World League (Rabitat al-ʿAlam al-Islami). Subsequently, decrees by additional institutions must be examined: the Fiqh Council of North America, the Indian Religious Law Union, the Sudanese Religious Law Union, the Religious Law Committee in al-Azhar, the Permanent Committee for Islamic Research and Fatwa in Saudi Arabia, the ECFR, and the General Presidency of Scholarly Research and Ifta' (Haya't Kibar al-ʿUlama') in Saudi Arabia, as well as protocols of professional conventions, conferences, and research by modern day religious scholars.

Another guideline for the adjudicator is that religious decrees are formulated together and not individually. The ruling has to be consistent and the adjudicators are bound by the council's previous rulings and decisions until such time that the assembly votes to alter a ruling. The adjudicator must quote his sources in full and note the positions of religious scholars regarding the authenticity of the hadith cited in the decree. The decree's conclusion must reference all the sources, including the name of the school, or the name of the religious law union that issued the religious decree upon which it was based.

The council prohibited the use of *talfīq* (pragmatic eclecticism) – for a law on a given topic or issue that is broken down into multiple subtopics, each subsection can be defined by a law originating from a different schools of thought. Thus, the final decree is labeled as an innovation that has yet to be passed by an acknowledged religious scholar. This form of ruling must meet three criteria: (1) The existing alleviations of the various schools should not be followed without justification, and any stipulations articulated by the school for the adoption of the alleviation should not be ignored (as this repudiates a religious code of constantly seeking for alleviations); (2) The decree cannot contradict a ruling by the shariʿa system in Israel or the council; (3) The council's rulings cannot dispute laws that are under the consensus of religious scholars (*ijmāʿ*).

In the adoption of alleviations from the various schools, the council stipulates the following conditions: (1) Alleviations should not be adopted merely for the pleasures of mankind; (2) They should be recognized by religious scholars and not be deviant; (3) They are conditioned on annulling a difficulty (*ḥarj*), whether individual or collective; (4) The adjudicator must possess the religious law knowledge to navigate between the various laws, and if he does not meet this criterion, he must rely upon a worthy religious scholar; (5) Adoption of the alleviation will not serve as a pretext for illicit results; (6) The adjudicator must be certain that the alleviation was borne out of reverence.

Working from the belief that the Muslim public in Israel has a strong desire to be acquainted with shariʿa laws and to adhere to them, the council strives to make religious adjudicators accessible to the public through daily assignments to a phone hotline. The public also submits questions via the printed newspapers, and the adjudicators respond on the council's website, which thus far has published about eleven thousand decrees on diverse topics. According to the council's secretary, it receives hundreds of questions each month. From the beginning of 2010 until the beginning of 2012, the website registered over 170,000 visits, out of which 45,000 were from Israel.[42] In addition, the council published collections and booklets on various topics, as well as two volumes of its religious rulings in 2005 and 2012.

Examining the aforementioned publications reveals that the adjudicators strictly follow the methodology they themselves have set. The vast majority of their *ijtihād* is transmitted *ijtihād (naqlī)* from religious scholars of the four schools, minimizing the innovation of new religious laws as much as possible. For example, regarding the validity of marriage between a Muslim man and a non-Muslim woman, the adjudicators first discussed the position of the family in Islam, the correct way to choose a partner, and the nature of the relationship that should exist between the couple. They presented the positions of the four schools relating to the permissibility of a man marrying a woman from the People of the Book in the lands of Islam, illustrating it with quotes from religious law literature and the religious evidence utilized by those religious scholars. Subsequently, they detailed the current circumstances of mixed marriages as depicted by modern scholars, quoting several religious decrees by Shaykh Mahmud Shaltut. In the conclusion, they presented a ruling which derives from the position of the previous scholars, adapting it to current times and circumstances.[43]

The adjudicators deviate from the directives of the four schools only on rare occasions. Such a case was in the prohibition of sexual relations between a man and a woman who, although they had entered wedlock, had not begun a joint life together as part of the ceremony customary

[42] See the council's general publications, website, and newspaper ads that were distributed to the public. The author received those from the council's secretary during an interview with him at the council's offices in Nazareth on July 22, 2012.

[43] *Fatwa al-Majlis al-Islami al-Ifta'* 2 (Nazareth, 2012): 190–3.

in Muslim society in Israel. This prohibition negates the position of the schools stating that after a marriage agreement is signed, they are considered husband and wife and are allowed to engage in sexual relations. In this case, the council rejected religious law in favor of social custom, basing its ruling on religious decrees published on Islamweb.[44] The council further decreed that women are allowed to undergo hymen reconstruction surgery in cases of rupture due to an accident, since this medical procedure is necessary to rectify the situation. They grounded their decree in rulings by the Islamic Fiqh Academy, affiliated with the Organization of Islamic Cooperation.[45]

The council's conservative approach is clearly manifested in permitting a Muslim man to marry of woman of the People of the Book; the ruling is based on the positions of all four schools that sanctioned these marriages, albeit their potential harm labels them as not preferable.[46] The council's adjudicators favored a decree issued long ago and under unfamiliar circumstances, rather than acknowledging the shift that has occurred, as did Qaradawi who prohibited Muslim minorities residing in non-Muslim countries from entering into such marriages due to the damage incurred by Islam and to Muslims interests.[47]

Building, digging, and planting in Muslim cemeteries is another intriguing religious ruling by the council. Upon reviewing the positions of the four schools, the adjudicators decreed that it is forbidden to damage the graves in any way as it disrespects the dead, even if the renovation is performed for a Muslim cause such as building a mosque. They argued that their position did not contradict the religious ruling by the *Ḥanafī* scholar Fakhr al-Din al-Zaylaʿi, which permitted one to dig and build in cemeteries after the bodies have disintegrated into dust. The council argued that a cemetery constitutes Muslim waqf and is intended solely for burial; thus, any other use is prohibited.[48]

To conclude, the religious law endeavors by the Northern Branch of the Islamic Movement represent conservatism rather than innovation in religious law. Nevertheless, they stand by their declarations that religious ruling must meet the unique challenges faced by Muslims in Israel, as they live under different circumstances than Muslims in the lands of Islam.

[44] Ibid., 24–5.

[45] Ibid., 30–2.

[46] Ibid., 190–3.

[47] Qaradawi, *Fi Fiqh al-Aqalliyyat al-Muslima: Hayat al-Muslimin Wasat al-Mujtamaʿat al-Akhra* (Cairo, 1st edition, 2001), 100–4.

[48] *Fatwa al-Majlis al-Islami al-Ifta'* 2, 299–301.

Their religious rulings illustrate a profound commitment to religious law tradition and consistent adherence to international Islamic organizations for religious ruling on modern and novel issues, alongside a handful of innovative religious law decrees.

Religious Decrees by the Sufi Order of al-Tariqa al-Khalwatiyya al-Qasimiyya al-Jamiʿa

The Sufi order of al-Tariqa al-Khalwatiyya al-Qasimiyya al-Jamiʿa was founded by the al-Qasimiyya family originating from Hebron. In the mid-nineteenth century, al-Shaykh Husni al-Qawasmi moved to Baqa al-Gharbiyye where he established the order, built its religious and affiliated institutions, and spread it throughout the north and the south.[49] Until the 1970s, the order flourished, and was followed by the majority of people residing adjacent to it – its heads serving as the religious authorities for their appeals. Following the resurgence of various political factions, nationalistic and Islamic, from the early 1970s onward, the order's influence dwindled and its supporters in Israel diminished.[50] In 1990, the order established a shariʿa college for Islamic studies that later became the al-Qasemi Academic College. In 1993, the college received the recognition of the Israeli Council for Higher Education, and could thus dispense academic degrees in teaching.[51]

The Shaykh heading the order is considered the mufti of all supporters who are bound by his decrees, yet in many cases he refers them to imams in mosques. In 2003, the *al-Iftaʾ* Center was founded by al-Qasemi Academic College to satiate the modern public need for an accessible and reliable scientific center for religious ruling.[52]

The center strives to strengthen the public's relations with the college, coordinate between its departments, and supply answers on the religious matters that are referred to it. The shariʿa department adds to the academic prestige of the center, emphasizing its role in instilling social and religious values, as well as dispensing religious knowledge and tolerance to promote

[49] More on the Sufi order, D. Ephrat, *Spiritual Wayfarers, Leaders in Piety: Sufis and the Dissemination of Islam in Medieval Palestine.* In *Harvard Middle Eastern Monograph* 40 (Cambridge, MA: Harvard University Press, 2008).

[50] Mahmood, Khaled. Interview by author. July 23, 2012. Vice-President of the al-Qasemi Academic College and deputy to the shaykh of the order. Hold a PhD in Shariʿa and Islamic Studies from the University of Jordan.

[51] See Al Qasemi Academic College, *al-Dalil al-Academy*, Al-Qasemi College, Baqa al-Gharbiyye 2009/2010.

[52] Elaborated by Khaled Mahmood.

such values. In the years 2004–2007, the center received approximately one thousand applications; however, the religious decrees by the Shaykh and the center were not documented, and tended to be dispensed verbally.[53]

The order and center's adjudicators have outlined a binding religious law methodology in which they first turn to the primary sources, the Qur'an, the sunna, and the *ijmāʿ*, then to the secondary sources, the *qiyās*. They take heed to avoid causing harm to Muslims, to permit what can benefit the public and is not forbidden by the primary sources, and to follow the proverbs of the *ṣaḥāba*.[54]

Believing that obligation to one specific school should be cast aside, they accept the religious law tradition of previous religious scholars from all four schools without favoring one over the other. Therefore, their rulings are defined by *ijtihād naqlī* that draws from all four schools in addition to other acknowledged religious scholars. Religious laws are chosen by the degree of authenticity and accuracy of their primary sources, their contribution to the attainment of shariʿa goals, the conditions and circumstances of the Muslim public in Israel, and the fulfillment of its interests (*maṣlaḥa*). They also adopt the local custom (*ʿurf*) as a source for religious ruling.

For novel issues, without precedents in religious tradition, they construct new religious ruling (*ijtihād inshāʾī*) through purposeful interpretation of the primary sources, aspiring to reflect in the new decree the same objective found in the religious law. For them, *ijtihād inshāʾī* is limited to adjudicators with advanced degrees in Islamic studies who are proficient in the field in which they seek to construct new decrees, and contingent on its acceptance by all members of the *al-Iftaʾ* Center.

The center's adjudicators adopt the maxim that religious law should be modified according to the developing times and circumstances. Thus, they believe that the adjudicator must be familiar with the conditions and reality of the public for which he constructs the decree. They further consider Muslims in Israel distinct in comparison with Muslims around the world.

Doctor Khaled Mahmood is cautious about applying the *fiqh al-aqalliyyāt* doctrine to the Israeli case. He maintains that religious law stemming from this doctrine can be applied to the Israeli case in some instances, such as the permission to take a mortgage to build or purchase a house. In other matters it is not applicable, demonstrated in the decree that a woman who converted to Islam can remain with her non-Muslim

[53] Ibid.
[54] Ibid.

husband. Nonetheless, he also criticizes Islamic activists who promote a highly conservative approach and reject religious decrees that mitigate life circumstances with shariʿa laws. Because they implement religious decrees by Saudi scholars who do not consider the unique circumstances of Muslims in Israel, he refers to them as "Wahhabis."[55]

Doctor Mahmood notes that new religious laws were introduced only on rare occasions. He points to the example of the religious decree that the divorce of a man who acted under a spell (*ṭalāq al-masḥūr*) is null and void because it was achieved without free will and under duress.

Accepting a bank mortgage to build or purchase a house is an additional topic in which a new religious decree was obtained. Upon arriving to the al-Qasemi college from the West Bank in 1992, Doctor Mahmood refused to rule on the matter and directed the applicants to adjudicators more familiar with the circumstances of Muslims in Israel. However, now that he has a deep understanding of these circumstances, he believes that Muslims in Israel are allowed to take a mortgage if they are unable to afford a house or land on which to construct a house. In his far reaching decree, Dr. Mahmood relied on the principle that necessity revokes a prohibition (*al-ḍarūrāt tubīḥ al-maḥẓūrāt*). The lands allocated to young Arab Muslim couples by the state are limited; while rented apartments, which are uncustomary as a long term solution for Muslims in Israel, are also in short supply. Thus, the issue of building a house to start a family has become a necessity for Muslims, without which the task becomes ever more difficult. He clarifies that this ruling is exclusive to Muslims in Israel due to their unusual circumstances, and for Muslims in the lands of Islam his decree would have been different.[56]

In terms of binding Israeli civil law, Dr. Mahmood believes that the civil legal norms that compel Muslims as citizens should not be questioned because they constitute a necessity that must be abided. In this sense, Muslims must be allowed to act according to a legally binding civil norm even if it is religiously forbidden. For instance, the Islamic validity of car insurance is immaterial because it is a state imposed requirement. He bases this understanding on the Prophet's hadith that Muslims are not religiously liable for anything they do as a result of oversight, forgetfulness, or necessity.[57]

[55] Ibid.
[56] Ibid.
[57] Ibid.

Comparing Religious Law in Israel and *Fiqh al-Aqalliyyāt al-Muslima*

The life circumstances of each minority group examined in the research, both in Israel and the West, are historically, geopolitically, economically, socially, and judicially dissimilar. However, comparing the *fiqh al-aqalliyyāt* framework for Muslims in the West with the religious law practiced by Muslims in Israel reveals that in both cases, the approach to imposed civil law is dependent on the circumstances. In instances where civil law contains elements that are also found in Muslim religious law tradition – thus making it possible to mitigate civil with religious law – both doctrines seek the common denominators, striving to mediate the two systems, and introduce religious content into civil arrangements. Furthermore, when a civil arrangement contradicts the pillars of religion and reconciling the two is impossible, both doctrines opt to ignore the civil arrangement and urge Muslims to passively object by not appealing to the civil judicial system.

While in Israel the practiced religious law by the various elements is consistently based on selective *ijtihād* (*intiqā'ī*) and does not result in *ijtihād inshā'ī* of constructing new religious decrees,[58] *fiqh al-aqalliyyāt* scholars have established a broader methodology. This methodology is also comprised of selective *ijtihād*, but goes further: incepting new religious laws that differ from classic religious laws through *ijtihād inshā'ī*, and creating religious law mechanisms that fulfil the objectives of shari'a beyond those of the specific decrees. Nevertheless, the bases and principles of both religious law methodologies indicate that they share a common goal: achieving Muslim interests through a possible deviation from the known and familiar array of shari'a laws, while maintaining the general principles of religious law and pillars of religion through accepted tools and mechanisms. In this sense, both *fiqh al-aqalliyyāt* and Israeli shari'a courts demonstrate significant innovation of religious law despite employing different *ijtihād*.

In both cases, the Islamist element that supports participation in the election process offers similar reasoning: (1) The obligation to commend the good and deny the evil; (2) The Muslim interest obtained by participating in the elections – that is to say, participation in the election produces

[58] Y. Reiter, "Judge Reform: Facilitating Divorce by Shari'a Courts in Israel," *Journal of Islamic Law and Culture* 11, 1 (2009): 35–36.

rights and thwarts harm to Muslims by inducting them into the political establishment.

Conversely, the justification of Islamists who oppose participation is, in both cases, based on the same rationale: participating in the elections constitutes an endorsement of the non-Muslim establishment, and requires Muslims to partake in the forbidden act of legislation reserved exclusively for God.

According to *fiqh al-aqalliyyāt*, the indigenous Muslim minority must act to establish shariʿa courts to rule on its affairs and not succumb to an exclusive civil judicial system as determined by al-Amrani. This is in contrast to the immigrant Muslim minority, which is unable to appoint a qadi from within the community to preside over their affairs according to shariʿa laws.[59] In Israel, shariʿa courts conform to the shariʿa, and Muslims can appeal to them on all matters pertaining to personal standing and waqf. Thus, the Israeli case falls under the religious law framework of *fiqh al-aqalliyyāt* since it is eligible for the requirement of establishing a religious judicial system for Muslim minorities.

Conclusion: Preliminary Trends in the Development of Local Muslim Religious Law in Israel

Despite officially being affiliated with either the *Shāfiʿī* or the *Ḥanafī* Schools, Muslims in Israel (following the state's inception) did not develop a consistent, conscious religious awareness guided by a single religious school. The religious awakening of the Muslim minority in Israel commenced a few decades later, and became more substantial only toward the late 1980s with the success of the Islamic Movement in the municipal elections.

Among the numerous reasons behind the several decades of stagnancy in Muslim religious law in Israel are: the exodus of the religious elite from Israel following the events of the 1948 war, depriving the country of educated religious authorities for decades; the severing of Muslims in Israel from their Islamic surroundings; a lack of access to religious adjudicators in Islamic countries; an inability to study in Islamic institutions in Muslim countries; the absence of such institutions in Israel. During that period, the religious perceptions of Muslims in Israel were obtained through

[59] Mohammed Al Amrani, "Al-Usra al-Muslima fi al-Gharb bayn al-Tashriʿ al-Islami wa-l-Qawanin al-Udʿiyya," *Al-Majallat al-ʿIlmiyya li-l-Majlis al-Urubi li-l-Ifta wa-l-Buhuth*, 7 (July 2005): 190.

inherited religious traditions in correlation with each generation's religious education and concerns.

Another potential explanation for the lack of development in Muslim religious law in Israel is that segments of the Muslim public accepted the religious law authority of the Jerusalem mufti. Shaykh Sarsur explicates that due to the religious authority of the Jerusalem mufti, the Southern Branch of the Islamic Movement did not record the decrees issued by its institutions and leaders, albeit some did appear sporadically in their internal publications. The Movement did not deem it essential to issue religious decrees for the general public, except in matters pertaining particularly to the Movement, such as participation in the elections. Shaykh Sarsur explains that this position was altered in the sixteenth convention that took place in Tira on December 28, 2013, with the decision to establish a department for *fiqh*, religious ruling, and documentation that would endeavor to develop religious laws for Muslims in Israel taking into account their unique circumstances. The Movement is planning to choose the members in charge of issuing religious decrees and documenting them.[60]

A significant shift in the religious awareness and activity occurred in the early 1990s. Several active religious elements within the Muslim public are responsible for this transformation: the shariʿa courts that spearheaded innovation and reform in shariʿa laws; the Southern and Northern Branches of the Islamic Movement that established institutions for religious studies and centers for religious ruling; the Sufi order al-Tariqa al-Khalwatiyya al-Qasimiyya al-Jamiʿa, which established a college for shariʿa studies and a center for religious ruling at the al-Qasemi college. Alongside shariʿa court qadis, the graduates of these institutions instigated developments in religious law, and launched a process of renewal and advancement of Muslim religious law in Israel.

Despite dissimilarities in detail, all of the previously discussed Islamic elements portray, whether consciously or subconsciously, innovative tendencies in religious law decrees that may lead to the development of local Muslim religious law. The developed practice originated from, and was a direct continuation of, general Muslim religious law, albeit different in details from the religious law practiced in even the closest Islamic countries. This evolution is not unique to the Israeli case, and is analogous to Muslim law developing in the West in light of *fiqh al-aqalliyyāt* – each case having its own conditions and circumstances.

[60] Sarsur, Ibrahim. Interview by author. January 17, 2014.

Analyzing the processes of renewal and reform in shariʿa laws pertaining to personal standing reveals that shariʿa courts uphold the shariʿa, albeit subjugated to Israeli law. Deviating from the Ottoman judicial practices, the courts developed new religious tools with which to cope with imposed civil laws and shifting circumstances. The manner in which shariʿa laws are implemented in Israel is a direct derivative of Israeli society and its constraints: shariʿa courts' obligation to conform to legal principles and norms dictated by civil and criminal legislation; the balance of power in the political system regarding the autonomy granted to the execution of shariʿa laws; the position of the Muslim community in Israel in relation to religion and the application of shariʿa laws. This application reflects the needs and constraints of the local individual upon encountering the general religious law principles. The principles, religious mechanisms, and methodology developed by shariʿa courts in Israel are similar to those developed by *fiqh al-aqalliyyāt*.

The ruling of shariʿa courts in Israel should be regarded as one of the test-cases for the implementation of Muslim law in non-Muslim countries in accordance with the local circumstances. Nevertheless, despite the propinquity in time, the advancement of religious law within shariʿa courts in Israel occurred separately from the emergence of *fiqh al-aqalliyyāt* in the West. Neither *fiqh al-aqalliyyāt* nor its scholars were mentioned in the drafts and final decrees of the shariʿa court of appeals. Moreover, Qadi Natur divulges that until the early 2000s he was unaware of the existence of the *fiqh al-aqalliyyāt* doctrine and not influenced by its thinkers.[61]

De facto, the Southern Branch adopted the religious methodology of *fiqh al-aqalliyyāt* as manifested in its religious decree on elections. In ruling that it is permitted and even obligatory to participate in the elections, it utilized the same argumentations and justifications used by Muslim minorities in the West.

The Northern Branch adopted a conservative approach, ruling according to the classic religious tradition and alongside international unions and centers for religious law ruling. Nevertheless, the Northern Branch's council for religious ruling acknowledged the distinct characteristics of the Muslim public in Israel, which must be taken into consideration upon constructing a religious decree. Even though Northern Branch adjudicators do not relate directly to *fiqh al-aqalliyyāt*, they explicitly accept the rulings of the ECFR, which promotes the doctrine of *fiqh al-aqalliyyāt* as one of the sources for constructing new religious laws. Furthermore, the

[61] In response to the author's query from November 8, 2012.

council subjugated its ruling to shariʿa courts, determining that *talfīq*[62] should not be used when a ruling contradicts a verdict by the shariʿa judicial system.[63]

The Sufi order al-Qasimi dedicated considerable energy to provide Islamic education through its academic college, and instruct the order's followers through unrecorded religious decrees based on comparable methodology to that employed by shariʿa courts. Although their methodology is quite similar to that of the *fiqh al-aqalliyyāt* doctrine, they do not recognize the doctrine as a binding source.

A comparison of developing Muslim religious law in Israel and *fiqh al-aqalliyyāt* reveals that despite the vast dissimilarities in a range of particulars, there is a noteworthy overlap in the methodology utilized for religious decrees and rulings. This similitude is not prevalent in all matters, nor is it applicable to the entirety of the Islamic public in Israel, which varies in nature and religious beliefs; however, its existence is undeniable for some factions and in certain matters.

[62] A religious law term relating to constructing a religious law from two different sources. One segment of the law relies on a certain school, and the other segment on another. Thus, one law integrates laws from two different schools.

[63] See supra note 41.

5

The Future of *Fiqh al-Aqalliyyāt*

Fiqh al-Aqalliyyāt's Approach to Diverse Minorities

Yusuf al-Qaradawi makes the distinction between indigenous minorities (*ahl al-balād al-aṣliyūn*) and immigrant minorities. According to his approach, the Islamic expansion transformed Muslim minority communities into part of their adopted lands. They are considered indigenous minorities, similar to the original inhabitants of a land conquered by Islam, who converted to Islam and remained Muslims after the wave of conquest had ebbed. Furthermore, there are regions where Muslims settled and integrated in a land, as well as Muslim regions annexed by non-Muslim countries. In comparison to the non-Muslim majority in those countries, Muslim communities are considered a minority, although they may be vast in terms of numbers.[1]

Immigrating Muslims who relocated from Muslim countries to Western Europe, North America, and Australia did so primarily for purposes of education and work, or in flight from their native countries as refugees. Among immigrant Muslim minorities, Qaradawi also incorporates the descendants of Muslims who were brought to the Americas, and particularly to the United States, to serve as slaves. He further expands this category to include West European, American, and Australian citizens who, following their interactions with Muslims, recently converted to Islam. Due to the fragility of their faith in the context of their non-Muslim surroundings, such converts are also considered immigrant Muslim minorities.[2]

In his book, *Fi Fiqh al-Aqalliyyat*, Qaradawi determines that the indigenous Muslims in Eastern Europe do not constitute a minority, much like Muslims in Albania, Bosnia, Kosovo, Macedonia, Croatia, Serbia, Montenegro, Bulgaria, and the European portion of Turkey. Since these

[1] ʿAbd al-Rahman ʿAbd al-Khaliq, *Awlwiyat al-ʿAmal al-Islami fi al-Gharb*, Kuwait, 1993, 5–7, http://d1.islamhouse.com/data/ar/ih_books/single5/ar_awlawiat_amal.pdf

[2] Ibid., 18.

countries are in fact Islamic, their Muslim inhabitants are not considered a minority in need of *fiqh al-aqalliyyāt*.[3] Qaradawi further draws a distinction between non-Muslim countries with which there exists a treaty and non-Muslim lands of war. Countries that have international agreements and diplomatic relations with the lands of Islam are not considered lands or war, which, by contradistinction, are at a state of war with Islam (e.g., Israel and Serbia).[4]

The bulk of Qaradawi's work on *fiqh al-aqalliyyāt* is dedicated to the Muslim minorities in Western Europe and North America. He relates to them with affinity and amity, claiming that had they not existed, they ought to have been invented in order to support Islam in those countries and bring them to support and cooperate with the causes of the Islamic world. Nonetheless, in his religious decrees, Qaradawi does not relate to indigenous minorities in relation to *fiqh al-aqalliyyāt*. In addition, he does not delve into the manner in which distinctions between them and immigrating minorities might affect how shair'a laws are applied to each case according to the divergent conditions and circumstances.[5] He does, however, argue that both minorities suffer from hardships and challenges in the fields of religious law and politics, because the majority group does not grant them the appropriate rights, nor recognize their religious distinctiveness. They also experience financial hardships that derive from the fact that significant segments of the minority have a limited income, putting them at odds with the financially stable majority. Cultural hardships stem from the majority's hegemonic culture that disregards the cultures of minorities. Overall, the adversities encountered by minorities originate from their diverse religious beliefs and the desire to cling to a Muslim religious identity.

The relative lack of discussion regarding the indigenous minorities vis-à-vis *fiqh al-aqalliyyāt* is a feature common to other thinkers and religious scholars of the doctrine from the *wasaṭī* faction. They categorize Muslim minorities as Muslims who immigrated to the West and Westerners who, upon associating with Muslim immigrants, converted to Islam. Each minority group lives under different historical, geo-political, social, legal, and financial conditions. Their commonality is their inability to rule the country and implement shariʿa law, particularly in the

[3] Qaradawi, *Fi Fiqh al-Aqalliyyat al-Muslima*,17.

[4] The text of the show can be found on Qaradawi's website, checked on May 24, 2011, http://www.qaradawi.net/new/

[5] Qaradawi, *Fi Fiqh al-Aqalliyyat al-Muslima*, 33.

field of personal standing, which is highly sensitive to Islamic tradition. Conversely, Taha Jabir al-ʿAlwani, who also refers to the doctrine mainly in relation to Muslim minorities in the West, seldom refers to indigenous minorities in this context. He outlines a list of guiding questions that enable each minority to examine whether it falls under the umbrella of methodological religious law offered by *fiqh al-aqalliyyāt*. Al-ʿAlwani's approach represents an essential novelty. It offers the methodology and principles of *fiqh al-aqalliyyāt* to any minority with the appropriate life circumstances, even to indigenous minorities or minorities that are in a state of conflict with their surroundings. Al-ʿAlwani outlines fundamental rules for the implementation of *fiqh al-aqalliyyāt* which take into account the unique circumstances of each country. His guiding set of questions can assist any minority to perform self-examination and determine the religious attitudes and religious law approach it will take towards its political, legal, public, and social surroundings:[6]

1. What is the minority's response to the questions "who are we?" and "how do we become aware of our identity?"
2. What is the nature of the political establishment that controls the minority: is it a democracy, monarchy, dictatorship, or a military regime?
3. What is the nature of the majority? Is it a domineering majority that seeks to assert the regime's hegemony and exclusivity, not wishing others to maintain their uniqueness or enjoy autonomy? Or is it a majority that strives to achieve a dynamic equilibrium based on tested rules that allow minorities to express their uniqueness? What guarantees are provided to safeguard this uniqueness? In what ways can religious expression be pursued?
4. What is the scope of the minority's human, cultural, political, and economic strength?
5. What is the nature of the reciprocal relations between the majority and the minority in terms of the economy and employment? Is there a sharing in resources, industry, professions, and businesses, or separation and discrimination in the aforementioned fields?
6. What is the nature of the settlement? Does a physical integration exist between the two communities? Or rather, is there separation and

[6] Taha Jabir al-ʿAlwani, "Mudkhal Ila Fiqh al-Aqalliyat (Long)," *Majallat al-ʿIlmiyya li-l-Majlis al-Urubi li-l-Ifta' li-l-Buhuth* 4–5 (June 2004): 79–81.

exclusion, either natural or manmade? Is there a partnership in housing and habitation?

7. Does the minority possess cultural depth and a unique identity that can potentially allow it to achieve hegemony? What are the effects of this cultural hegemony on the majority?
8. Do the minority's roots transcend the borders of the joint state, or is it an independent minority devoid of external ties? What are the influences of these two options on the minority?
9. Does the minority differentiate itself through various activities? If so, what are these activities and how are they received by the majority?
10. Can the minority routinely perform the aforementioned activities, or does it require leaders and institutions to assist it?
11. What role do the leadership and institutions take upon themselves in the lives of the minority? Do they go to great lengths to preserve its cultural identity and uniqueness?
12. Do minority institutions and organizations transform into an interest group that promotes the distinct features of the minority, persuading it that its cultural qualities are what identifies it as a minority? What sentiments are associated with the distinctiveness of the minority? Are they positive or negative?
13. Do the institutions and organizations that preserve its uniqueness lead the minority members to consider the value and importance of said uniqueness? Or perhaps, do they not accept their uniqueness and discard any claims of distinct features about the minority? What are the effects of each of these approaches?
14. In cases where the minority has distinct historical roots and a different ethnic origin, how can its cultural delineation be drawn without causing its members to withdraw inwardly or assimilate into the majority?
15. How can one raise awareness to defend the minority against negative sentiments from the majority?
16. How can joint activities for majority and minority communities be established? And in what fields?
17. How can one safeguard the unique cultural identity of the minority, while at the same time, pursue a joint majority-minority cultural identity?
18. How can the minority discern the portion of its unique culture that can become part of a joint culture? What can it gain from the majority culture? What role does the majority play in this?

19. Does the struggle between the cultures of majority and minority have historical roots? If so, what are they?
20. Do minority interests come into conflict with majority interests? What should the minority do in such a case?

The answers supplied by each minority should enable it to examine whether its circumstances label it a minority that is subject to, and bound to act by, the religious law methodology of *fiqh al-aqalliyyāt*. If it is not considered such a minority, the population should adhere to the general religious law customary in the Muslim world. Al-ʿAlwani's approach empowers minorities – in addition to immigrants and Western citizens – to act as a minority, whether indigenous or in conflict with its surroundings and still in the formulation stage, as is the case in Israel. Salah Sultan,[7] a religious scholar of Egyptian descent, concurs with this position. He believes religious law should correspond to the reality of Muslim minorities that suffer infringement of their legal rights, such as the predicament of Muslims in Kashmir or Chechnya.[8]

In this sense, the divergence of Qaradawi's and al-ʿAlwani's attitudes represents differing approaches to *fiqh al-aqalliyyāt*. Qaradawi regards it as a religious law solution to individual cases, whereas al-ʿAlwani sees it as a comprehensive, innovative approach to religious law on the principle level, which constitutes a renewed reading of religious law. Without favoring one approach over the other, in my opinion, the doctrine developed more on the principle level than on the individual case level. Thus, it has transformed into an innovative Islamic philosophy amalgamating observance of the Islamic religion, the fulfillment of the objectives of shariʿa, preservation of Islamic identity, and life in a civil society which subjugates Muslims to legal arrangements and norms that at times contradict Muslim religious law. Therefore, the question whether the doctrine is applicable to the Muslim minority in Israel is a declaratory question, rather than one of religious law.

Fiqh al-Aqalliyyāt al-Muslima – Comprehensive and Systematic Religious Law

Fiqh al-aqalliyyāt scholars have determined that Muslim minorities residing outside the lands of Islam require *fiqh al-khāṣ*, a specialized religious

[7] Born 1959, resides in Bahrain, holds a PhD in Shariʿa Studies, is a lecturer in several universities, hosts a television show on "Al-Nas."

[8] Sultan, Salah, "Al-Dawabit al-Manhajiyya li-fiqh al-Aqalliyyat al-Muslima," without a date, http://www.islamselect.net/mat/89446

law based on a true sharīʿa *ijtihād* that takes into consideration their location, time, and unique circumstances. This perception is based on the notion of the universality of Islam (*ʿālamiyyat al-Islām*); the linkage between originality and modernity (*aṣāla wa-muʿāṣara*); the rule that sharīʿa laws alter according to the time, place, and circumstances; and the acknowledgment that Muslim minorities in the West are in a unique position that justifies altering sharīʿa laws in such a manner.

They believe that Muslim minorities are unable to subjugate the surrounding society to their religious laws, or resolve their affairs according to sharīʿa, separately from the state's legal system. Therefore, they are forced to cope with society's rules and regulations, some of which negate Muslim religion. In this respect, *fiqh al-aqalliyyāt* compels the adjudicator to dedicate in-depth study to several factors: the everyday realities of the Muslim minority in non-Muslim countries; the development and changes they undergo, as well as the associated repercussions; and the distinct features of the minority in question. The decree should convey to the public the influences of the environmental factors so they can respond to such factors in a cognizant fashion, rejecting the negative elements and exploiting the positive ones. This adjudicating approach will protect Muslims from undesired influences and strengthen family units such that they are able to educate the next generation according to Islamic values, preserving their religious identity.

Through the methodology illustrated by *fiqh al-aqalliyyāt* thinkers and scholars – as well as in conjunction with the aforementioned sharīʿa principles and frameworks – muftis have decreed on the affairs of Muslim minorities from all walks of life, taking into account their unique circumstances. This religious jurisprudence allows them to maintain and display their world views, integrate, and preserve their Islamic identity, thus serving as role models for the general public, and promoting the call to Islam (*al-daʿwa*). Analyzing *fiqh al-aqalliyyāt* religious decrees suggests that the doctrine is not based on ad-hoc alleviation of sharīʿa laws and granting religious permits to Muslim minorities, but rather constitutes a comprehensive methodology. The methodology of *fiqh al-aqalliyyāt* is based on sharīʿa principles and frameworks that coincide with the foundations of religious law (*uṣūl al-fiqh*): the objectives of the sharīʿa (*maqāṣid al-*sharīʿa); Muslim interest (*maṣlaḥa*); alleviation and flexibility in religious law (*al-taysīr bi-l-fiqh*); elimination of hardship (*rafʿ al-ḥaraj*); establishing religious rules that, in case of necessity, revoke a prohibition (*al-ḍarūrāt tubīḥ al-maḥẓūrāt*). Examination of research and religious rulings by *fiqh al-aqalliyyāt* adjudicators reveals consistency in the implementation of the doctrine. All research and fatwas first examined the relevant shariʿa laws pertaining to the topic in question by the four schools. They further defined the conditions and circumstances of the Muslim minorities to which their rulings applied. Consequently, they utilized the framework and religious law principles of the methodology to implement shariʿa laws in light of the distinct situation of the minority. All rulings have commonalities – alleviation of the burden placed on the believer (*taysīr*), promotion of the Islamic religion in the West, and preservation of Muslim identity and interests among Muslim citizens.

Analyzing *fiqh al-aqalliyyāt* rulings in the field of personal standing reveals that the developed methodology coincides with the distinct conditions of minorities. As discussed, this distinction is manifested in living under non-Muslim rule, the need to face temptations, isolation of the family, educational burden, and serving as the messengers of Islam. In rulings over matters of personal standing the methodology strives to fulfill the objectives of the shariʿa: preservation of the human race, closeness and devotion between husband and wife, sexual pleasure, and familial cohesion, alongside the shining example presented by Muslim family life. This has bred new religious law on matters of personal standing that differ from the religious law customary in the Islamic world. On occasion, muftis have adjusted the priorities, clout, and significance of each shariʿa objective in order to better suit the unique conditions of each minority. Such modification was attained through alleviation and mitigation of some decrees, while adopting a hardline approach in others. For example, the preservation of the human race becomes even more imperative in the West due to prevalence of phenomena such as bachelorhood, abstaining from marriage and children, and the disintegration of the family. Consequently, the objective of the preservation of the human race, which is of a lesser consequence in the lands of Islam (some Islamic countries even call for restrictions on family size due to extensive, unsupervised growth in population), is imperative to minority communities in order to encourage Muslims to start families and raise children. The attainment of this objective necessitates lenient religious decrees in terms of procreation in conjunction with a stricter approach toward bachelorhood or abstention from having children. Analyzing the various decrees and research produced by the doctrine's scholars and adjudicators, particularly on matters of personal standing, proves that this methodology is both systematically and consistently implemented through numerous religious decrees. Among the most prominent of these decrees is Qaradawi's decree allowing a woman who converted to Islam to remain married to her non-Muslim husband.

The decree relied on Muslims' interests (*maṣlaḥa*) and the desire to bring women closer to Islam, namely in promotion of the *daʿwa*.

Achieving other principles within the methodology is also evidenced in al-ʿAlwani's decree permitting Muslims to adopt Muslim children in non-Muslim countries if it is the only apparent way to preserve their Muslim identity. This is based on the sharīʿa rule that minor harm is preferable to substantial harm; as well, it upholds general sharīʿa objectives which emphasize that the preservation of religion among Muslim minorities in non-Muslim countries supersedes the prohibition against adopting children.

Fiqh al-aqalliyyāt's point of departure can be found in the notion that the civil law enforced upon Muslim minorities does not necessarily contradict religious law. At times, civil legislation can coincide with divine law, as both aspire to achieve identical principles – the benefit of society and the individual. However, in other instances the two systems contrast in their tendencies and elements. *Fiqh al-aqalliyyāt* advocates for the pursuit of common ground as frequently as possible, thus bridging the two systems. In this way, Muslims are not driven to transgress, on the one hand, while, on the other, society at large is not provoked into fearing that Muslims break state laws and threaten society's foundations and well-being. The points of intersection between civil and Islamic laws produce a common ground that can be utilized to mitigate the disparity and attain stability in the lives of Muslim minorities. Conversely, when there is an irreconcilable contradiction, Muslim adjudicators are ordered to harden their line of ruling in order deter Muslims from civil laws that negate religion's decrees. Under these circumstances, Muslims must attempt to refrain from turning to civil proceedings. Nevertheless, adjudicators must find an applicable solution for Muslim minorities to assuage this contradiction.

Another manner through which *fiqh al-aqalliyyāt* copes with the chasm between Islamic tradition and state law is the sterilization of non-Muslim customs that havc infiltrated the heritage and tradition of Muslim communities, thus marring them as seemingly primitive cultures. These blemished traditions should be abandoned in favor of enlightened Western traditions, particularly in matters of personal standing. The starkest example is the inferior position of women and their designation as capricious. This outlook is manifested in women's lack of freedom to decide for themselves as they are forced to abide by their parents or husbands; in many cases, violence is a possible tool of achieving said obedience. With this in mind, upon ruling, adjudicators are asked to grant women their appropriate standing according to religious law, filtering out the non-Muslim customs that are detrimental to women's position and rights. Through their ruling, they must strive and enable women to partake in minority public life; furthermore, by emphasizing the importance of the marriage institution, they ought to ensure appropriate education for the younger generation, reinforcing family values.

In coping with civil law, the *fiqh al-aqalliyyāt* methodology is manifested in the religious decree that validates divorce verdicts by non-Muslim judges issued in a state civil court and based on civil law, which on this matter, diverges from shariʿa law. The implication of this decree is that by marrying according to non-Muslim law, the husband has knowingly delegated authority over divorce to the state's legal system, and accepted the potential annulment of his marriage by a non-Muslim judge as a possible repercussion of this decision. Although the husband may not have declared it forthright, *fiqh al-aqalliyyāt* scholars rely on the rule that a widely known and accepted custom is equivalent to a preexisting condition. Religious acknowledgment of a verdict issued by a non-Muslim judge is designed to prevent injustice to one of the parties under the distinct Western circumstances. Thus, through interpretation of religious law, the doctrine has mitigated religious law with civil law. Determining the personal standing of the individual in this way spares Muslims unmanageable hardships. Another case is al-ʿAlwani's ruling that encourages Muslims in the West to adopt the *Mālikī* School's approach to divorce, granting the wife a divorce in cases of harm that befell her, conflict, or the husband's absence. This religious approach simplifies the separation process and sequesters the husband's right to divorce, transferring it to the arbitrators. This form of ruling demonstrates freedom from commitment to one school and acceptance of all schools, thus facilitating the choice of the most appropriate religious law based on the case. In shariʿa, this is referred to as *takhayyur*, adopting the approach of another school, in this case, the *Mālikī* School. This religiously validates civil separation procedures and assuages the contradiction between religious law and civil law, which in such cases annuls the marriage even without the husband's consent.

In this sense, *fiqh al-aqalliyyāt* represents a systematic method of constructing religious law through predetermined and fairly unambiguous religious principles. It displays an innovative approach toward religious law; at the core of this methodology lies the fulfillment of the objectives of shariʿa and the realization of Muslims' interests–*al-maṣlaḥa*. This is not to say that any transgression should be condoned. The authority to determine whether the matter in question constitutes a *maṣlaḥa* lies with the trustworthy religious scholars, *ahl al-ʿilm al-thiqāt*, who are knowledgeable and experienced in the pillars of the Qur'an and the sunna, as well as in the lived reality of the nation of Islam. The proviso is that the *maṣlaḥa* is collective, *jamāʿiyya* – determined by the *mujmaʿ fiqhī mukhtaṣ*, an assembly of religious law experts, and not by a single person. The union should consider the reality of the nation and not that of the individual. Each *mujmaʿ* has its own method to evaluate the *maṣlaḥa* and to determine that the digression serves a benefit, provided that there is no unequivocal text in terms of meaning and authenticity in the Qur'an or the sunna (*naṣ qaṭʿī al-thubūt wa-l-dālāla*).

It is important to note that shair'a laws by classic religious law are valid and binding. They were not altered nor substituted with other laws, and the revision is in their application, not on the religious level. For instance, the prohibition on interest-incurring loans is a binding religious prohibition also for Muslim minorities. The ECFR ruling permitting Muslim minorities to take a mortgage in order to buy a house does not annul this shariʿa law nor alter its principle. However, the execution of the law under the unique circumstances of Muslim minorities has resulted in an unusual ruling that permits loans under specified circumstances and without hindering the validity of the law. In this sense, this exceptional ruling by the ECFR does not revoke the law, but rather implements it in a different way based on the *maṣlaḥa* of the Muslim minorities. In addition, in order to fulfill shariʿa objectives in the case of Muslim minorities, a new religious law was created, which derives from general law.

The *Fiqh al-Aqalliyyāt* Framework for Relations between the Muslim Minority and the State

Fiqh al-aqalliyyāt is not a religious law framework designed exclusively for Muslim minorities' internal affairs, such as religious rites or personal standing. Rather, it outlines a model for relations in the public sphere between the Muslim minority and the majority and state institutions, based on the Quranic verse (8:60): "God does not forbid you from being kind and acting justly towards those who did not fight over faith with you, nor expelled you from your homes. God indeed loves those who are just."[9] This verse allows Muslims to interact, cooperate, be loyal to, and support non-Muslims, provided that the latter act with decency toward Muslims and not infringe on their rights, that is, take arms up against their religion and drive them from their homes. The doctrine calls upon nations to act

[9] Ahmed Ali, trans. *Al-Qur'an* (Princeton, NJ: Princeton University Press, 1993), 480.

with decency (*qisṭ*) toward Muslim citizens and allow them to uphold their religion and preserve their rights. In this vein, *fiqh al-aqalliyyāt* calls for civil integration among the general public, and acceptance of common norms while maintaining the distinct Muslim tradition (contingent on the circumstances). This approach regards the state as a just and enlightened entity; there is no need to alter it, nor create a parallel public system in its stead. The doctrine's thinkers reject the division adopted by classic religious law between the land of Islam (*dār al-Islām*) and the land of war (*dār al-ḥarb*), considering the West as a land of treaty (*dār al-ʿahd*) or land of acceptance of Islam (*dār al-ijāba*). Furthermore, this approach adopts legal norms that take into account everyday life in the modern world.

The doctrine's thinkers believe that the attaining of Muslim interests and the serving as role models that draw other nations closer to Islam, will be achieved through integration into general society. The doctrine displays a multi-cultural model that enables every citizen to receive his civil rights, on the one hand, while realizing his religion and culture within his communal sphere, on the other. *Fiqh al-aqalliyyāt* calls for a multi-cultural society under which all cultures, and in this instance Islamic culture, can flourish. Such a society would facilitate the advancement of Islamic culture in non-Islamic countries, establishment of its unique religious identity, and development of a Muslim communal sphere that fulfills its members' needs. Muslim society must sustain an active and industrious participation in general society, in order to promote it as a shared field where all cultures can strive together according to societal rules and norms.

Fiqh al-aqalliyyāt also calls for legal pluralism that acknowledges the legal frameworks of the various groups comprising society, and the existence of parallel legal systems. This pluralism enables Muslim minorities to establish institutions for arbitration or ruling in intra-Muslim disputes, mainly in the field of personal standing, allowing Muslim minorities to litigate according to shariʿa. This approach further enables the state to accommodate shariʿa laws that pertain exclusively to the affairs of the Muslim community, ensuring its survival and facilitating its development.

To achieve this pluralism, the doctrine operates in two veins: one is calling upon the state to acknowledge Muslim minority's religious laws and to allow them to uphold these laws within the general legal system; this may be through civil courts that pass judgment on intra-Muslim disputes that conform to the shariʿa, or through referring these cases to religious tribunals within the community that rule according to the shariʿa. The other vein is calling for the institution of shariʿa arbitration centers that Muslims would turn to willingly, and with the consent of all parties involved. These voluntary arbitration centers coexist alongside the general legal system. Allowing minority communities autonomy on matters of marital relations through courts that uphold religious and personal law constitutes a practical solution for minorities without harming the general public. In addition, it does not oppress the Muslim individual, especially when there is a civil legal system in which the public can litigate according to civil laws. This legal pluralism can ease tensions between the community and the state whose civil law differs from religious law. This applies to instances where religious marriages are not registered with the civil authorities, civil divorces are not recognized by religious law, and paternity tests are performed.

Beyond applying *fiqh al-aqalliyyāt* to solve specific problems, particularly when anticipating the future, it can serve as a comprehensive theory that provides an outline for the ideal relationship between minority and the state. The doctrine's multicultural vision acknowledges the right of the group to preserve its cultural and religious characteristics, and the right for fair treatment and cooperation in the public sphere. This is based on a covenant (*ʿaqd al-wafāʾ*) that in exchange for safeguarding their rights that derive from being citizens, Muslim citizens proclaim their loyalty to the non-Muslim sovereign. On the one hand, *fiqh al-aqalliyyāt* calls upon the state to treat Muslims with decency – not harm them, their religion, or their civil, financial and social rights, nor cause them to lose their homes or property. Failing to do so will brand the state as a land of war with which coexistence is impossible. On the other hand, the doctrine calls upon Muslims to fortify their religious identity, create a vibrant and lively religious cultural space, and establish independent institutions to officiate their religious affairs, such as shariʿa arbitration centers and educational institutions for the study and development of Islamic culture. In order to thwart any form of religious oppression or discrimination against Muslims by the state, *fiqh al-aqalliyyāt* calls to uphold and respect the democratic laws of the state. The doctrine regards each law or regulation as a necessity that must be met with a religious approach in order to contain it and ensure continued harmonious coexistence. Nevertheless, so long as their existence and preservation of their religion is secure, the doctrine calls on Muslims to actively participate in the public sphere, vote, join political parties, and run in elections to try and influence the state's treatment of Muslim minorities and Islam.

Fiqh al-Aqalliyyāt – between Theory and Application

Despite its robust religious law approach and affiliation with the *wasaṭī* faction which is prevalent in the lands of Islam, *fiqh al-aqalliyyāt* is not accepted by many Muslims in the West, and it encounters impediments that prevent its implementation.

The vast diversity among Muslim minorities in the West – comprised of the secular, Islamic liberals, *wasaṭī*, *salafi* and other factions – is the main impediment for the reception of the doctrine as a religious authority for Muslim minorities. Secular Muslims perceive religion as a cultural element. Hence, religious methodology, albeit liberal, is not applicable to them and does not influence their decisions and religious and civil perceptions.

Islamic circles in the West also do not receive *fiqh al-aqalliyyāt* as a religious authority. Claiming it deviates from, and transgresses against the pillars of religion, the *salafi* faction vehemently opposes it, and wishes to prevent its scholars from obtaining a hegemonic status. Traditional Islamic believers, chiefly from the Indian Peninsula, adhere to the tradition of Islam as it was developed in India over the last two hundred years, not regarding *fiqh al-aqalliyyāt* as a religious authority. Other segments within the Islamic world who accept their reality, its rules and regulations, adopt a religious law approach more liberal than that offered by the doctrine. They adhere to a broader implementation of the objectives of shariʿa than classic religious law or *fiqh al-aqalliyyāt*.

Lack of public awareness is another challenge faced by *fiqh al-aqalliyyāt*. Many Muslims in the West, including dominant Islamic activists, are unaware of the doctrine, albeit when it is conveyed to them they identify with it. The doctrine's scholars and thinkers as well as the ECFR do not do enough to disseminate the doctrine, and the majority of their literature is written in Arabic rather than in English. It is therefore inaccessible to Muslims in the West; in Europe and the United States, the doctrine is far less common than in the Islamic world in the East, including the pivotal role enjoyed by al-Qaradawi in Arab media.

Another impediment to its wide reception as a religious authority is the diversity of conditions and circumstances in each country. Civil law differs from country to country; thus, a successful solution for a Muslim minority in one country does not necessarily coincide with the laws and circumstances in another. This disparity results in an inability to implement unified religious law for all Muslim minorities. Due to these impediments, Muslims in the West are not unified religiously, and are unable to conform to a uniform religious perception and religious law methodology, even one that strives to resolve religious conundrums deriving from their unique predicament in the West. This stark lack of cohesion deems it impossible to bridge the gaps without considerable flexibility in the religious perception. However, such moderation seems unlikely in the foreseeable future. Hindered by these limitations, *fiqh al-aqalliyyāt* is not received as a binding religious law doctrine. In the Fiqh Council of North America, each scholar can rule independently, based on his beliefs. The same is applicable to Europe. For instance, in Britain, shariʿa councils decree according to each adjudicator's perception and the ruling is accepted by a majority of adjudicators, many of whom unfamiliar with the doctrine.

Despite its robust religious approach and affiliation with the popular *wasaṭī* faction, the *fiqh al-aqalliyyāt* doctrine is unlikely to be implemented in the lives of Muslim minorities in the various Western countries. In this sense, *fiqh al-aqalliyyāt* may be a hypothetical religious law perception that showcases a fundamental religious law theory, yet its tangible application is restricted.

Fiqh al-Aqalliyyāt: An Outline for Innovative Religious Law

Researchers such as Andrew March, Alexandre Caeiro, Uriya Shavit, and Shammai Fishman regard *fiqh al-aqalliyyāt* as a religious law methodology based on a utilitarian approach. March claims that *fiqh al-aqalliyyāt* stems from the intersection of liberalism and Islam, and is founded on a strategy of profitability in religious law (*maṣlaḥa*), allowing for a more flexible approach to Muslim religious law according to the principles of *wasaṭiyya*. Shavit concurs with March, maintaining that the *wasaṭī* approach utilizes theological concepts that enable assuagement of shariʿa laws according to the principles of *wasaṭiyya*, which employs a liberal application of religious principles to alleviate Muslim minorities and promote the *daʿwa*. Fishman draws the same conclusion, claiming that *fiqh al-aqalliyyāt* integrates al-ʿAlwani's notion of the universality of Islam (*ʿālamiyyat al-Islām*) and rules according to the objectives of shariʿa (*maqāṣid al- shariʿa*) in order to promote the *daʿwa* and the propagation of Islam. Caeiro believes that Islamic *fiqh* is based on dialectical relations between Holy Scripture and context – a notion that, according to al-ʿAlwani, lies at the heart of *ijtihād*. Therefore, Caeiro claims that decrees by *fiqh al-aqalliyyāt* scholars deviate from classic religious law, and the standing of *fiqh* has shifted from holy law to one of individual rationalism. Al-ʿAlwani and Qaradawi offer diverse views of *fiqh al-aqalliyyāt*: Qaradawi regards it as religious law for specific cases, whereas al-ʿAlwani views it as religious law on the principle level. The conclusions of the aforementioned researchers notwithstanding – and without choosing between Qaradawi's and al-ʿAlwani's approaches – I believe that the doctrine has developed on the principle level of religious law, and constitutes more than a judicial approach designed to rule on specific cases. In my opinion, *fiqh al-aqalliyyāt* presents an innovative religious law perception that differentiates between *fiqh* that is implemented in religious law as it is manifested in the primary sources of shariʿa, and the implementation of shariʿa law in unique circumstances bound by place and time. This implementation is obtained through the assimilation of shariʿa law with reality and its conditions as perceived by Muslim groups, anywhere and at anytime.

In this sense, general *fiqh* becomes the desired, sought-after ideal. However, upon attempting to solve problems that are specific to time and place, local solutions must be found that take into consideration the power balance between shariʿa laws and the obligatory laws and prevailing circumstances of the location, mitigating them with religious laws. Various practices have been formulated in every culture and society, resulting in the establishment of diverse ruling arrangements and norms. Thus, the context of the local application, i.e. the norms and measures that developed in a certain community, cannot be severed from religious law tradition and the sources of the shariʿa. This is substantiated by the fact that the doctrine's religious principles are flexible and enable modification of religious law according to the shifting circumstances and conditions. For example, in a ruling that contradicted an explicit source, such as the prohibition on interest in a mortgage, the doctrine's thinkers relied on the Muslims' interest, the *maṣlaḥa*, among other factors. This mechanism is flexible and its definition is case specific. In addition, the attainment of the objectives of the shariʿa (*maqāṣid al-sharīʿa*) allows for a different interpretation of religious texts in relation to diverse conditions and situations in order to achieve the objective of shariʿa in any field and under any circumstance. Concurrently, in certain cases, priorities in jurisprudence (*fiqh al-awlawiyāt*) and balance in jurisprudence (*fiqh al-muwāzanāt*) enable favoring one interest or a decree over another, or rejecting an interest in order to prevent harm by adhering to the rules of *fiqh*, such as opting for the lesser of two evils (*akhaf al-ḍararayn*), or favoring the prevention of harm over the reaping of benefit. This also applies to annulling a decree in case of necessity (*ḍarūra*), or under certain circumstances when a need becomes a necessity, thus overruling a decree or religious law (*al-ḥājiyāt al-munazila manzila al-ḍarūrāt*).

BIBLIOGRAPHY

ʿAbd al-Kadir, Muhammad Khalid. *Min Fiqh al-Aqalliyyat al-Muslima*. Doha: The Qatari Office of Waqf and Islamic Affairs, 1997.

ʿAbd al-Khaliq, ʿAbd al-Rahman. *Awlwiyat al-ʿAmal al-Islami fi al-Gharb*. Kuwait: 1993. http://d1.islamhouse.com/data/ar/ih_books/single5/ar_awlawiat_amal.pdf

Abdelhaleem, Tariq. "Al-Wasatiyya al-Muhaditha wa-Athruha al-Dar ʿala Din al-Ama." Mawqʿ al-Maqreze, 2010. http://webcache.googleusercontent.com/search?q=cache:q9DJjwpM8sAJ:http://www.almaqreze.net/ar/news.php?readmore%3D859%2B%D8%B7%D8%A7%D8%B1%D9%82+%D8%B9%D8%A8%D8%AF+%D8%A7%D9%84%D8%AD%D9%84%D9%8A%D9%85+%D8%A7%D9%84%D9%88%D8%B3%D8%B7%D9%8A%D8%A9+%D8%A7%D9%84%D9%85%D8%AD%D8%AF%D8%AB%D8%A9&hl=iw&gbv=2&&ct=clnk

Abu al-ʿAta, Islam Muhammad. "Anqisamat Hawl Shariʿa Baqaʾ al-Zawja al-Kitabiyya al-lati Aslamt maʿ Zawjiha al-Ghayr Muslim fi al-Dul al-European."2010. http://www.masress.com/misrelgdida/23577

Abu Sayeed, Shaykh. *Polygamy and Islam: Seminar on Shariʿa as a Way of Life*. London: Islamic Culture Center, 2008.

Abu Zuhra, Muhammad. *Ibn Taymiyya, Hayatuh wa-ʿAsrutuh- Arawʾuh wa-Fiqhuh*. Beirut: Dar al-Fikr al-ʿArabi, 1991.

Ali, Ahmed, trans. *Al-Qurʾan*. Princeton, NJ: Princeton University Press, 1993.

Ali, K. "Progressive Muslims and Islamic Jurisprudence: The Necessity for Critical Engagement with Marriage and Divorce Laws," in *Progressive Muslims: On Justice, Gender and Pluralism*, ed. O. Safi (pp. 89–163). Oxford: One World Publications, 2003.

Al-Abyani, Muhammad Zayd, *Sharh al-Ahwal al-Shakhsiyya*, 9th ed. Beirut: Maktabat al-Nahda, 2002.

Al-ʿAlwani, Taha Jabir. *Fi Fiqh al-Aqalliyyat al-Muslima*. Cairo: Nahdet Misr, 2000.

"Mudkhal Ila Fiqh al-Aqalliyat (short)." In *Maqasid al-Shariʿa* (1st ed., pp. 95–120). Beirut: Dar al-Hadi, 2001.

"Nazrat Taʾsisiyya Ila Fiqh al-Aqalliyyat." http://www.onislam.net/arabic/madarik/politics/89619-2001-02-11%2014-50-15.html

Toward a Fiqh for Minorities: Some Basic Reflections, with an introduction by Shaikh Zaki Badawi (London and Washington: The International Institute of Islamic Thought, 2003).

"Mudkhal Ila Fiqh al-Aqalliyat (long)." *Majallat al-'Ilmiyya li-l-Majlis al-Urubi li-l-Ifta' li-l-Buhuth* 4–5 (June 2004).

"Aslah al-Ta'lim al-Dini." Al-Jazeera, December 4, 2005. Interview with shaykh al-'Alwani. www.aljazeera.net

Al-Amrani, Mohammed. "Al-Usra al-Muslima fi al-Gharb bayn al-Tashri' al-Islami wa-l-Qawanin al-Wad'iyya." *Al-Majallat al-'Ilmiyya li-l-Majlis al-Urubi li-l-Ifta' li-l-Buhuth* 7 (July 2005): 175–227.

Al-Ansari, Shamsu al-Din. *Nihayat al-Muhtaj ila Sharh al-Minhaj*. Beirut: Dar Ihya' al-Turath al-'Arabi, 3rd edition, 1992 (1413 according to the *hijri* calendar).

Al-Ashqar, Umar Sulaiman. *Ahkam al-Zawaj*. Jordan: Dar al-Nafa'is, 1997.

Al-Bakr, Muhammad 'Abd al-Rahman. *Al-Sulta al-Qada'iyya wa-Shakhsiyya al-Qadi*. Egypt: Al-Zahra' li-l-I'lam al-'Arabi, 1988, 1408 according to the *hijri* calendar.

Al-Bayzali, Abd al-Hamid. "Bahth fi Kitab Muhammad bin Mahmud al-Asrushini Jami' Ahkam al-Sighar." Master's Degree Thesis, Cairo, 632 according to the *hijri* calendar.

Al-Bichri, Shaykh Al-Arabi. "Shira' al-Buyut 'an Tariq al-Qard al-Banki." *Al-Majallat al-'Ilmiyya li-l-Majlis al-Urubi li-l-Ifta'* 6 (January 2005): 159–78.

Al-Bist, al-Imam Abi Sulayman. *Ma'alim al-Sunan wa-huwa Sharh Sunan al-Imam Abi Dawud*. Beirut: al-Maktaba al-'Ilmiyya, 2nd edition, 1981.

Al-Buti, Muhammad Sa'id. *Al-Salafiyya Marhala Zamaniyya Mubaraka La Madhhab Islami*. Damascus: Dar al-Fikr, 1998.

Al-Dumyati, al-Sayyid Muhammad Shata. *I'ana al-Talibin 'ala Hal al-Faz Fath al-Mu'in li-l-'Alama Zayn al-Din al-Malibari*. Beirut: Dar al-Fikr li-l-Tiba'a wa-l-Nashr wa-l-Tawzi', 1997.

Alexa. Traffic date for "Islamonline" website. http://www.alexa.com/siteinfo/islamonline.net

Al-Ghalayini, Mohammed. *Al-Marakiz al-Islamiyya fi North America*. Jordan: Dar Amar li-l-Nashr wa-l-Tawzi'a, 2009.

Al-Ghannouchi, Rached. "Al-Islam wa-l-Muwatana." Al-Jazeera. http://www.aljazeera.net/NR/exeres/81878E28-53C4-4638-9F9B-008B572B7197.htm

Al-Ghazali, Muhammad. *Mustaqbil al-Islam Kharij Ardih Kayf Nufakr fih*. Cairo: Dar al-Shuruq, 1997.

Al-Hawari, Muhammad. "Waqi' al-Wujud al-Islami fi Europe." *Al-Majallat al-'Ilmiyya li-l-Majlis al-Urubi li-l-Ifta' li-l-Buhuth* 12–13 (July 2008): 176–254.

Al-Husayni, 'Ala'. *Al-Islam fi Britain. Beirut*. Beirut: al-Ilm li-l-Nabihin, 2007.

Al-Jawziya, ibn Qayyam Muhammad ibn Abi Bakr ibn Ayyub ibn Sa'ad ibn Hariz. *Ahkam Ahl al-Dhimma*. Beirut: Dar al-'Ilm li-l-Malayin, 1993.

Al-Jundi, Ahmad Nasri. *Mabadia' al-Qada' fi al-Ahwal al-Shakhsiyya*. Nasr: al-Matbaʿa al-Haditha, 1992.

Al-Kasani,ʿAla' al-Din Abi Bakr bin Masʿud al-Hanafi. *Bada'iʿ al-Sana'iʿ fi Tartib al-Shara'ʿ*. Beirut: Dar al-Kutub al-ʿIlmiyya, 2nd edition, 1986, vol. 9, 4079.

Al-Khatib, Muʿtaz. "Fi Naqd al-Qawl bi-l-Wasatiyya wa-l-Aʿtidal." Islamonline, without a date. http://www.kalema.net/v1/?rpt=754&art

Al-Lubnani, Salim Rustam Baz. *Shirh al-Majla*. Dar Ahya' al-Turath al-ʿArabi, 3rd edition, 1986.

Al-Madkhali, Rabee bin Hadi. *Sharh Usul al-Sunna li-l-Imam Ahmad bin Hanbal*. Cairo: Dar al-Minhaj, 2007.

Al-Mahdi, Tahir. "Tahadiyat Tuwajih al-Usra al-Muslima fi al-Gharb." *Al-Majallat al-ʿIlmiyya li-l-Majlis al-Urubi li-l-Ifta' li-l-Buhuth* 8–9 (June 2006): 53–64.

Al-Marghinani, Abi Bakr bin ʿAbd al-Jalil. *Al-Hidaya Sharh Bidayat al-Mubtada'*. Cairo: Dar al-Islam, 2000.

Al-Mtiri, Shaykh Hakim. "Al-Huriyya aw al-Tufan." Without a date. http://www.dr-hakem.com/Portals/Content/?info=TXpRMkpsTjFZbEJoWjJVbU1RPT0rdQ==.jsp

Al-Najjar, Abdul-Majeed. "Malat al-Afʿal wa-Athruha fi Fiqh al-Aqalliyyat." *Al- Al-Majallat al-ʿIlmiyya li-l-Majlis al-Urubi li-l-Ifta'* 4–5 (2003). http://www.e-fcr.org

"Nahwa Ta'sil Fiqh li-l-Aqalliyyat al Muslima fi al-Gharb." January 14, 2004. http://www.onislam.net/arabic/madarik/culture-ideas/89695-2004-01-14%2018-59-54.html

"Maqasid al-Shariʿa fi Ahkam al-Usra Muwajahha li-Ahkam al-Usra al-Muslima fi al-Gharb." *Al-Majallat al-ʿIlmiyya li-l-Majlis al-Urubi li-l-Ifta' li-l-Buhuth* 7 (July 2005): 67–102.

"Takdim," *Majallat al-ʿIlmiyya li-l-Majlis al-Urubi li-l-Ifta' li-l-Buhuth* 18 (July 2011): 67–102.

Al-Nashmi, Ajeel Jasem. "Al-Taʿliqat ʿala Bahth Madkhal ila Usul wa-Fiqh al-Aqalliyyat li-l-Ustadh al-Duktur Taha Jabir al-ʿAlwani." *Al-Majallat al-ʿIlmiyya li-l-Majlis al-Urubi li-l-Ifta' li-l-Buhuth* 7 (June 2005): 17–63.

Al-Qasimdar, Mujahid al-Islam. *Al-Nizam al-Qada' al-Islami*. Dar al-Kutub al-ʿIlmiyya, 2001, 1422 according to the *hijri* calendar.

Al-Qatan, Mannaʿ. *Tarikh al-Tashriʿ al-Islami*. Cairo: Maktabat Wahba, 5th edition, 2001.

Al-Qinawi, Ahmad Hanafi. *Al-Jawahir al-Hasan fi Tarikh al-Habshan*. Cairo: 1902–03.

Al-Rawi, Omar. "Al-Islam wa-l-Muslimun wa-l-ʿAmal al-Islami fi Europe-al-Waqiʿ, al-Mawʿiqat, al-Amal." Islamonline, 2003. http://www.islamonline.net/arabic/daawa/2003/12/article05.shtm

Al-Razi, Fakhr al-Din. *Al-Tafsir al-Kabir aw Mafatih al-Ghayb*. Beirut: Dar al-Kutub al-ʿIlmiyya, 1990.

Al-Sarakhsi, Shams al-Din. *Kitab al-Mabsut li-l-Sarakhsi*. Beirut: Dar al-maʿrifa, 1910, 1331 according to the *hijri* calendar.

Al-Shanqiti, Muhammad bin al-Makhtar. "ʿAn Fatwa al-Muslimin fi al-Jaysh al-Amriki." Without a date. http://alarabnews.com/alshaab/GIF/19-10-2001/Mokhtar.htm

Al-Sharqawi, Jamal. "*ʿAn al-Fatwa al-Amrikaniyya, Majallat al-Sunna*." Vol. 110. Britain (2003).

Al-Shashuki, Badr al-Din. *Al-Mujaz fi al-Qanun al-Dawali al-Khas*. Jedda: Maktab al-Khadmat al-Haditha, 1973.

Al-Shaykh, Mamduh. "Hal Yatbalwar Mafhum Jadid li-ʿAlamiyyat al-Islam?" 2008. http://www.nashiri.net/articles/intellect-and-philosophy/2075–v15-2075.html

Al-Tarabulsi, ʿAlaʾ al-Din. *Maʿin al-Hukam*. Damascus: Dar al-Fikr, without a date.

Al-ʿUthaymin, Muhammad bin Salih. *Al-Asl min ʿIlm al-Usul*. Egypt: Maktabat al-Iman al-Mansura, without a date.

Al-Wansharisi, Ahmad. *Tahqiq Muhammad Hajji wa-Zara al-Awqaf wa-l-Shuwun al-Islamiyya li-l-Mamlaka al-Maghribiyya wa-Dar al-Gharb al-Islami*." Morocco: 1981.

Al-Zaylaʿi, Fakhr al-Din, *Al-Hidaya Sharh Bidayat al-Mubtadaʾ*, 939. Dar al-maʾarfa, vol. 3, 46 in "Al-Hadana fi al-Sharʿ."

Al-Zaylaʿi, Fakhr al-Din. *Tabyin al-Haqaʾiq Sharh Kanz al-Daqaʾiq*. Vol. 3.Beirut: dar al-maʿrifa, 1892, 1313 according to the *hijri* calendar.

Al-Zuhayli, Wahba. *Al-Fiqh al-Islami wa-Adillutih*. Damascus: Dar al-Fikr, 2007.

Amara, M. H. "The Collective Identity of the Arabs in Israel in the Era of Peace," *Israel Affairs* 1/2 (2003): 249–62.

Anderson, J. N. D and Coulson, N. J. "Sharia." In *The Encyclopedia of Islam*, 2nd edition, ed. H. A. R. Gibbs, B. Lewis, Ch. Pellat, C. Bosworth et al., vol. 11 (Leiden: E.J. Brill, 1960–2002).

Bin ʿAshur, Tahir. *Maqasid al-Shariʿa al-Islamiyya*. Jordan: Dar al-Nafaʾis, 2nd edition, 2001, 1421 according to the *hijri* calendar.

Bin Bayyah, Abdallah. "Al-Farq bin al-Drura wa-l-Haja Tatbiqa ʿala Baʿd Ahwal al-Aqalliyyat al-Muslima." *Al-Majallat al-ʿIlmiyya li-l-Majlis al-Urubi li-l-Iftaʾ* 4–5 (July 2004): 95–145.

"Al-Hadana fi al-Sharʿ." *Al-Majallat al-ʿIlmiyya li-l-Majlis al-Urubi li-l-Iftaʾ li-l-Buhuth* 8–9 (June 2006): 273–86.

"*Wa-Madha ʿan Fiqh al-Aqalliyyat al-Muslima*." 2006. http://www.binbayyah.net/portal/artciles/274

"Al-Walaʾ bayn al-Din wa-l-Dawla." *Al-Majallat al-ʿIlmiyya li-l-Majlis al-Urubi li-l-Iftaʾ* 12–13 (July 2008): 99–113.

Bin Fawzan, Saleh. *Sharh al-ʿAqida al-Wasatiyya li-Shaykh al-Islam Ahmad bin Taymiyya*. Riyadh: Maktabat Dar al-Islam, 1994.

Bin-Qasim, bin Muhammad. *Majmu' Fatawa Shaykh al-Islam Ahmad ibn Taymiyya*. Saudi Arabia: Majma' al-Malik Fahid li-Tiba'a al-Mushaf al-Sharif, 2004, 1425 according to the *hijri* calendar.

Bitshun, Shirin. "Nafaqat al-Zawja wa-Mabada' al-Musawaa bina al-Mara'a wa-l-Rajul." *Al-Siwar al-Haraka al-Nasawiyya al-'Arabiyya li-Da'm Dahaya al-I'tida'at al-Jinsiyya*. 37 (2010).

Bowen, J. R. *Can Islam be French? Pluralism and Pragmatism in a Secularist State*. Princeton, NJ: Princeton University Press, 2010.

Bunt, G. *iMuslims: Rewiring the House of Islam*. Chapel Hill: University of North Carolina Press, 2009.

Caeiro A., al-Saify, M "Qaradawi in Europe, Europe in Qaradawi? The Global Mufti's European Politics." In *Global Mufti: The Phenomenon of Yusuf al-Qaradawi*, eds. Bettina Graf, Jakob Skovgaard-Petersen, 109–48. London: Hurst & Company, 2009.

Caeiro, A. "The European Council for Fatwa and Research", Paper presented at the Fourth Mediterranean Social and Political Research Meeting, European University Institute, Florence, Italy, March 19–23, 2003.

"European Islam and Tariq Ramadan," ISIM244 Newsletter, June 14, 2004a https://openaccess.leidenuniv.nl/bitstream/handle/1887/16930/ISIM_14_European_Islam_and_Tariq_Ramadan.pdf?sequence=1

"The Social Construction of Sharia: Bank Interest, Home Purchase, and Islamic Norms in the West." *Die Welt des Islams* 44/3 (2004b): 353–4.

"The Power of European Fatwas: The Minority Fiqh Project and the Making of an Islamic Counterpublic." *International Journal of Middle East Studies* 42/3 (2010): 435–49.

Capotorti, F. "*Minorities*," in Encyclopedia of Public International Law, Bernhardt R., ed. (1985), 385–395.

Decisions and Fatwas issued by the European Council for Fatwa and Research. Cairo: Dar al-Tawzi' wa-l-Nashr al-Islamiyya, 2002.

Dilwar, H. "Muslim Political Participation in Britain and the 'Europeanisation' of Fiqh. *Die Welt Des Islams*, 44/3 (2004): 376–401.

Edge, I. D. "Family Law, Minorities and Legal Pluralism: Should English Law Give More Recognition to Islamic Law?" *Temple Church, DRAFT*, November 12, 2008.

Ephrat, D. *Spiritual Wayfarers, Leaders in Piety: Sufis and the Dissemination of Islam in Medieval Palestine*. In "Harvard Middle Eastern Monograph" 40. Cambridge, MA: Center for Middle Eastern Studies, 2008.

Fatwa al-Majlis al-Islami al-Ifta'. Nazareth: vol. 1, 2005.

Fatwa al-Majlis al-Islami al-Ifta'. Nazareth: vol. 2, 2012

Fadl, K. Abou El. "Islamic Law and Muslim Minorities: The Juristic Discourse on Muslim Minorities from the Second/Eighth to the Eleventh/Seventeenth Centuries." *Islamic Law and Society* 1/2 (1994): 141–87.

Fishman, S. "Ideological Islam in the United States: 'Ijtihad' in the thought of Dr. Taha Jabir al-Alwani." *Jamaa* 11 (2003): 51–81.

"Some Notes on Arabic Terminology as a link between Tariq Ramadan and Shaykh Dr. Taha Jabir al-Alwani, Founder of the Doctrine of 'Muslim Minority Jurisprudence' (Fiqh al-Aqalliyyat al-Muslima)." December 2003, www.e-prism.org/images/tariqfinal291203.doc

"The Fiqh al-Aqalliyyat Doctrine in the Writings of Taha Jabir al-Alwani and Yusuf al-Qaradawi." Master's Thesis, Jerusalem: Hebrew University of Jerusalem, 2006.

"Fiqh al-Aqalliyyat: A Legal Theory for Muslim Minorities." *Research Monographs on the Muslim World.* Hudson Institute, Series 1 (Paper no.2, 2006).

Ghadban, R. "Fiqh al-Aqalliyyat and Its Place in Islamic Law." *Orient* vol. 2 (2010): 56–63.

Goiten S. D. and A. Ben Shemesh. *Introduction to Muslim law: Basic principles and laws.* (Faculty of Law of the Hebrew University. Legal Studies, No. 3.) Jerusalem: Mif'al Hashichpul and Gvilim Publishing Co. Ltd., 1957.

Goren, A., and N. Nachmani. *The Importance of Being European: Turkey, the EU & the Middle East.* Jerusalem: The Hebrew University of Jerusalem, 2007.

Griffiths, J. "What is Legal Pluralism?" *Journal of Legal Pluralism and Unofficial Law* vol. 24 (1986): 1–55.

Halawa, Hussein Mohammed. "Al-Talaq wa-Ahkamuh." *Al-Majallat al-'Ilmiyya li-l-Majlis al-Urubi li-l-Ifta' li-l-Buhuth* 8–9 (June 2006): 133–208.

Hallaq, W. B. *A History of Islamic Legal Theories.* Cambridge: Cambridge University Press, 1997.

Hasan, S. "Sharia: A Way of Life." Seminar on Sharia as a Way of Life (London: The Islamic Culture Centre, 2008).

Hasan, Suhaib. "Al-Tafriq al-Qada'i min Khilal Qanwat al-Shari'a al-Islamiyya." *Al-Majallat al-'Ilmiyya li-l-Majlis al-Urubi li-l-Ifta' li-l-Buhuth* 8–9 (June 2006): 245–270.

Huntington, Samuel P. "The Clash of Civilizations?" *Foreign Affairs*, vol. 72, no.3 (Summer 1993): 22–49.

Hutchinson, A. M. "*Arbitration/Mediation in Family Law and Children's Cases in the UK.*" Seminar on Arbitration First. London: The Islamic Culture Centre (2005).

Ibn 'Abidin, Muhammad Amin.*Hashit ibnu 'Abidin Rad al-Muhtar 'ala al-Dur al-Mukhtar Sharh Tanwir al-Absa.* Beirut: Dar al-Kutub al-'Ilmiyya, 4th edition,1994.

Ibn Hazm, Ali bin Ahmad. *Al-Ihkam fi Usul al-Ahkam, Tab'a Muhqqaqa.* Beirut: Dar al-Afaq al-Jadida, without a date.

'Imara, Muhammad. "Khamsun 'Am 'ala Istishhad Hasan al-Banna, Mashru' Islami li-l-Nahda al-Hadariyya." *Al-Mujtam'* (Kuwait) 1337, 1999.

Jaballah, Ahmad. "Al-Asra al-Muslima fi Europe bayn Ta'thirat al-Bi'aa al-Ahtima'iyya wa-l-'Adat al-Murutha." *Al-Majallat al-'Ilmiyya li-l-Majlis al-Urubi li-l-Ifta' li-l-Buhuth* 7 (July 2005): 231–48.

Jackson, S. "Legal Pluralism between Islam and the Nation-State: Romantic Medievalism or Pragmatic Modernity?" *Fordham International Law Journal* vol. 30 (2006): 158–76.

Jad al-Haq, ʿAli Jad al-Haq. "Fatwa fi Baʿd Ahkam Tatʿalliq bi-l-Aqalliyyat al-Muslima fi Ghayr Diyar al-Muslimin." *Majallat al-Azhar* 6, year 63 (December–January1991).

Kedourie, E. *Nationalism*. London: Hutchinson University Library, 1966.

Khadduri, M. *War and Peace in the Law of Islam*. Baltimore: Johns Hopkins Press, 1955.

Kymlicka, W. *Multicultural Citizenship: A Liberal Theory of Minority Rights*. Oxford: Oxford University Press, 1995.

"Multicultural States and Intercultural Citizens." *Theory and Research in Education* 1/2 (2003): 147–69.

Laurence, J. and P. Strum, eds. *Governments and Muslim Communities in the West: United States, United Kingdom, France and Germany*. Proceedings of a workshop and conference on March 3–5, 2008. Washington, DC: Woodrow Wilson International Center for Scholars, 2008. http://www.wilsoncenter.org/sites/default/files/govtsmuslimcommun_0.pdf

Lauziʾere, H. "The Construction of Salafiyya: Reconsidering Salafism from the Perspective of Conceptual History." *Ijmes* 42 (2010): 369–89.

Layish, Aharon. "The Transforation of the Shariʿa from Jursits' Law to Statutory Law in the Contemporary Muslim World." *Die Welt des Islams* 44 (2004): 85–113.

Malik, M. "Accommodating Muslims in Europe: Opportunities for Minority Fiqh." *ISIM* Newsletter, December 13, 2003, http://www.isim.nl/files/newsl_13-10.pdf

Mallat, Hassan. "Tayyar al-Wasatiyya," Mokarabat website, 2009, http://www.mokarabat.com/s5938.htm

March, A. F. "Sources of Moral Obligation to Non-Muslims in the 'Jurisprudence of Muslim Minorities' (Fiqh al-Aqalliyyāt) Discourse." *Islamic Law and Society* vol. 16 (2009): 34–94.

Masud, M. K. "Islamic Law and Muslim Minorities." ISIM Newsletter vol. 11, December 2002 http://www.isim.nl/files/newsl_11.pdf

Mawlawi, Faysal. "Al-Mafahim al-Asasiyya li-l-Daʿua al-Islamiyya fi Balad al-Gharb." 2005. https://uqu.edu.sa/files2/tiny_mce/plugins/filemanager/files/4230042/dawa_magreeb.doc

"Al-Khulʿ wa-Ahkamuh al-Shariʿa maʿ Tatbiqat ʿala al-Aqalliyyat al-Muslima." *Al-Majallat al-ʿIlmiyya li-l-Majlis al-Urubi li-l-Iftaʾ li-l-Buhuth* 8–9 (June 2006): 211–42.

Modood, T. "British Muslims and the Politics of Multiculturalism." In *Multiculturalism, Muslims and Citizenship*. Tariq Modood et al. eds. 37–56. Oxon: Routledge, 2006.

Still Not Easy Being British: Struggles for a Multicultural Citizenship. London: Trentham Books, 2010.

Mursi, Ahmad. "Al-Muwasasat al-Islamiyya fi Mujtamaʿ al-Jaliyat wa-l-Aqalliyyat Nazrat Mustaqbaliyya." *Multaqa Khadim al-Haramayn al-Sharifayn al-Malik Fahd bin ʿAbd al-ʿAziz al Suʿud al-Islami al-Thaqafi*, Copenhagen, 2001.

Nachmani, A. *Europe and Its Muslim Minorities*. Sussex Academic Press, 2009.

Nafi, B. M. "Fatwa and War: On the Allegiance of the American Muslim Soldiers in the Aftermath of September 11th." *Islamic Law and Society* 11 (2004): 78–116.

Nielsen, J.S. *Towards a European Islam*. London & New York: Macmillan press and St. Martin's Press, 1999.

Nizam, al-ʿAllama al-Hammam al-Shaykh Nizam wa-Majmuwʿa min ʿUlmaʾ al-Hind al-Aʿlam. *Al-Fatawa al-Diniyya, fi Madhhab al-Imam al-Aʿzam Abi Hanifa al-Nuʿman*. Damascus: Dar al-Fikr, 2nd edition, 1430 according to the *hijri* calendar.

Orhun, O. "Intolerance and Discrimination against Muslims (Islamophobia)." *Security and Human Rights* vol. 3 (2009): 192–200.

Özyürek, E. "The Politics of Cultural Unification, Secularism, and the Place of Islam in the New Europe." *American Ethnologist* 32/4 (2005): 509–12.

Pew Research Center. *The Future of the Global Muslim Population: Projections for 2010–2030*. The Pew Forum on Religion & Public Life, January 2011. http://www.pewforum.org/The-Future-of-the-Global-Muslim-Population.aspx

Polka, S. "Between liberalism and Fundamentalism: The Political Thought of Mainstream Islam (Wasatiyya) in Contemporary Egypt." PhD diss., Ramat Gan: Bar Ilan University, 2000.

"The Centrist Stream in Egypt and its Role in the Public Discourse Surrounding the Shaping of the Country's Cultural Identity." *Middle Eastern Studies* 39/3 (2003): 39–64.

"Constructing Muslim Identity in Western Society: The Rulings (Fatawa) of Shaykh Yusuf Al-Qaradawi for Muslims in the West." In *Muslim Minorities in Non-Muslim Majority Countries: The Islamic Movement in Israel as a Test Case*. Elie Rekhess and Arik Rudnitzky eds., 43–62. Tel Aviv: Tel University, and The Konrad Adenauer Program for Jewish-Arab Cooperation, 2011.

Qaradawi, Yusuf al. *Ghayr al-Muslimin fi al-Mujtamaʿ al-Islami*. Beirut: Muasisatur-Risalah, 1997.

Al-Halal wa-l-Haram fi al-Islam. Cairo: Maktabat Wahba, 22nd edition, 1997.

Al-Siyasa al-Sharʿiyya fi Dawʾ Nusus al-Shariʿa wa-Maqasidha. Cairo: Maktabat Wahba, 1998.

Al-Ijtihad al-Muʿasir bayn al-Indibat wa-l-Infirat. Cairo: al-Maktab al-Islami, 2nd edition, 1998.

Al-ijtihad fi al-Shariʿa al-Islamiyya maʿ Nazarat Tahliliyya fi al-ijtihad wa-l-Muʿasir. Cairo: Dar al-Qalam, 1999.

Taysir al-Fiqh li-l-Muslim al-Muʿasir fi Dawʾ al-Qurʾan wa-l-Sunna. Cairo: Maktabat Wahba, 1999.

Fi Fiqh al-awlawiyat wa-Dirasa Jadida fi Daw' al-Qur'an wa-l-Sunna. Cairo: Maktabat Wahba, 2000.

Taysir al-Fiqh li-l-Muslim al-Mu'asir fi Daw' al-Qur'an wa-l-Sunna. Beirut: Muasisatur-Risalah, 2000.

Fi Fiqh al-Aqalliyyat al-Muslima: Hayat al-Muslimin Wasat al-Mujtama'at al-Akhra. Cairo: Dar al-Shuruq, 1st edition, 2001.

Kalimat fi al-Wasatiyya. Kuwait: Al-Markaz Al-'Alami li-l-Wasatiyya, 2007.

"Al-Watan wa-l-Muwatana fi Daw' al-Usul al-'Aqadiyya wa-l-Maqasid al-Shar'iyya." *Al-Majallat al-'Ilmiyya li-l-Majlis al-Urubi li-l-Ifta'* vol. 12–13 (July 2008): 20–98.

Qudama, Shaykh Imam al-'Allama Muwafaq al-Din Abi Muhammad 'Abdullah ibn Ahmad bin Mahmud, al-Mughni 'Ala Mukhtasar al-Ayman Abi al-Qasim 'Umar bin al-Husayn bin 'Abdallah bin Ahmad al-Kharqi, al-Shaykh al-Imam Shams ad-Din Abi al-Farj 'Abd al-Rahman binu Abi 'Umar Muhammad binu Ahmad binu Qudama al-Maqdisi, al-Sharh al-Kabir 'ala Matan al-Maqna', Kalahuma 'ala Madhhab Imam al-A'imma Abi 'Abdallah Ahmad binu Muhammad binu Nubul al-Shibani ma' Bayan Khalaf Sa'ir al-A'imma wa-Adilatihum Radi Allah 'Anhum. Beirut: Dar al-Kutub al-'Ilmiyya, without a date, vol. 10.

Quraishi A. and N. Syeed-Miller "No Stars: A Survey of Islamic Family Law in the United States." In *Women's Rights & Islamic Family Law: Perspectives on Reform*. Lynn Welchman ed. 179–219 London: Zed Books Ltd, 2004.

Ramadan, T. *Western Muslims and the Future of Islam*. Oxford: Oxford University Press, 2004.

Reiter, Y. "Judge Reform: Facilitating Divorce by Shari`a Courts in Israel." *Journal of Islamic Law and Culture* Vol. 11, Issue.1 (2009): 35–6.

Rekhes, E. "Resurgent Islam in Israel." *Asian and African Studies* 27/1–2 (1993): 189–206.

Rida, Rashid. *Yusr al-Islam wa-Usul al-Taysir al-'Am*. Cairo: 2nd edition, 1956.

Rohe, M. "Islamic Law in German Courts." *Hawwa* 1/1 (2003): 46–59.

"Application of Sharia Rules in Europe: Scope and Limits." *Die Welt des Islams* vol. 44/3 (2004): 323–350.

"Islam and the Law in Europe." *Orient* vol. 2 (2010): 23–36.

Schacht, J. *An Introduction to Islamic Law*. Oxford: Clarendon Press, 1964.

Shaham, Ron. "Enjoying from all the Worlds: Legal Forum Shopping in Islamic Societies." *The New East* 46 (2006): 54–78.

Shaham, R. *The Expert Witness in Islamic Courts: Medicine and Crafts in the Service of Law*. Chicago: University of Chicago Press, 2010.

Shahar, I. "Legal Pluralism and the Study of Shari'a Courts." *Islamic Law and Society* 15/1 (2008): 112–41.

Shah-Kazemi, S.N. *Untying the Knot: Muslim Women, Divorce and the Shariah*, London: University of Westminster, 2001.

Shavit, U. "The Wasati and Salafi Approaches to the Religious Law of Muslim Minorities." *Islamic Law and Society* 19/4 (2012): 416–57.

Shkedi, Asher. *Words of Meaning: Qualitative Research – Theory and Practice*. Tel Aviv: Tel Aviv University, 2007.

Siddiqi, Faiz-ul-Aqtab. "Family Law, Minorities and Legal Pluralism: Should English Law Give More Recognition to Islamic Law?" http://www.wynnechambers.co.uk/pdf/Shaykh_Faiz_Speech.pdf.

Sinclair, Kirstine. "Muslim Organizations in Denmark – Five Years after the Cartoon Controversy." Syddansk Universitet, 2011. http://static.sdu.dk/mediafiles//8/0/9/{80922C6E-1D2B-455D-9A98-7BC29829098D}1106KS.pdf.

Sivan, Emmanuel. *The Clash Within Islam*. Tel Aviv: Am Oved, 2005.

Stendel, Ori. *Arabs of Israel: Between the Rock and the Hard Place*. Jerusalem: Academon, 1993.

Sultan, Salah. "Al-Muwatana fi Ghayr Diyar al-Islam bayn al-Nafin wa-l-Muthabitin."*Al-Majallat al-ʿIlmiyya li-l-Majlis al-Urubi li-l-Iftaʾ* 12–13 (July 2008): 135–72.

"Al-Dawabit al-Manhajiyya li-Fiqh al-Aqalliyyat al-Muslima." Without a date. http://www.islamselect.net/mat/89446

Tamanaha, B. Z. "The Folly of the 'Social Scientific' Concept of Legal Pluralism." *Journal of Law and Society* vol. 20 (1993): 192–217.

Takruri, A. *Al-Wajiz fi Sharh Usul al-Muhakmat al-Sharʿiyya*. Amman: Dar al-Fikr li-l-Tibaʿa li-l-Nashr wa-l-Tawziʿ, 1997.

The Center for Security Policy. *Shariah Law and American Courts: An Assessment of State Appellate Court Cases*. Version 1.2. May 18, 2011. http://www.shariahinamericancourts.com

Thomson, Hajj A. "Applying Islamic Fiqh in UK Arbitration Law." Seminar on Arbitration First. London: The Islamic Culture Centre, 2005. 16–23.

"Accommodating the Islamic Dissolution Law of Marriage within English Law." Seminar on Dissolution of Marriage, London: The Islamic Culture Centre, 2006.

"How Some Elements of Shariah Can be accommodated in British Legal System." Seminar on Sharia: A Way of Life, London: The Islamic Culture Centre, 2008.

Tubuliyak, Sulaiman. *Al-Ahkam al-Siyasa li-l-Aqalliyyat al-Muslima fi al-Fiqh al-Islami*. Jordan: Dar al-Nafaʾis, 1997.

Voll, J. O. "Religious Diversity in the United States." *Al-Shajara: Journal of the International Institute of Islamic Thought and Civilization (ISTAC)* vol.14/1 (2009): 1–18.

Warwick, T. *Legal Pluralism: Toward a Multicultural Conception of Law*. Aldershot, UK: Ashgate, 1999.

Woodman, G. R. "Ideological Combat and Social Observation: Recent Debates about Legal Pluralism." *Journal of Legal Pluralism* vol. 42 (1998): 21–59.

"The Idea of Legal Pluralism." In *Legal Pluralism in the Arab World*. B. Dupert, M. Berger and L. al-Zawaini eds. 3–20. The Hague: Klewer Law International, 1999.

Yilmaz, I. "Muslim Law in Britain: Reflections in the Socio-Legal Sphere and Differential Legal Treatment." *Journal of Muslim Minority Affairs* 20/2 (2000): 353–60.

Zahalka, Iyad. *Shari'a Courts: Between Identity and Adjudication*. Tel Aviv: Israel Bar Association Press, 2009.

Zidan, Abd al-Karim. *Madkhal li-Dirasat al-Shari'a al-Islamiyya*. Beirut: 16th edition, 1999.

Nizam al-Qada' 'ala al-Shari'a al-Islamiyya. Beirut: Muasisatur-Risalah, 2002, 1422 according to the *hijri* count.

Interviews and Lectures

Abdul Rauf, Feisal. Interview by author. New York City, October 18, 2012. Head of the Cordoba Initiative in New York.

Amin, Mohammed. Interview by author. London, October 16, 2011. British Muslim of Pakistani descent, board member of the Islamic Council of Britain.

Bone, Amra. Interview by author. London, October 13, 2012. Islamic activist of Pakistani descent, the only female shari'a judge in Britain, in Birmingham.

Edge, Iyan. Interview by author. London, October 13, 2012.

Fishman, S. Lecture given by Fishman at a conference and personal communication with author. Tel Aviv University, March 18, 2010.

Halawa, Hussein Mohammed. Interview by author. ECFR offices in Dublin, Ireland, February 12–13, 2012. General Secretary of the ECFR.

Suhaib, Hasan. Interview by author. Leyton Shari'a Council, London, October 15, 2012.U

Hathout, Maher. Interview by author. Islamic Center, Los Angeles, April 1, 2012.

Hendi, Yahya. Interview by author. Washington, DC, November 1, 2012. Member of the Fiqh Council of North America, a religious councelor and lecturer at Georgetown University.

Johansen, Karen-Lise. Presentation given at a conference "Muslims, Citizenship and Community Participation: on Ideological Extremism," 2008. Danish researcher working for the Danish government.

Khalil, Asim. Interview by author. New York City, October 23, 2012. Head of the Muslim Bar Association of New York.

Muhammad,Shams ad-Duha. Interview by author. London, October 13, 2012. Member of Jama'at al-Tabligh, and founding director and principal of the Ebrahim College in London

Qaradawi, Yusuf al. Minutes of his show. Checked on May 24, 2011, http://www.qaradawi.net/new/

Ramadan, Tariq. Interview to "Islamonline," September 10, 2003, http://site.matariaonline.com/dindetail.asp?id=29

Sarsur, Shaykh Ibrahim Abdullah. Interview by author. Januray 17, 2014. Former head of the Southern Branch of the Islamic Movement.

Shanqiti, abu Bakir al. Interview by author. Virginia, November 2, 2012. Head of the International Institute of Islamic Thought in Virginia.

Verdicts by the Jordanian Shari'a Court of Appeals

Maḥkamat al-Asti'nāf al-Shari'a fi Amman- Case no. 409/2004–59704, Na'im al-Sahli v. 'Abir al-Tahir wa-'Iysa Abu Murad. Personal communications with Qadi al-Rawajba, a qadi at the Jordanian Shari'a Court of Appeals.

Maḥkamat al-Asti'nāf al-Shari'a fi Amman- Case no. 336/2007–66725, Musa Khabbas Wafa' al-Khatib versus Ahmad Qasim. Personal communications with Qadi al-Rawajba, a qadi at the Jordanian Shari'a Court of Appeals.

Fatwa (Religious Ruling)

Al-Albani. Without a date. For more on Shaykh al-Albani's fatwa on Muslim emigration from Israel, al-Salafiyya Manhaj wa-Hayat, see http://mosafer10.arabblogs.com/archive/2007/10/362298.html

Al-Lijnna al-Da' ima li-l-Buhuth al-' Alamiyya wa-l-Fatwa. Without a date. The Permanent Committee for Islamic Research and Fatwa in Saudi Arabia prohibits taking a loan with an interest for purchasing a house: http://islamqa.info/ar/ref/105331

Al-Majlis al-Urubi li-l-Ifta' wa-l-Buhuth (2008). Ruling 17/1 of the ECFR (which reiterated ruling 16/3) *in Al-Majallat al-'Ilmiyya li-l-Majlis al-Urubi li-l-Ifta'* 12–13 (July 2008): 498–9.

Al-Majlis al-Urubi li-l-Ifta' wa-l-Buhuth. Ruling 8/3 by the ECFR permitting a woman who converted to Islam to remain with her non-Muslim husband: http://articles.islamweb.net/media/index.php?page=article&lang=A&id=4527

Al-Majlis al-Urubi li-l-Ifta' wa-l-Buhuth. ECFR fatwa regarding participation in elections: https://islamicfatwa.wordpress.com/2009/04/06/%D8%AD%D9%83%D9%85-%D8%A7%D9%84%D9%85%D8%B4%D8%A7%D8%B1%D9%83%D8%A9-%D8%A8%D8%A7%D9%84%D8%A7%D9%86%D8%AA%D8%AE%D8%A7%D8%A8%D8%A7%D8%AA-%D8%A8%D8%A7%D9%84%D8%AF%D9%88%D9%84-%D8%BA%D9%8A%D8%B1-%D8%A7/

Research conducted on election participation, and running within a non-Muslim political party: https://islamicfatwa.wordpress.com/2009/04/06/%D8%AD%D9%83%D9%85-%D8%A7%D9%84%D9%85%D8%B4%D8%A7%D8%B1%D9%83%D8%A9-%D8%A8%D8%A7%D9%84%D8%A7%D9%86%D8%AA%D8%AE%D8%A7%D8%A8%D8%A7%D8%AA-%D8%A8%D8%A7%D9%84%D8%AF%D9%88%D9%84-%D8%BA%D9%8A%D8%B1-%D8%A7/

Al-Majlis al-Urubi li-l-Ifta' wa-l-Buhuth (2009). ECFR fatwa permitting to purchase a house with loans that incur interest: http://muntada.sawtalummah.com/showthread.php?1908-%CD%DF%E3-%D4%D1%C7%C1-%C7%E1%E3%E4%C7%D2%E1-%C8%DE%D1%D6-%C8%E4%DF%ED-%D1%C8%E6%ED-%E1%E1%E3%D3%E1%E3%ED%E4-%DD%ED-%DB%ED%D1-%C8%E1%C7%CF-%C7%E1%C5%D3%E1%C7%E3

El-Awa, Mohamed Selim et al. Fatwa that permits partaking in war against Muslims within the United States Army: http://www.aawsat.com/details.asp?section=4&article=61545&issueno=8356http://www.onislam.net/arabic/madarik/politics/89594-2002-03-01%2012-53-34.html

Al-Odah, Shaykh Salman bin Fahd. A Fatwa that unequivocally prohibits Muslim soldiers from fighting against Muslims in Iraq in 2003: http://www.onislam.net/arabic/newsanalysis/3008%D9%88%D8%AB%D8%A7%D8%A6%D9%82%20%D9%88%D8%A8%D9%8A%D8%A7%D9%86%D8%A7%D8%AA/82843-2003-03-08%2000-00-00.html

Bayyah, bin Abdallah. Bayyah's fatwa on settlement in a non-Muslim country: http://www.binbayyah.net/portal/fatawa/374

Bin Baz, Shaykh ʿAbd al-ʿAziz. A speech given at the Sixteenth International Conference of Young Muslims, *Majallat al-Buhuth al-Islamiyya 6, 346.*

Buhuth wa-Darasat. "Quebec Tarfud Iqamat Mahakim Shariʿ a li-Muslimi Canada," 2005: http://islamtoday.net/bohooth/artshow-12-57707.htm

Islamweb. Without a date. A fatwa prohibiting loans in order to purchase a house: http://www.islamweb.net/fatwa/index.php?page=showfatwa&Option=FatwaId&Id=49918

Islamweb. Without a date. Fatwa that prohibits Muslim men to marry women that are not from the People of the Book: http://www.islamweb.net/fatwa/index.php?page=showfatwa&Option=FatwaId&Id=2974

Israel, Al-Athad al-ʿAlami li-ʿUlma' al-Muslimin (International Union of Muslim Scholars), without a date: http://www.iumsonline.net/ar/default.asp?MenuID=11&contentID=4210

Majmaʿ al-Fiqh al-Islami. Third convention, *Majallat Majmaʿ al-Fiqh al-Islami, 3, 1987, vol.2, 1152.*

Nimr, Kamal Kamal ʿAbd al-Hamid. Majallat al-Buhuth al-Islamiyya 22, 250.

Qaradawi, Yusuf al. Al-Qaradawi *Yadʿu al-Muslimin li-l-Astʿadad li-Yawm Zawal ma Yusamma Isla'il.*

INDEX

Lightning Source UK Ltd.
Milton Keynes UK
UKOW05n1811120916

282833UK00003B/46/P

9 781107 114586